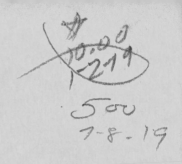

Also by Hays Gorey

NADER AND THE POWER OF EVERYMAN

"MO"

a woman's view of watergate

BY

MAUREEN DEAN

WITH

HAYS GOREY

SIMON AND SCHUSTER · NEW YORK

DESIGNED BY EVE METZ
MANUFACTURED IN THE UNITED STATES OF AMERICA

1 2 3 4 5 6 7 8 9 10

LIBRARY OF CONGRESS CATALOGING IN PUBLICATION DATA

DEAN, MAUREEN.
"MO" A WOMAN'S VIEW OF WATERGATE.

INCLUDES INDEX.
1. WATERGATE AFFAIR, 1972–   2. DEAN,
MAUREEN.   3. DEAN, JOHN WESLEY, 1938–
I.   GOREY, HAYS.   II.   TITLE.
E860.D4   973.924   75-22058
ISBN 0-671-22161-2

For Irene and John

Contents

1

A Parting
Stream of Consciousness

It's our last day and night in our own home before John . . . goes away, and the atmosphere is charged.

I know what he's going through, and I wonder how he can stand it. He's the one who's going to prison. He's the one who spent years studying law and utilizing his knowledge of it. Now he will never be allowed to practice law again.

We will be apart for at least a year, probably more. Today is August 27, 1974. On September 3, he goes in, and he won't be out until . . .

But we promised not to think in those terms.

I still can't accept the fact that John is going to prison. I never have. It's unreal.

I keep hoping something will happen, but if it doesn't, this is not the kind of a last day at home we should have to remember. John is grumpy, preoccupied. He's fussing about all sorts of little things that don't need fussing over. I think he's avoiding me.

And I have to pretend I can play that game, too, but I'm not very good at it. I hang a picture, and then another, and every five minutes I sit down in the kitchen, and I imagine he has already gone. There will be hours and months like this, when I'll be sitting right here, thinking and thinking, and wondering how he is, and if prison life will finally break his spirit even though nothing else has, and what life for us will be like when he finally returns.

One thing we both know—and if we didn't know it, maybe neither one of us could endure this—we know that whatever is in store, it's for us together. We've both known failed marriages, which may be why we both recognize that this marriage—our marriage—will not fail. I'm amused when people ask me how I can be so certain. There's no way to explain it, except to say that we have discovered the secret, and the secret is truth. We can and do always tell each other the complete and unvarnished truth. And having dealt with truth, we have discovered so much else, including that the way we feel about each other won't ever change. Our love, some say, was strengthened by John's troubles and we'll have to be careful when the usual strains and stresses return to our marriage. Return? They've never left.

Even on this his last day we're piqued with each other. John is trying at the last minute to get every detail of our financial affairs in order, so everything will be as easy as possible for me. Yesterday he gave an interview to *Playboy* for $5,000, which will help to take care of expenses for part of the time that he is away.

I dread every second that ticks away on the clock. The day goes on: John on the phone, John in and out of the house, John ordering this, John suggesting that. It's almost as if nothing at all unusual is about to happen. That's the way he wants it. It *isn't* the way I want it.

The bright sun is sinking now. The orange glow in the sky has turned to pink. The doorbell rings, and it's good, good friends, Gene Adcock and Cameron Keller, stopping by for a final drink with us. The thought that this is really farewell for who knows how long—as far as John is concerned—brings that choked feeling into my throat again, and I'm aware that my eyes are moist, but I don't break into tears, because everyone is being so "normal," no matter how much of a strain it is, and, oh God!—if I break now, so will Gene, and then we'll have just the kind of last evening John doesn't want. Biting my lower lip has worked before, and, please, let it work now. Miraculously, it does work for a moment, and now there is another ring of the doorbell, and somehow I find the strength to greet a new visitor and submerge the thoughts that are about to overwhelm me.

This time it's a short, slender, lithe figure that could easily be mistaken for that of a Boy Scout. But this is no Boy Scout. This is another of the lawyers ruined by Watergate, another whose name will never be forgotten, another who did wrong and who will pay and pay for as long as he lives, and then pay still more because his name is linked to scandals that will never be forgotten.

It is Donald Segretti, and I think, as I look at him, that even though his name will always be synonymous with political dirty tricks, everyone should see him as I am seeing him now—shy, polite, a trifle embarrassed to be who he is. Of course, everyone won't see him this way. I realize how vicious some of those pamphlets he distributed were—but he went to jail to pay for his mistakes and that should be enough. But it won't be.

Segretti is here because John engaged him to draw up wills for both of us, and Segretti seems so grateful for even this little bit of legal business while he still has the right to practice law. He seems uncomfortable and doesn't stay long, and, in fact, everyone leaves early, sensing that John and I should have much of this last night alone.

And so we sit, and we sip our cocktails and look at each other, and I want to tell John that I feel there has been something so wrong about this last day. But he is so intently businesslike that I realize he has determined to be this way. "Normal." What was it he said? "I don't want anything dramatic when the time comes." And now the time has come, and he thinks this is the way to avoid dramatics: act as if today is just another day, and tomorrow and all the tomorrows will be just other days.

Matter-of-factly he is saying, "Let's get packed and get up early, because we'll be leaving the house tomorrow at eight o'clock," and I think how ridiculous this is, because we have no reason to be in Washington at any particular hour, and how much nicer it would be to sleep a little later and have a leisurely morning and some additional precious hours in our own home together. But when I ask John to make reservations on a later plane, he snaps that he will not because two U.S. marshals are going with us, and all of us would have to change our reservations and our plans, and he isn't about to put anyone to that. It isn't very tender, but John isn't being very tender about anything.

I am put out because this doesn't make any sense, and when I tell him I probably won't even fly there with him because it is stupid to leave so early, we argue, and I run into the bedroom and let the tears flow. I don't do any packing. I don't sleep either, but I set the alarm for six o'clock so I will have time to pack if I should change my mind. Now the alarm is ringing, and through my blurry and still teary eyes I see it is 6:04, and I'm so emotionally and physically exhausted that I just want to stay in bed and avoid reality.

But I cannot. I can't think of John flying back alone. So I get up and pack, and now John and I are making the bed together one last time, and one of my long red fingernails breaks, and he says something about long red fingernails—something snide—and now we are angry again. I suppose we are both near our breaking points—too much emotion held inside, too much feeling and sadness not expressed, too much caution about hurting the other, too much reluctance to talk about what is happening to us.

But I can't understand John's being so "normal," and again I decide that I will not go with him, and he just says,

"Suit yourself." I storm off into the living room, with tears in my eyes and the determination that I will not really break down and cry. I sit alone on the huge sofa, and I wish John would come in and hug me and say, "I'm sorry," but he won't. So I say to myself, What the hell? You know you're going anyway, you know you want to be with him every moment, every second now. I ask the marshals to help with my bags, and I climb into the car and sit there in silence. And I think how much turmoil and pain there is for two people who love each other, and why, I wonder, must it be like that?

Flying east we talk a little, but not much. President Ford is holding a news conference that has been specially picked up on the movie screen; we watch, and I wonder how they can beam such a clear telecast to a swiftly moving jet. I watch the second President of the United States I have met, and I notice how open he is, and how calm, and that there is no perspiration on his upper lip. He says there will be no amnesty or pardon for Richard Nixon until after Special Prosecutor Leon Jaworski has taken whatever action he deems appropriate, and John and I look at each other, and his eyes are big question marks, but he says nothing, and we look back at the screen.

Washington, D.C., is below us, and I know our emotions are really mixed. "There's nothing there for us any more," John has said so often, and that's almost all right with me, because I prefer to live in Los Angeles anyway. But Washington will always evoke the sense of what might have been and the awful thing that was. After we land, I go through the motions of getting settled in the apartment of my close friend Heidi, because again John is away all day long being interviewed by the special prosecutors. They are questioning him again, as investigators have been doing for fourteen months now, and I wonder how he can still have more new things to tell them.

I shop for groceries and discover how recognizable I still

am. The checker knows who I am and wishes me luck, and a man in the supermarket says, "I know you are someone famous, but . . ." and I smile sweetly and point to that day's *Washington Post* with John's picture on the front page, and the man says, "Oh." This is how the waning days of August are spent. Friends telephone, and so do such people as Charley Shaffer, John's attorney. And now it is September 2, another "last night" together, only this one will be for such a long, long time.

We have dinner at Poor Richard's in the Chevy Chase Holiday Inn, and there isn't much to say. All I can think of is that my husband is going to jail and that he is really not a criminal, but how can I make everyone see that, and, of course, I know I can't.

Every so often I wonder what John is thinking, but I don't ask. Then on the morning of the day I have dreaded for so long, I awake to find a note he has put on the mirror before leaving the apartment on our last day together. "I wanted to tell you why I'm going to jail. Why the 'system' has—or is—pulling us apart. Something we're not used to being. But I shall carry with me the thoughts in my head—and will share them with you later. Because you must know that we've got our pride. We've stood the hardest test—truth in love and in explaining what happened during my days, weeks, months, and years at the White House. We'll talk later so you'll have my every thought. So escape in peaceful sleep. Because you're too good to suffer the pain of all this."

John plans to be home early in the afternoon of September 3, 1974, and knows that he does not have to surrender until five o'clock, but it is one-thirty when he does his last-minute packing and two o'clock when the marshals arrive. "No!" I shriek, and then John says: "It's best, dear, really it's best," and I slump and say weakly, "Maybe it is," and then the last kiss is a quick one.

"I love you. I miss you already" is all I have time to say

before he is gone. In thirty seconds he is back because he has forgotten his sunglasses. Another quick kiss and he is gone—really gone—and I call after him and the marshals: "See you all on the news tonight," because I want John to know that I, too, can keep it light, if light it has to be.

Completely alone, strangely I don't cry, and I call Mom and Junie and Heidi and Pete and talk without a crack in my voice, but then suddenly I have called everyone I should call and I feel empty. A glass of wine helps, and then I flick on the radio and Fred Graham of CBS is saying that John looked pale and shaken as he was ushered into the courthouse to be fingerprinted and photographed, and of course I know that John was not pale, and "shaken" is simply newsman's jargon to inject drama. But all that is of little concern compared to the thought of John's being fingerprinted and photographed and issued standard clothing, all of which hurts me deeply, because under the law John Dean is now a common criminal, even though to me he is a man of courage and one who tried to save his country and without whose efforts his country might not have been saved at all.

Friends drop in to comfort me, and other friends telephone, and some people bring wine and cigarettes. We watch NBC News and David Brinkley says that John Dean has begun serving a "light" sentence.

A light sentence? One to four years—light?

John went away five hours ago.

Already it seems like five months.

2
Lucky Friday the Thirteenth

What my life is now and will be forever really began on November 13, 1970—for me a very lucky Friday the thirteenth.

There are days—even moments—in everyone's life that each of us looks back on and asks, "What if . . . ?" What if I hadn't gone some place, met someone, forgotten something, remembered something? What if I hadn't answered the telephone, missed the plane, lost my key? It's frightening. Is life charted according to some divine plan? Or is it just random and chaotic happenstance? On my fortunate Friday, the day that John Dean and I met, I like to think there was a plan at work.

The day began like most days back then—uneventfully. I would have enjoyed sleeping late, but I couldn't, because I had to go to my office. I was an insurance broker, and to make a living in that business, you have to work at it. It was a sheer delight to sell a big policy, not only because you knew you could pay the bills for a while, but because you might be able to coast—just a little. But this was not the time for coasting. It was a time for starting early and quitting late, working hard every single minute.

For night people like me, morning is a time of struggle. I go through my ritual, but it is as if I am wading through tar. First there is the bath, then coffee, then dressing, followed by tidying up the two-bedroom apartment I shared with Pat Hornung, the estranged wife of former football star Paul Hornung. Then I applied my makeup, did something to my hair, and headed for the office, running a little late this morning, which I confess was not unusual.

I ran quickly down the stairs from my second-floor apartment, stepping over my neighbor's newspaper, not bothering to glance at the headlines or to check my horoscope. Years later, I just had to go back to see what the stars said was in store for me that fateful day. My horoscope:

"LIBRA (September 23 to October 22) : You want to run away from those duties ahead of you, but perseverance will bring fine results. Use good judgment instead of following hunches today, which are apt to be erroneous. Take time for social activities."

The previous month I had turned twenty-five—a quarter of a century! I had already been through one marriage that was annulled, then a second marriage that left me a widow. My first "husband" had neglected to divorce his wife before marrying me. My second husband died tragically in an automobile accident while we were living apart. I had traveled throughout the United States and Europe, I had had a taste of college and a brief stint as an American Airlines stewardess, and now I was earning my own living in the insurance business. All that was quite a bit to pack into those few, fleeting years between high school graduation day and birthday No. 25.

The drive to work that morning took me through the winding pass of Coldwater Canyon from Beverly Hills to the Wilkinson Insurance Agency in the San Fernando Valley. Mastering the intricacies of life insurance and health insurance programs had been a real challenge to me. Like so many women, I wanted a challenge. I wanted to prove something about myself. I felt I had to do something that required study, diligence, and some degree of intelligence. Daddy was no longer around to take care of little Mo, and I had no inclination to try marriage again—

not immediately, anyway. So I worked and I studied and I earned my license to sell and to assist clients with insurance-oriented estate plans. I felt competent, and I felt good about being able to help people.

Just the night before, Bill Wilkinson, the agency owner, and I had worked very late on a major group insurance proposal, and he had some finishing touches to apply to it on Friday. I had to be there in case I was needed, but I knew it would be a slow day for me. Just another day—one to devote to staring at the walls of my office, thinking about the crucial ingredients missing from my life: love, the security that love can bring, the sense of really and truly belonging somewhere and to someone.

By four-thirty I was more than ready to get back to my apartment. Pat was out of town, and I had a date. But by the time I had wound my way back through the canyon in my five-year-old T-bird, the mind, spirit, and the heart had had it. Any woman knows the feeling: you just can't bear the thought of going through all that a woman must do to be ready to go out at night—a bath, any one of a number of rituals having to do with hair, choosing the right clothes to wear, rushing like a whirlwind, and still managing to be sweet, smiling, and to all appearances unruffled by the time the doorbell rings and "he" walks in, having changed his shirt and shaved—maybe—all set for a swinging evening.

My date was with Hugh O'Brian, and I know the script for Beverly Hills bachelor girls requires them to swoon before every celebrity who deigns to invite them out to dinner (and whatever may come after). I liked Hugh. We had dated often before. But it was not my habit to swoon over celebrities simply because they are celebrities. Nor is it now. Actors who crave and receive adulation are tiresome, simply because they are always acting. Politicians— as I was to learn later—are much the same. In fact, most politicians are *always* performing. If they stop and become normal, natural human beings, it must be only in front of their wives or mistresses.

Hugh O'Brian is a likable, gentle, decent person, but I never could develop any romantic interest in him. He was fun to go out with because we always went to interesting places. Once we flew up to Las Vegas and flew back the same evening. We often went to the Ontario Motor Speedway, to dinner at the Bistro, a posh Beverly Hills restaurant, or to parties with lots and lots of fun people. But Hugh never seemed to me totally comfortable with a woman. He believed his image required that he have an attractive woman on his arm when he appeared in public, and so I felt less like a person than like an appendage—or a prop.

Hugh is a very difficult person to really know or understand. He tells you about his life, especially his generous interest in helping orphan boys, but he has no real interest in the lives of the women he dates. This is not my conclusion alone—friends who have dated him feel the same.

After five I arrived home. I just sat, trying to figure out what to do about the evening ahead. From the outside, my apartment resembled a large house more than a six-unit apartment building. There was a certain homeyness about its well-kept lawn and hedges. But best of all it was in Beverly Hills—where I'd always wanted to live. If you are brought up in a poor or struggling middle-class environment in the Los Angeles area, a Beverly Hills address becomes a badge of distinction, something to strive for, something that announces—like a Mercedes Benz or a Rolls Royce in the driveway—that you have arrived, even if you haven't.

Beverly Hills is also clean, protected, and convenient. It is tree-lined and filled with parks. For whatever reason—genetic inheritance, astrological influence, or childhood training—without a clean house and attractive surroundings I am simply miserable. In addition to the cleanliness,

Beverly Hills is blessed with an efficient police department, whose cars patrol regularly and frequently enough to convey a sense of security to all its residents, single or married, male or female. And living there, reasonably close to my office, I could travel the winding canyon road and avoid daily encounters with the chaotic and frightening California freeway traffic.

On this Friday evening, the apartment seemed ever so much more appealing than an invitation to dinner. Deciding not to leave it, I plopped down on the bed by my telephone and wondered what to tell Hugh. I hate to hurt anyone's feelings, and I'm passionately opposed to disrupting any one's plans, no doubt because I am so easily bruised myself. Finally I eliminated all options but one: I would tell Hugh the truth.

He was very sweet. He said he fully understood why I was simply too exhausted to venture out that night. Get some rest, he told me. Once before I had broken a date with Hugh, and that time he sent me flowers. Then he thoughtfully stopped by to see if I needed anything—and I wasn't home! I remember thinking: well, if he sends me flowers *this* time, at least I'll be here. I was determined to vegetate for the entire weekend.

After pouring myself a vodka and water, I sank into the cushiony folds of the sofa, luxuriating in the quiet and the blessed aloneness.

The telephone rang.

Should I answer?

No.

It would be Hugh, persuading me to reconsider, and I would not reconsider.

But if I didn't answer, Hugh would assume I had broken my date with him to go out with somebody else. I think being stood up hurts a male ego even more than it hurts a female ego.

The call could not have been for Pat. One of the luxuries we had allowed ourselves was separate, private telephones. I *had* to answer it.

There was no chance that I would change my mind. Now I was no longer concerned about hurting Hugh's feelings! The original refusal is the most difficult.

I answered—in a voice that I hoped sounded as if I might be in need of a resuscitator: "Hello."

But it wasn't Hugh. The voice was deep and unfamiliar. The conversation went very much like this:

"I'd like to speak with Maureen, please."

"This is Maureen." No more whispering. I was curious.

"Oh, hi," the unfamiliar voice went on. "My name is John Dean. Bill McClain gave me your number and suggested I might call you. I'm a friend of Barry's." (Bill McClain was a California-based aide to Congressman Barry Goldwater, Jr. I had met Bill when I was dating Barry.)

"I'm in from Washington, and Bill said of all the single girls he knows, you're at the top of the list."

For a few seconds, I said nothing. This deep voice sounded rather old for me. I shrugged. One of Goldwater's playboy pals, with a most unoriginal line.

"So what else is new?" I responded, also unoriginally, but I was annoyed. How many other girls had Bill McClain suggested to this fellow? Where did I really fall on the list? How many others had he tried to date?

"I know it's late," he said, ignoring my gibe, "but I was hoping you'd be free for dinner. I know this may sound odd, but I've decided to cancel another blind date another friend here in Los Angeles fixed me up with—some starlet. I didn't really cancel it. I just didn't call after I talked with Bill and he told me I really ought to call you first."

That deep, resonant, ever so polite voice sounded sincere. At a minimum, I was still curious.

"How is Bill? I haven't seen him for some time." (I was testing him. Did he really know Bill McClain?)

"He's fine. He's planning to go to law school. He told

me to tell you hello when I called. (Pause) Do you have any plans this evening?"

"Well . . ." I hesitated. Then something made me say: ". . . not really. I did earlier, but I don't now. I'm kind of . . ."

He interrupted.

"You'd do me a great honor to have dinner with me."

I came to my senses. This was ridiculous.

"I'll be joining the friend I mentioned and his date first for cocktails, and then we'll go to a restaurant near where he lives. I don't know the name of the place."

I didn't want to have dinner with anyone. I had just broken a date. Why on earth would I go out with a perfect stranger? I couldn't even remember the last time I had had a blind date, which is a risky business. I'd never really had to take such a risk.

But I said: "Yes."

I'll never know why.

There is no logical explanation. Every circumstance, even in retrospect, argues against it. His voice was charming, and he was polite and considerate, but for all I knew he could have been sixty years old or weighed 250 pounds. For some reason, I suddenly, miraculously and unconsciously gained a second wind, and the evening of television and reading that had seemed so appealing earlier quickly lost its attraction.

He told me he'd come by in an hour. I had to move fast to get myself together. And then—real panic hit me. What had I done? I couldn't even remember his name. Well, whatever-his-name-was would probably be going back to Washington the next day, so it would be an early evening. I picked out a dress—a camel-colored knit midi—and dark brown boots. As I was scrubbing my face, I looked at myself in the mirror and realized: My God! This is Friday the thirteenth! What in the world am I doing—going out on a blind date on Friday the thirteenth?

I am not superstitious, I always tell myself. But I am not brave enough in my disbelief to flout superstitions. I do not walk under ladders. Nor do I put a hat on a bed or accept a salt shaker from someone before it has been placed on the table. If salt spills, I play it safe and toss some over my shoulder. I *may* be more superstitious than I am willing to admit, even to myself. And even though I do not believe in astrology either, I regularly check my horoscope. And I am not prepared to say it is all hokum. Friday the thirteenth was not a night to venture out with a total stranger. I just had to remember his name! He had mentioned he was staying at the Statler-Hilton, but I couldn't call if I didn't know his name.

Perhaps I should call Bill McClain, but what could sound sillier than my saying: "Bill, I want to break a date with someone you told to call me. What's his name?" I was desperate, but my pride prevailed over my desperation. And I realized that he would be on his way by now.

Nothing could help—except possibly another vodka and water. I had time only for a sip when he knocked.

My apprehensions dissolved like ice cubes dropped into a volcano. There he stood: handsome, medium height, slender, Brooks Brothers glen plaid suit, blue shirt with a button-down collar, wing-tip shoes, a slight tan. (And he wasn't wearing those owlish-looking tortoiseshell glasses I dislike. I didn't see those until later.)

Suddenly it occurred to me that I was in a momentary trance, probably staring at him. I offered him a drink. It had to be vodka, because I seldom drank, Pat didn't drink at all, and there was nothing else to offer.

John (thank goodness he reintroduced himself) strolled around the apartment while I fixed his drink. He said he liked it, and I warmed to that. Pat and I had spent weeks trying to make our living quarters as comfortable and attractive as possible. It was nice to have a stranger perceptive and thoughtful enough to comment favorably on our labors. I felt good about it—and him.

I turned on the stereo. I just knew that something was happening very swiftly. I wanted to be appealing to this man who already was so appealing to me. For the first time in what seemed to me a very long time, I was flirting, and weighing in my mind the various feminine wiles I once employed by design but which I was now allowing to rush out. I remember demurely adjusting the cutaway seam in the front of my midi dress to expose a suitably modest amount of leg.

It was time to make conversation.

"What do you do in Washington?" I asked.

"I'm a lawyer."

"In a law firm?"

"No, I'm . . ."

"On your own?"

"No. I work for the government."

I'm no better at drawing people out than John is at volunteering personal data.

In fact, John turned the conversation from himself to talk about Bill McClain and Barry Goldwater, Jr. This was my first clue to something about John that I was to notice again and again: in social situations, John Dean was most reluctant to talk about where he worked and what he did, even when there was no stigma attached to either. On the other hand, when John had difficulty getting a flight res-ervation or a check cashed, he was not at all bashful about mentioning the White House. And it worked like magic—then.

John told me that he and Barry had been roommates in prep school and close friends ever since.

But I didn't want to dwell on Barry—not that night—I wanted to know more about John.

"Are you a congressman, too?"

"No. Actually, I work at the White House. I'm the counsel to the President."

He said it modestly, but obviously with great pride.

I was impressed. Impressed, but not bowled over. Washington was not a strange, awe-inspiring scene to me. I had lived there for several months, long enough to sense that Washington and Los Angeles are not just different worlds. They're different planets. In Washington, I knew, a person's title and his proximity to power are everything. What you do is more important than who you are. Everyone is interested in the former, hardly anyone in the latter. And when the power is gone, the men who held it and were fawned over yesterday have been forgotten today. And if it's true that Washington is too obsessed with government, it is equally true that Los Angeles is too disinterested. Certainly that was true of me.

John looked too young, I thought, to be a *real* power in the government. But his title—counsel to the President—convinced me that he had to be very bright.

John then asked me about my business, something few men do when they are with women who are considered physically attractive. He listened to me. He appeared to be interested in what I told him. He was certainly different from most of the men I had been dating. He made me feel that I was a person, not an arm piece for the evening, not just another blonde who should be in the chorus line, or an office secretary who wouldn't run too fast if the boss started chasing her.

After a half-hour, we drove in my Thunderbird to an apartment building that was familiar to me—I had dated a man who lived there. We went to the apartment of Paul Frees, a TV and movie figure, and the voice of many animated characters, including the Pillsbury dough boy. Frees, about forty-five, an amusing man and accomplished artist, was interested in media facets of the Nixon administration's drug abuse program. John had met him in Washington.

His much younger girl friend took an immediate interest in John, and I immediately felt jealous, which I didn't understand at all. It seemed ridiculous—I had just met him. She quickly engaged John in conversation, and he displayed more enthusiasm for what she was saying than I thought was warranted. She was working for former Governor Edmund G. (Pat) Brown, who had sent his regards to John, with whom he had worked on a government commission in Washington.

My attempt to divert John with my own sparkling conversation was, initially, a failure. After a drink at Paul's apartment and talk of having another, I knew I had reached my quota. I nudged John, told him I was starving, and thank goodness the four of us left for Stephanino's, a small, dimly lit Italian restaurant operated by Steve Crane, one of Lana Turner's ex-husbands. I told John the story of their daughter (Lana Turner and Steve Crane's), who had gained notoriety years before in connection with the fatal stabbing of one of her mother's lovers. I thought John would be fascinated.

He had no idea what I was talking about.

Why hadn't I ever worked for Pat Brown?

I worried needlessly.

At last, John took over the conversation, and he directed it to me. We talked and talked and talked. We both seemed to realize there was a special magic, and occasionally we found ourselves totally ignoring our host and his friend—who plainly was no longer a threat. We made studied efforts to launch four-way conversations, but managed to fool no one. Seeing what was happening to us, our companions smiled and told us to forget them. At one point Paul said he knew what we were feeling, and was jealous. Then John and I turned and looked into each other's eyes and let the world disappear all over again, including Hugh O'Brian, who, I learned the next day, had dined at the same restaurant. Soon John and I were holding hands under the table. Then there were discreet kisses.

I probably should have objected.

I didn't.

I was falling in love with a man I didn't even know. Hours earlier, I would have said there was no such thing as love at first sight, other than a teenager's first infatuation with a member of the opposite sex. Now, at twenty-five, I knew better.

The beautiful night ended late. We didn't want it to end at all. When we stood at the door of my apartment, I couldn't let him go. Would he care for coffee? He declined. A drink? No. But he made no motion to leave, either. Suddenly and helplessly, we were embracing and exchanging tender, meaningful kisses.

It was too late for John to call a taxi and expect to get one. And we had already agreed to spend the next day together. So I reluctantly told him he could sleep in Pat's bedroom, but that the limits of my generosity extended no further. Frankly, I was surprised at myself for having gone that far. But I wasn't worried. There was something about John that told me I could trust him.

Wondering, worrying, I fell asleep. Nothing I had done all evening made any sense. And yet—in a way I could not then define—everything made perfect sense.

3
The Prelude

She was Irene Kelly Kane to her friends and relatives and neighbors. To me she was once Mommy, then Mom, and sometimes, "Oh, Mother!" In 1962 this stern, demanding, yet always loving woman took my brother Ronnie and me to one side and calmly announced that after thirty-three years of marriage, she and Daddy were getting a divorce.

They were both strong in their Catholicism. But they had grown so far apart that divorce was the only course. Daddy—Sidney Charles Kane—weakened by tuberculosis, had never been strong physically. During six years of their marriage he had been in a hospital, and one of his lungs had been removed. So they had been through difficult times together. But it was time to part.

I can understand now, though I could not then, how mismatched these two wonderful people really were. To me, they seem like two precious stones that sparkle in settings of their own, but somehow lose luster when they are brought together.

Of course, I wept. I loved both parents dearly. But divorce was not exactly a new phenomenon to anyone living in southern California, and Mom was so down-to-earth, matter-of-fact, and resolute. I was sixteen at the time. We were grown up now, Mother said. Soon we would be living our own lives. She was determined to live hers.

As far as luster is concerned, Mother had an enormous

advantage over Daddy. His was a subdued glow: solid, dependable, durable. But to me, he was the greatest. He was an avid reader who retained all that he read, and his major interest was world politics. When he was younger, he had won a scholarship to the University of California at Berkeley. After working as a soda jerk and a runner on Wall Street, he got a job as a dancer in a Broadway show, which is how he met Mom. After they were married, he became an apprentice diamond setter at the suggestion of his older brother, Frederick. When my uncle moved his business to California, Daddy followed. From then on he always worked as a diamond setter, never earning a great deal of money.

Mother was a Ziegfeld Follies beauty in the 1930s. She could have had a career as an actress, stage or screen, but the life simply did not appeal to her. What a beauty she was! I still have some of her photographs and newspaper clippings. The photographs show that she was—there is no other word for it—a knockout. A natural blonde, with her hair pulled back in a bun, she was statuesque, wore a sweet, vivacious expression on her face, and had a gorgeous figure.

She attracted more eyes than just Ziegfeld's, I'm sure. In fact, she went on to appear in a musical on Broadway, starring a young comedian with an absurd ski-slope nose—named Bob Hope. In the chorus line, great beauty is absolutely essential; talent is helpful, but not necessary. Mom had sufficient beauty to land in the first row of the chorus, but she was not the star. She was such formidable competition, however, that the female lead insisted she be removed from the front row and relegated to a position where her physical attributes would distract fewer eyes from the star performer. Mother was furious, but she couldn't quit. She needed the job. Later, she captured a part in a play starring Alfred Lunt and Lynn Fontanne.

But Mom felt there was something missing in show business life. She dated a lot, but never got caught up in the party swirl. Most often when the show was over, she would head straight for home. When Daddy came along, she fell in love. After they were married and moved to California, she began a new career: housewife.

Different forces must have been at war within Irene Kelly. There was the strong hold of her Catholicism, which obliged her to marry a Catholic, and to have children, and to bring them up in the Catholic religion. Yet religion did not bring her the sense of security it brings to some— security for herself and her family. Daddy's uncertain health made insecurity a permanent dweller in our home. Mother could have married a wealthy actor or producer, but she happened to fall in love with a diamond setter. She willingly gave up riches and the chance to escape into that world where economic and social struggle had already resulted in victory.

For many years, ill fortune seemed to dog her footsteps. During the period of Daddy's illness, her own father and two of her sisters were killed in an automobile accident. She had to return to New York to be with her mother, and for many years she helped my grandmother financially and in every other possible way.

Ronnie did not come along until after fifteen years of marriage. I was born three and a half years later. Until I was four years old, I had no hair, the result of a scalp disease I was born with. I remember Mother rubbing olive oil on my head daily, massaging my scalp, and providing me with an assortment of bonnets to wear when she took me any place. Then suddenly, all my hair just popped out.

Perhaps it was a result of all that scrubbing, but somehow very early in life I acquired a fetish for cleanliness. Every time I got a spot on my clothes, I would change them, which sometimes meant five or six changes a day. I'm still the same way.

Mom and I were always very close. When Ronnie and I

were small, she took us with her every place she went. We never had a baby sitter in our lives. It was clear that she valued her children more than anything, and that she never regretted having given up a glamorous career. She always thought her children were the reward she received for having done so.

Other than my mother, my environment played the major role in forming my character and personality—particularly in instilling a dreadful feeling of insecurity that has so often plagued me.

My upbringing took place in circumstances I can best describe this way: We Kanes and our immediate neighbors lived in Mar Vista, California, the hole in a doughnut of affluence. Granted such a situation is not unique, it nonetheless gave some of us who simply glimpsed the glitter, glamor, and gloss a deep sense of inferiority and insecurity. Our home in Mar Vista was small, Spanish-style, comfortable. Had it been located in Topeka, Kansas, or Brownsville, Texas, my feeling about it probably would have been entirely different. Then it would have been the same as most other homes. And had it been in Topeka or Brownsville, perhaps I would have acquired a different set of values.

But it *was* in Mar Vista, and it *was* near Beverly Hills, an area dominated by vast estates, where private swimming pools are commonplace, where Cadillacs and Lincolns and Mercedes Benzes and even Rolls Royces fill the parking areas, or glide grandly down Sunset Boulevard, often with a uniformed chauffeur at the wheel. This was a nearby world that we definitely were not a part of, and yet we could not avoid seeing it daily. I still remember seeing the magnificent limousines pull up to the occasional mansion that was not hidden by shrubbery, and peering intently as the glamorous and finely plumed women (how many were movie stars?) alighted.

Irene Kelly Kane was not spellbound by this world that

was so near at hand and so far beyond her grasp. She could have been part of it, but she had made her choice. What she did want, however, was security for her children. So one day she accepted a humdrum job with the Hughes Aircraft Company, and worked hard at it for twenty years, so that her children could attend good private schools and enjoy other advantages. Her motivations were the best, but for me there was one adverse and lasting effect.

I suppose I became most keenly aware of my family's comparatively deprived state when Mother took me out of the Grandview Boulevard public school and enrolled me at the Notre Dame Girls' Academy in Beverly Hills. I liked school—the classes—moderately well, but the affluence of so many of my classmates completely intimidated me. They were the children of the economically well-to-do, and being among them did nothing for my sense of self, my self-confidence, or my sense of values.

I had always been shy. Now I was literally looking for a place to hide. All-girls slumber parties were the rage, but how could I ever have one at my home after seeing what really went on inside the doors of those magnificent estates? —servants to prepare and serve your meals, huge rooms with huge beds, intercom systems so the girls in one bedroom could chat and giggle with the girls in the others, swimming pools and tennis courts, sometimes even small movie theaters. I could never invite these friends to my humble home—never.

This atmosphere had a strong impact on me. When I was among moneyed people, I was miserable. But I was also becoming aware of how nice it would be to *be* one of them.

I don't remember the exact year when boys first paid attention to me—probably around the seventh or eighth grade—but I do remember their names: Billy Kirkham and Jimmy Webb. They liked me, but I pretended not to notice. It was the year I finally got the braces off my teeth.

My first date was with—literally—the boy next door, Jimmy Miller, when I was about fourteen.

I did not then—and don't now—consider myself a great beauty. In fact, I suspect that Jimmy probably dated me at the urging of his mother. But to my complete astonishment, I was once named "best-looking" in one of those silly little contests held at school. When I first heard there was to be such a contest, I knew exactly who would win it: Laura Montalban, now a model for Bill Blass, whose classic beauty was evident to me even then. Later Laura was recognized for her grace, poise, and features so fine they could have been carved from stone. She had the same qualities then, but few noticed them.

The "best-looking" (I can't call it beauty, and neither could they) contest was about the extent of my extracurricular activities at Notre Dame Girls' Academy. I never stayed for field hockey or basketball games or to work on student publications, dance committees, or anything of the sort. I had to get home right after school so Mom wouldn't worry about me. My grades were all right, but no more than that—mostly C's and B's. I had no time for anything extracurricular. During the Christmas holidays one year, I worked as a wrapper in a jewelry store. Then I got a job as an assistant in the dietary department of a hospital, setting up trays for patients whose ailments required that they eat only special kinds of foods. It was hard work, wedged in between classes I had to attend in the daytime and homework I was assigned to do at night. I was almost fired for consistently showing up late, but someone was needed, and there weren't too many applicants, so I managed to stay on.

After being graduated without honors, I didn't really know what I wanted to do next. I would have liked to have gone away to college, but I was only seventeen, and Mother wouldn't hear of it. I also knew that there were very few vocations that I was equipped for. I was clearly not qualified to do anything really challenging or exciting, and it was a little early for Sir Galahad to appear on the horizon. Like so many young, restless, dissatisfied high school graduates, unable to make decisions about the future, I "drifted," working that summer as a telephone information operator, until the sheer boredom of it compelled me to do something with myself. I enrolled at Santa Monica City College, somewhat to my own surprise.

During my freshman year, my father died. I found his death terribly difficult to accept. But it had happened. I had always wanted, needed, and had a daddy, and now, even though he hadn't been living with us, he was really gone. I know Mother loved him until the end, although they could not communicate with each other and live together.

After Daddy's death, I was again plunged into unhappiness and indecision. Finally I decided that even though I was completely unprepared for a career, I could not remain in college for long. The money was not there. I would have to find whatever work there was, save my money, and return to school when I could afford it.

"Whatever work there was" turned out to be a job as a part-time secretary with the Wilkinson Insurance Agency. I loved it.

Having few options, I stayed with the job and managed to save a little money. A year earlier I had wanted to enroll at College of the Desert in Palm Desert, California. This desire was not dictated by academic standing, excellence of faculty, or quality or variety of the curriculum. The major attraction was Michael Biner, a very sweet and thoughtful young man who was president of the student body and whom I had met on a blind date—I think on a Friday the thirteenth. I never did enroll, and so for a while Michael Biner disappeared from my life. And while he was out of it, I dated another Michael. His last name was Schwab, and his greatest claim to fame was that his father owned the Hollywood drugstore where Lana Turner was "discovered" and quickly converted into "the sweater girl," the image that gained her instant movie fame and fortune.

But Michael Schwab was wealthy and moved in some of the "better" Beverly Hills social circles. I put "better" in quotes because my association with these West Coast "socialites" brought me the most frightening and possibly the stupidest episode of my life.

At one of those Beverly Hills parties I attended at this time, I met an older man, older to me because he was in his early forties and I was only eighteen. He had been married before, was apparently quite wealthy, and he quickly became infatuated with me. After a comparatively short time he asked me to marry him.

He certainly was no Sir Galahad, but he seemed to me to be a person who could provide the kind of security that I must have been looking for. Of course, I was confused. I didn't love this man, but Mom had married for love and had spent her life struggling to keep her home and family together. After thirty-three years, she had been divorced. And Beverly Hills, where the divorce rate must be as high as anywhere in the world, is not a place where the classic storybook romance is a tale that carries much credence. It's difficult to convince children whose parents are getting divorced that true love exists, and is enduring.

Of course, I realize that there were many happy marriages in Beverly Hills, but children in Beverly Hills do not usually grow up expecting to find the perfect mate and to live happily ever after. Marriage and marriage-for-love are not accorded the veneration they receive in middle America, nor are they looked upon as so lasting.

I took a look at myself and my prospects, and it was obvious that I was not about to embark on a promising career, nor was I in love with anyone my own age. I guess I was also fascinated by jet travel and the world on whose fringes I had dwelt but never belonged to. When my not quite Sir Galahad insisted that I fly to New York with him to buy an engagement ring and to do some other shopping for the wedding, Mom thought I should say yes. I did too.

I had never been on an airplane before, and the thought of the flight east excited me more than the prospect of marriage. It is clear now that I was blinded to what became disaster by the dazzle of the world that I thought I—at long last—was about to enter.

In New York we had a suite at the Regency. We looked at rings, and he bought one for me. We had dinner and a rather pleasant evening, at the end of which I think he fully expected me to go to bed with him. I did not. The next day he gave me back my airline ticket and some money, and I made my second airplane trip, this one—thank God—to home.

Mother was beside herself. She could not believe she had sent her daughter off on something so awful.

About one month later, he telephoned, sent flowers, and was very apologetic. He said he could not explain his behavior, but wanted to be forgiven. After several calls, I finally agreed to go to dinner with him. He was wearing a 9½-carat diamond ring on his little finger, which struck me as odd, to say the least.

On my nineteenth birthday, he took me to a party at Patti Page's home, and then to the Daisy, an exclusive private club in Beverly Hills, where, in front of several people, he gave me the diamond ring as a birthday present.

Of course, he kept insisting that I marry him, and I kept telling him not now—wait. I can see now I was in a situation from which I could not extricate myself—I just didn't know how. He even went ahead and ordered a wedding dress specially designed for me.

But finally I decided I just couldn't go through with it, no matter how much money he had or how much security he could provide. Even though nothing similar to the New York experience ever recurred, I couldn't put it out of my mind. The world of "glitter" I had looked upon all my life—like a child with her nose pressed against the candy store window—was missing a few essentials. I stopped returning his telephone calls.

Years later, this same person was quoted in one of those horrible national weekly gossip papers as saying that John Dean's wife had stolen a ring from him. He also said that I had once lived with him. Neither story is true.

I did keep the ring on the advice of an attorney who told me it was a gift and I was entitled to it. It was an $18,000 ring, insured for $25,000, that I sold for $12,000, of which $4,000 went to the attorney. I gave $5,000 to my brother to open a business, made a $1,500 downpayment on a Thunderbird for myself, and gave $1,500 to Mom to help with bills. There was a lawsuit over the ring, and I gave a deposition. He lost the case, and I thought that a sordid chapter of my life was over. Except for his late attempt to cash in on some cheap publicity when John and I were in all the newspapers and magazines and on television, it was.

Michael Biner's timing was always perfect. He always seemed to be there when I needed him most. Just as I was escaping from this nightmare, Mike called and we became good friends again after several years of silence. We dated several times and had loads of fun. But I needed to get away from unpleasant memories. I applied for a job as a stewardess with American Airlines, and was sent to Fort Worth, Texas, for training. I felt as if I were back at a girls' school again.

Though I liked what I was doing—as an interim activity —I never became really fond of flying. But at least I was earning a living for myself, and I was also *away* from the nightmare of the previous year. After receiving my wings, I was based at Dallas, flying to Memphis, Nashville, and New York. For a while I also flew the late-night flight (the "red eye special") from Dallas to Phoenix. The only really famous passenger I ever served was Van Cliburn, the celebrated concert pianist. I never dated pilots—or anyone, for that matter, until . . .

Again my life became a hopeless tangle. Some friends I had met at the swimming pool where we lived in Dallas invited me to have lunch with them. They asked if I would like to bring a male friend and I said no. Would I mind if they invited a friend of theirs and made it a foursome? No.

And that is how I met George Owen, who was then a scout for the Dallas Cowboys professional football team, which was owned by his friend Clint Murchison. George was forty years old. He was great fun, and we got along famously. And then we got very serious—*very* serious. On April Fools' Day 1967, we were married.

We had no major problems for six weeks, and then we had a really major problem: I learned that George was still married to singer Diane Wisdom. The matter of divorcing her before marrying me apparently had not struck him as being of vital importance, but it was terribly important to me. I moved out immediately and flew back to mother.

In California again, I threw myself back into the arms of Michael Biner. Never in my life had I been more hurt and confused. I thought I had been through enough, and nothing had worked out well at all. But rather than solve my problems, I compounded them.

Mike and I drove to Tia Juana, Mexico, where he begged me to marry him. I told him I couldn't—I didn't know the status of my marriage to George, for one thing. Mike had warned me against marrying George in the first place, and he convinced me that the marriage was null and void anyway since George was already married when he married me.

All right. Michael was the one—the only one—who had truly loved me through the years. I didn't want to be alone and on my own again. So I said yes. Mike and I were married in a quickie ceremony in Tia Juana.

When we arrived back home, Mike was afraid to tell his parents that we were married. I couldn't believe it. He said they would object and maybe disinherit him because they thought he was too young for marriage, and because they would be outraged at not having their son married in a big wedding befitting their social status. And perhaps they would not be overly pleased at Michael's having married me, a woman who already had a tangled marital history.

We argued and argued, and again I went back to mother, in tears. I was beginning to feel like a yo-yo, and I certainly was behaving like one.

George had been calling me frantically from New Orleans, where he was then working with the New Orleans Saints, and I agreed to talk to him. He could straighten everything out, he said, and he begged me to return. Believe it or not, I did.

I suppose I thought I was getting back at George by marrying Michael, and getting back at Michael by returning to George. But in reality I was wounding myself more than anyone else.

I went back to George Owen, and for at least one reason I'm glad I did. In New Orleans, I met Paul and Pat Hornung, and Pat became one of my dearest friends.

I stayed with George for a few weeks, not knowing for certain if I was Mrs. Owen or Mrs. Biner. George traveled a lot—without me—so while he was on one of his trips, I decided this was not the life for me and I left, returning once again to Los Angeles. George still hadn't managed to get a divorce, and I was beginning to realize that he wasn't trying very hard.

Mike and I talked only briefly. I told him I could not resume our life together, that I had to go away and try to get my head together. I chose Lake Tahoe, where I stayed with a new and good friend I had met through George, Heidi Rikan. I skied, swam, gambled, played tennis, and hiked. I lost weight, going from 115 to 98 pounds, and from a size 6 to a size 3. George saw me once during this period and handed me $200. "My God, you're starving," he said. "Go fatten yourself up."

After several months with Heidi, I finally decided that I had to straighten out my tangled marital situation, so I sought and got an annulment of my marriage to George Owen.

At my invitation, Michael came up to Tahoe and we talked everything out. Then we returned to Los Angeles, told his parents that we were married, and they accepted the fact. We rented an apartment, and I vowed to live a "normal" life from then on.

And for a while life was normal, comparatively speaking.

We lived together quite happily for about a year, then we began quarreling. Something negative had seemed to hover over our relationship from the beginning. Maybe part of the problem was that I knew Michael would always be there to fall back on. I didn't treat him as well as I should have. He deserved much better.

In the summer of 1969, I left Mike. I didn't want it to be a permanent separation. We were just two angry young people, neither sufficiently mature to handle the situation. Rather than face up to and resolve our problems, I took my usual route—escape.

Heidi, the friend I had stayed with in Lake Tahoe, now lived in Washington, D.C., and she had often invited me to visit her. Since Mike and I were having such a rocky time, going to visit Heidi seemed the wisest thing to do. I spent a month in Washington with Heidi, and then persuaded her to drive back to California with me. Heidi was single, well-to-do, and had plenty of spare time, so we piled into her new Corvette and headed west.

On July 4, 1969, we were both frightened nearly to death

by a close brush with an oncoming automobile. Both cars were traveling at high speeds in opposite directions, and how we missed a head-on collision, I'll never know.

On that same day, at almost the same hour, Michael Biner was not so fortunate.

Driving a 1969 Corvette identical to Heidi's, he collided with another automobile on a California highway.

Michael Biner died instantly.

4
How to Succeed
in Government
Without Trying at All

It had been almost two years since Michael's death, and now on Saturday morning, the day after John Dean and I had met and shared an apartment, though not a bed, John said he had to see some people concerning property the Nixon Foundation was interested in acquiring for a presidential library. I was disappointed. Saturday was the day we had planned to spend together, since John had to return to Washington on Sunday. Darn! This was to be only the first of many experiences—including our first and second honeymoons—when John's duties would intrude on my plans to be alone with him. I never won any of these unequal contests.

John rejoined me later on Saturday, but the time and where we were going, I don't recall. I do remember that as we drove along in my Thunderbird, John turned up the volume on the car radio and tenderly, somewhat shyly, asked me to listen. I did. Neither of us has ever forgotten the lyrics of the popular song that was being played:

> This morning I woke up with this feeling
> I didn't know how to deal with . . .
> . . . . . .

> I think I love you,
> So what am I afraid of?
> I'm afraid that I'm not sure of
> A love there is no cure for.*

The song said it all for both of us. We did think we loved each other, but we both knew that love lies along a terribly rocky path, and we had both stumbled along it before. Individually we both knew how easy it is to confuse infatuation with love, because in the beginning they are the same. But one falls away, and the other becomes strong and durable.

The feeling I had toward John was different from any I had experienced toward anyone before. Still, I already had two strikes against me, and I didn't want a third. John had told me the night before that his marriage to Karla Hennings, the daughter of former United States Senator Thomas Hennings of Missouri, had failed, so I knew he wanted to be very cautious also. Neither of us wanted to call our feelings love and not infatuation, although even then we suspected that that is what they were.

We weren't entirely truthful with each other that day—the way we are now. John told me he had been married to Karla and that they had a son, John W. Dean IV (true), and that they were now divorced (false—the decree did not become final for several months). I think I skipped over some of the details of my background, too. Who wouldn't have?

The men John was working with in Los Angeles were Mike Sonnenreich, a brilliant young attorney who had arrived from Washington, and Frank DeMarco, a partner of President Nixon's personal attorney, Herbert Kalmbach.

John asked Mike to join us for dinner that evening, and assigned me to get him a dinner companion. I invited my former next-door neighbor, Evelyn Miller, and the four of us had dinner at a Japanese restaurant in the Hollywood

---

* "I Think I Love You," Tony Romeo. Copyright © 1970 by Screen Gems-Columbia Music, Inc. Used by permission. All rights reserved.

Hills. This second evening John and I had together was a repeat of the first, only worse. I mean *better*. More hand holding. More stolen kisses. More staring into each other's eyes. More conversations that shut out not only our guests, but the whole rest of the world. I remember Evelyn saying (who can blame her?):

"Can you believe those two? They're so obnoxious."

It was true.

That night, Evelyn stayed with me, and John took my car back to the hotel. Our goodbyes were loving and warm, but most important they were full of assurances that we'd see each other again—in just a few weeks. On Sunday morning, Evelyn drove me into town to pick up the T-Bird. John had left the key in an envelope at the desk, and as I opened it, I really felt the full force of an unpleasant fact: he was gone! How I had *not* wanted him to leave. But there had been so much talk of "When are you coming west?" and "When are you coming east?" that I had temporarily put the reality of our separation out of my head. Now it was there.

With everyone I meet I form an immediate and very strong impression, and ninety percent of the time I'm right. I just knew I couldn't be wrong about John Dean. It is true that I was very ready to fall in love, anxious to fill that terrible void, that emptiness in my life.

As I drove alone back to Beverly Hills, I thought about Michael Biner. Our marriage had failed because of my shortcomings, not his. I thought at the time that he was the immature one, but in reality I was. Mike was an over-the-counter stockbroker. He had to leave home very early in the morning because the stock market opens in the east at 10 A.M., which is only 7 A.M. in Los Angeles. So Mike arose early, came home early, and needed to go to bed early. I wanted to—and did—sleep late, and I wanted to stay out late at night and have fun. We were both very young, just into our twenties, and we had little money and few luxuries. Mike's parents lived a block and a half away, and my mother was only a mile away. Mike was his parents' "baby," and I suppose that's why I felt he was immature.

But my own immaturity was of a different sort. I couldn't bear the thought of living a routine existence, with dullness and financial struggle the main characteristics; and Mike was so possessive I developed a feeling of claustrophobia. Instead of appreciating his love, I felt suffocated by it. It wasn't his fault; he was being kind, loving, and gentle—qualities too rare to be spurned. But I didn't understand and I spurned them.

As I drove along, I began to compare John with Mike, thus confirming to myself what serious thoughts I was having about John. Even then I realized that the two men were not at all alike. In the first place, John was seven years older than I. When John took me into his arms, I felt so secure—the way I'd felt when my father held me. He was like my father in other ways—a Brooks Brothers type, someone who read everything he could lay his hands on, someone who knew so much about what was going on in the world. Maybe I should not be the way I am, but there's no helping it—I *need* someone. A father. A husband. Someone to depend on. I have no wish to be independent. To me, being independent is being lonely.

As these thoughts were going through my mind, John was flying east. I'm sure I was several leagues ahead of him in mentally mapping out a future for us. But I'm like that, and I think many women have to be like that.

For two days, I waited for John to telephone. I literally waited on the edge of my chair, but every time the phone rang, the wrong party was on the other end of the line.

Well, I had to say to myself, you weren't making as much progress as you thought you were. It was distressing. I really worried, because I really cared.

At last the phone rang, and the caller was John.

He asked me to come east for the Thanksgiving holidays. I suppose I should have expressed shock, but I didn't feel it. Perhaps I should have said something demure, but I did not feel demure. I think I am honest because dishonest words always seem to get stuck in my throat. There was something very beautiful developing between this man and me, and I knew it whether he did or not.

So I said: "Yes, yes, yes!"

John made reservations for us to fly to the Virgin Islands, and we spent seven absolutely heavenly days there. The legendary Aunt Mamie of Dubuque and several of my own real aunts would hope that at this point I would explain that we were chaperoned every moment, and that we stayed at different hotels, but there's that terrible problem of dishonest words. It carries over to my pen.

Days that I cherish as I do those days in late November 1970 just can't have anything really wrong about them. Yes—we made love, and it was beautiful. There was nothing cheap about it. We knew we cared for each other in a very special way. In my own mind, there was not the slightest doubt that we would be married some day. We simply had to be together—totally together. I wished the week would never end. But of course it did.

All the way back to Washington we talked of nothing except when we would see each other again. Christmas? Of course, although it seemed terribly far away. But it was the best we could do. John would come to Los Angeles for the holidays.

As I flew west alone, I did not feel lonely—for the first time in years and years. That terrible void in my life had been filled.

Not at that time nor at any other time did I think that it would be thrilling to be with a man who was close to the President of the United States. I rarely gave a thought to President Nixon, the White House, the famous people, and the centers of power in Washington. All that I wanted was to be with John Dean, whether he was counsel to the President or a lifeguard on the beach at Santa Monica. This may clash sharply with my acknowledged fondness for material comforts, but perhaps I was growing up—or just changing.

I didn't really know then and don't know for certain now when romance ripened into love for me, but I did know that it had happened, that it was more wonderful than anything that had ever happened to me before and even more wonderful than anything I could ever have imagined. I was flying back to California in a plane—but I think I could have done all right without one. I know how great I felt, and I was sure I looked a lot better, too. A woman does when she loves a man—and is loved by a man. You can see it in her eyes, her face, her smile. My mother saw it all, and it even made her feel and look better. Since Ronnie and I were born, there had never been any way for Mother to be happy unless we were happy. And she knew I had not been happy in a long, long while.

Now every day was thirty hours long. I didn't think Christmas would ever come.

I was right.

For me, it never did.

John let me down gently. He would not be able to come to California for Christmas. Business, he said. Karla and JWD IV, I thought. I was correct, though John didn't admit it for months.

But there was also some good news. He would visit me in Los Angeles for New Year's. Well, I wanted him for both holidays, but I consoled myself with the half-loaf.

I also made up my mind that when John returned to Washington, I would fly back with him, move in again with Heidi, find a job—and during my off hours make certain that my interests in John were fully protected.

When I told Mom, she did not chide me—she could see how happy I was. But Ronnie was terribly angry. He accused me of being slightly flaky to consider giving up my job and rushing off to the unknown in Washington in pursuit of a man I scarcely knew.

Ronnie labored under a misapprehension common to most men: that the male should pursue the female and not vice versa. I think Ronnie was disturbed also because he had been close to Michael Biner, and because my past track record had been so poor. He argued that I knew too little about John, and he had no reason to assume that John's intentions were honorable.

Ronnie's thinking was sensible, but sensible thinking is no match for a woman's intuition.

John came west for New Year's, and we had glorious times together. My next-door neighbors, the Millers, gave me a farewell party, and Mom came over to meet John for the first time. She liked him immediately, as I'd known she would. But Ronnie refused to come to the party at all. During the evening, I became terribly upset and telephoned him, but he wouldn't even talk to me. His wife Jayne said that he was "very upset" with me. I don't like having anyone upset with me, and when it is someone I love, like Ronnie, I can barely stand it. Even when Mom invited John to spend the last night before we left in her home, Ronnie refused to drop by or even call to say goodbye to me.

That was the only sad note in a life that was newly melodious for me, but it was an especially sad one. Some day, Ronnie would know I was right, I told myself.

On January 4, 1971, my new life really began. John and I flew to Washington, and I "moved in" with Heidi. But I stayed with John. That was inevitable, but it was not the original intent. My mail came to Heidi's apartment, most of my clothes were deposited there, but I kept running out there to pick up more things that I needed where most of my time was spent—at John's two-bedroom town house on Princess Street in Alexandria, Virginia, just across the Potomac River from Washington.

At heart I'm an interior designer. I just love to choose furniture, draperies, carpeting, and make everything blend and look just right together. John had only recently bought the house, and there was so much to be done—all of which I loved doing. While he worked in the White House, I looked all around the area for the dozens of things he needed and became more familiar with Washington, a city I really had known only slightly from past visits.

Then—as now—John and I were enough company for each other. Then—as now—we most enjoyed being together, just the two of us, and so we did very little socializing. Larry Higby (he was Bob Haldeman's top White House assistant) and his wife came to dinner once with Bruce Kehrli (another Haldeman aide) and his wife. And we saw quite a bit of John's deputy White House counsel, Fred Fielding, and his wife Maria, who lived nearby. But for a long time we avoided the big cocktail parties and embassy parties that White House people are always invited to.

Most nights John would get home between seven and eight o'clock, though sometimes it was later. We would have cocktails, then dinner. We'd talk and talk, and then maybe we would listen to music, depending on our mood. We called these our "two-person parties," and it went on like this for months. A few of our very close friends knew we were living together, but most people did not. John's parents knew and I'm sure disapproved, but they said nothing.

I just always assumed John was going to marry me. Later —much later—I discovered we had some difference of opinion on that subject, but during those first months of living together, it was just understood.

At least *I* understood it.

After about six weeks, the town house looked just right, and it was time for me to find a job. A government job. It was unbelievably easy. My experience—repeated thousands of times every year—may say something about why our government does not function more efficiently than it does.

I had absolutely no qualifications for a job in Washington—though I think I acquired some rather quickly. But the point is that often in Washington it isn't what you know but who you know that determines whether or not you work, and to what level you rise and how swiftly.

There are hundreds of jobs one can get without having to take a civil service examination. Recognizing my limitations, I decided to try for one of those. I called Mike Sonnenreich, who had had dinner with John and me and Evelyn that night in Los Angeles. Mike was then deputy chief counsel for the Bureau of Narcotics and Dangerous Drugs, and he was able to help me get a temporary appointment as a clerk, at very low pay. It was to last only three weeks, but a new commission was just about to be organized—in Washington, new commissions are always being organized —and perhaps there would be something for me there. My chances were not at all impaired by the fact that I was highly recommended by the counsel to the President of the United States, who also had named Mike to his job, and had named the presidential appointees to the commission. In fact, my chances might otherwise have been zip.

At the end of three weeks, Mike told me that I had been hired to organize the new National Commission on Marihuana and Drug Abuse. "But Mike—I don't know how to organize a commission," I cried. "What do I do?"

Said Mike: "Just do it."

"But I don't even know where to start."

Mike told me where to start. In order to arrange for office space and furniture, I should contact the GSA.

"The GSA? How can I contact the GSA when I don't even know what the GSA is?"

Washington is like that. It's a city of acronyms. Everyone who has been there for some time talks in a foreign language. It's "send this over to DOD" or HUD or DOT or

DOS or HEW or OEO. The people I worked with used to panic when I'd have to ask what DOD or HEW was. It was as if someone had wandered into an Elks Club headquarters and asked what B.P.O.E. stood for. It was weeks before I knew instantly that DOD was the Department of Defense, HUD was the Department of Housing and Urban Development, DOS was the Department of State, HEW was the Department of Health, Education and Welfare, and OEO was the Office of Economic Opportunity.

And, oh, yes—GSA was the General Services Administration.

While learning the language, and the ropes, I smiled, batted my eyes a lot—and found that people really were very helpful. My title was executive assistant to the executive director—titles are terribly important in Washington, and that one wasn't bad. I hired several secretaries for the office, including one for Mike, but she and I had a personality conflict almost from the start and that did not work out. I was paid $10,000 a year, and I really worked hard "mothering" everyone.

It was up to me to have everything in perfect order for meetings that were held, and for luncheons and dinners involving the director and the commissioners. And when they traveled—as they frequently did, to meetings and conventions in the United States and abroad—I would "advance" the trips, much in the manner that a political campaign advance team does. I would travel to the designated city ahead of the commissioners, select the hotels for them to stay in and the hotel dining rooms for the luncheons and banquets, decide on the menus, organize schedules, make all the arrangements. I was astonished at how quickly I caught on. In the next fourteen months I made several trips—to Los Angeles, Dallas, Chicago, San Francisco, New Orleans. I also traveled to London, Amsterdam, Paris, Madrid, and Geneva.

These were business trips, but there were others I took

for pleasure. For me they were also a test. I don't like to go places alone, and yet that is what I had to do. I flew alone, stayed alone, shopped alone, dined alone, went sight-seeing alone. I didn't like it at all, but I had to prove something to myself, and to John. My love for John forced me to *manage*, and I did. At the time it didn't surprise me in the least. Now I don't know how on earth I did it.

Another part of my assignment took an ironic twist later in my life. Mike Sonnenreich asked me to do a report on some of the drug rehabilitation programs being conducted in various prisons around the country. I visited both Danbury in Connecticut and Terminal Island in California, sat in—as the only woman—at encounter group sessions, and examined other facets of the programs. I never expected to use my knowledge of federal prisons in the way that I eventually did: later describing them to my husband when he realized he could be imprisoned in one of them some day.

Wherever I went, my job always included attendance at large embassy parties. I got to meet a number of United States ambassadors, including James Mittendorf, who was our ambassador to the Netherlands, and Walter Annenberg, then the ambassador to the Court of St. James. Mittendorf was very kind, and I think Annenberg would have been. But an odd coincidence touched off a strange incident during a party at the embassy in London in the fall of 1971.

My hairdo and dress made some people comment that I resembled the women in the impressionist paintings that decorated the walls of several rooms of the embassy. After meeting me, Annenberg almost seemed to think that I must really have been a character in one of the paintings, and that somehow I had come to life and was wandering around the embassy, looking at other paintings.

Or perhaps he didn't think that at all. If he did not, then I don't know what he thought. But I don't believe I would have liked whatever it was.

I would step from one room to another. Within seconds, the ambassador would be by my side. I would step out of that room and into another. Then I would steal a glance over my shoulder and see—right! Annenberg. Then I would double back into the first room, smile demurely, pretend that I was not self-conscious, and know he would soon be there.

I couldn't avoid him short of fleeing the party, which I had no intention of doing, so I just stood there, waiting for him to strike up a conversation, which he very quickly did.

This was not my first experience with important men who somehow believe that their positions of power make them irresistible to young women. Nor was it to be my last. There are different ways to handle such situations, which arise with "government girls," because high-ranking officials think government offices and commissions are staffed with women noted less for their skills than for their compatibility.

On a previous commission trip, for another example, I had a problem with another high government official. He seemed to assume that his prominence entitled him to grab me, one of the commission's minions, and hold me so tightly I was afraid he would break my ribs.

We were in London, so the mix was explosive: a middle-aged man away from home and drinking a bit too much, a young single woman on the payroll, and a big hotel where "no one will ever know." After dinner was over, I returned to my room and prepared to go to bed. Then there was a knock on the door.

"Who is it?" I called out.

"Me," he answered.

Oh. Well, what could he want? I had an idea, but I wasn't sure. Besides, technically he was my boss.

So I opened the door.

My memory is of what seemed to be a pair of disembodied arms flying through the door. They were very long arms, and they grabbed me and held me tight.

"Stop, stop!" I cried. "You've got the wrong idea."

Eventually, he got the right idea, and relaxed his grip. After trying a little "friendly persuasion," which didn't work, he left. I heaved a sigh of relief, secured the door from the inside, and went to bed.

Annenberg's intentions were not so lacking in subtlety, and for all I knew they were perfectly innocent. But after several months in government I had become exceedingly leery of important men, so many of whom assume that special privileges go along with their importance. I said something very haughty—perhaps even rude—and, perhaps coincidentally, that was the last I saw of Ambassador Annenberg.

My European business and pleasure trips had consumed several weeks, and I was anxious to get back to John. Sometimes when I was sent on trips, I had a vague suspicion that John was not all that unhappy about being left alone. Occasionally I would return to find all of my possessions neatly hidden away, out of sight of anyone who might have been in the house during my absence. When confronted, John wouldn't lie, but he wouldn't really respond either. He'd change the subject, speak in generalities, or otherwise put me off.

But I never had an experience quite like the one that hit me like a bolt of lightning when I returned from a vacation trip to Europe.

My plane landed in New York, and I immediately telephoned John in Washington to give him the glad tidings— I was back! He was not exactly ecstatic. In the past, John had occasionally seemed aloof and distant from me, but this was something more serious. I felt it. Was he angry because I had stayed away so long? That must be it. I had gone in part with the intent of making him realize he could not live without me. With a growing sense of panic, I realized that the trip had had the precise opposite effect.

When I told John I would be home that evening, he suggested I not come to his place. I couldn't believe it! What could have happened? John told me, as gently as he could on the telephone, that he was going to try to make a go of it with Karla. There was no gentle way to tell me something like that!

"What will I do?" I cried. "Where will I go? Can't I just stay with you for a little while until I can sort things out?" He said he thought it best that I not.

I felt lost. My new life—the life that was to go on forever —was over. Every morning since I had met John I had awakened with a certain zest for life, an anticipation of something good happening that day—seeing John, or getting a telephone call from him. He had come to be my reason for living. Now I couldn't be sure there was any reason.

In a daze, I flew back to Washington and arranged to stay with Candy Cowan, who had become a very close friend.

After unpacking my suitcases at Candy's, I telephoned Maria Fielding, told her what had happened, and that John and I were through. Maria somehow arranged to have John as a dinner guest at her home that night—before, during, and after which she gave him a piece of her mind. She insisted that he see me—it was the very least he could do. But by then, he told Maria, he was "afraid" to see me.

"Well, have another drink, and then go see her," she suggested.

He did.

John knew I would be going to Candy's—I had no place else in Washington to go. That night he telephoned, and then came over. I didn't know if I wanted to see him or not—until I saw him.

We both knew then. For a long time, we just stood and looked at each other. Candy had left us alone for a reunion that could have turned out much differently. For all she knew, I might have screamed and yelled and tried to scratch John's eyes out. Maybe she stayed nearby for the first few minutes, thinking she might be needed—to rescue John.

When we stopped staring and turned to hugging and kissing, a strange sense of reality gripped me. Of course, John loved me, and for a very long time there had been no question about my loving him. My intuition told me that John was not thinking at all about returning to Karla. (Much later, when we started telling each other nothing but the full truth, he admitted this was so.) It was something else. And I knew what that something else was, too. John, who had not been able to enjoy much freedom in a great many years, was now enjoying it so much that he simply did not want to give it up. So to him I was not only someone he loved—I was also a threat. He knew from long conversations at those two-person parties we used to have that I wanted to be married. He knew he wanted to be with me, but he had yet to recover fully from one failed marriage, and he had yet to make his mind up about what meant most to him—me, or his freedom.

Suddenly, a tingling feeling ran through my whole body. I no longer felt depressed, nor did I wonder if there were anything really worthwhile left in life for me. I had a clear sense of what my opposition was, and I had supreme confidence that I could overcome it. I had time to play the "waiting game." John could enjoy his "freedom" to the fullest, but one day he would come to realize that what we meant to each other was something more durable, more meaningful, and infinitely more wonderful than the "freedom" that can leave a young man confused, aimless—and, eventually, alone. One can go to the supermarket every day, sample this and sample that, but eventually the moment comes when one must buy. That moment would come for John, and I knew what his decision would be.

Now that we were back in each other's arms, we were again blissful. There was no more talk of "trying to make a go of it" with Karla. But neither did John intend to start making plans for a wedding as soon as his divorce decree became final.

In retrospect, I can see what John was trying to do, and I even had some sense of it then. He was trying to preserve the best of two worlds—the one in which we would be together, and the one in which he would be "free." Accordingly, he insisted that we become engaged. This was a large step toward marriage, but it was not an irrevocable one. Our engagement was something of a ploy by John. He could not make a decision between me and "freedom," and yet he could not stand the thought of losing me. The engagement ring would keep me "on the reservation," to borrow a Watergate expression, and yet without a wedding ring or even a firm commitment of one, John would be able to enjoy his cherished freedom, particularly when I was away on trips.

And I knew what he was doing. We went back to living together, and to our two-person parties, during which I made it very clear to John that this was not the kind of life I had in mind for the long run—that it would come to an abrupt end without marriage or a firm commitment of marriage.

After several months of agonizing, and after a great many futile talks, I realized that John was not ready to marry me and would not be for some time. There was only one course for me: to quit my job, return to Los Angeles, and disappear.

I told John that that was what I intended to do. I also made it clear to him that if he ever decided to come looking for me, it should be with marriage license in hand. It was his privilege to decide between "freedom" and me. He had had both long enough. Now he could have one, but not the other. With that I returned to Los Angeles, with the vague feeling that some day—I had no idea when—I would be coming back.

It was summer 1972, and to my great surprise, I was able to enjoy myself in Los Angeles and away from John. It still amazes me that I was able to date a great deal and somehow keep my mind off John for the first time in almost two years. It must have been because I knew in my heart that some day the telephone would ring, and that deep voice would say: "Come home, honey. I just can't live without you."

It happened almost that way.

First there were a number of love notes—brief ones.

Then came one that seemed to signal something.

"I love ya—more than anything in the world—my wonderful Mo!"

Of course, it was written in pencil, and it wasn't signed, except with an unrecognizable drawing of himself. But John Dean is nothing if not super cautious.

A day or two later, he telephoned. He had recently returned to the White House from the 1972 Republican National Convention in Miami Beach, Florida, which had renominated Richard Nixon and Spiro Agnew.

"I can't be without you any longer," he said. "Will you please hurry back? Will you marry me?"

I told him I'd have to think about it. I couldn't believe the sound of my own voice!

The next day I called him back. Very early.

As soon as he came on the line—with no preliminaries—I sputtered, "Yes, yes, yes!"

We were married two weeks later.

5

A Watergate Wedding
as Storm Clouds Gather

October 5, 1972

VERY SENSITIVE/PERSONAL ATTENTION
MEMORANDUM FOR: H. R. Haldeman
THROUGH: The Society of Single
White House Secretaries
FROM: John Dean
SUBJECT: *Missing in Action*

There comes a time in a bachelor's life when he inevitably gives serious thought to the institution of marriage. For this bachelor, that process commenced several months ago when I became engaged to a beautiful "California girl." Well, after having reviewed and re-reviewed innumerable mental option papers with all the care and caution that my legal training and Libra instincts could muster, I have concluded that this bachelor is ready, able, and extremely anxious to marry his lovely California girl!

Having made this decision—and having had my decision-making/implementation/and follow-up procedures stropped and honed by the Haldeman management team—I plan to marry Maureen on October 13th (subject only to technical problems of arrangements for the ceremony) and would like to take a few days out of the city by way of a quick honey-

moon. While I cannot fully predict what might break with
regard to my office activities, the 13th–18th appears to be good.
Thus when Higby makes his daily morning call to determine
if I have survived the preceding night and discovers my absence—I want you to know that I am "missing in action" and
not a POW, i.e., prisoner of (a) woman.

I hope the foregoing meets with your approval.

No objection————
No objection, but————
Comment—or other observation————

bcc: Counsel's staff

Historians probably will depict the Nixon White House
as one lacking in warmth, friendly relations, and humor,
and certainly it was short on all three. But not devoid of
them, as the above memo from John shows.

And it came back to him from Bob Haldeman with one
word written across it in very large letters:

"Reconsider."

Of course, at that time the White House had not yet
become the grim "paranoia palace" it would be in 1973.
It was about as happy a place in October 1972 as it had been
or would be during the Nixon years. President Nixon was
assured of reelection by an overwhelming margin, and
everyone was making plans for a big victory celebration,
a glittering second inauguration, and a historic second
term. Looking back on those days and those people, it is
difficult to understand how swiftly the euphoria was dis-
sipated, even though I am married to the man who was in
such a large measure responsible.

When I returned to marry John, the excitement of
arranging the wedding completely occupied both of us. I
couldn't really have concentrated on Watergate even if I
had had a reason to do so; but it would be untrue to say
I didn't have some perception of it.

I knew about the break-in. I knew about the arrests of the five burglars and E. Howard Hunt and G. Gordon Liddy. I knew that the *Washington Post* and some other publications were suggesting that there was involvement by higher-ranking people on the Committee for the Re-election of the President, and other people in the administration. I knew that the President had said last August that there had been an investigation by John Dean that showed that no one on the White House staff, "presently employed," had had any involvement in Watergate.

I also knew something the public did not know, and that was that John Dean was very surprised when the President told a press conference about the Dean investigation. He was surprised because there had been no Dean investigation. This disturbed me slightly, but really not very much, because like most Americans, I was convinced that there was no White House involvement. The Committee for the Re-election of the President, perhaps, but not the White House.

At the time of our wedding, just before the election, Watergate seemed to be fading as an issue. The Democrats had tried to make it a factor in the election, but there were few people who were very concerned about it. John had told me earlier, and just before we were married he told me again: it was important to keep certain aspects of the Watergate matter secret, and that if he managed to do that until after election day, there might be something very good for him in the second administration—an ambassadorship, perhaps, or maybe even attorney general some day. But he also warned me that things could go the other way and then the future would not be bright at all.

The need for secrecy until after the election didn't strike me as so unusual. I assumed there were national security or other legitimate reasons for John and the others to be acting as they were.

And I must confess, our wedding plans occupied virtually all of the available space in my mind.

Naturally, the date we chose for our wedding was a Friday the thirteenth—October 13, 1972, to be exact, almost two years after the lucky Friday the thirteenth on which we had met.

The wedding took place in the evening in a new town house John had bought in Alexandria—at 100 Quay Street, alongside the Potomac River. (He had also sold the place on Princess Street, which I had so carefully helped decorate, for a nice profit.)

We had seventy guests. I bought all of the food for the party that was to follow the ceremony, and cooked it all myself. We had roast beef, turkey, corned beef, breads, salads, and, of course, hors d'oeuvres, which I also made myself. We hired only a bartender.

John wanted William Rehnquist, an associate justice of the Supreme Court, to marry us. They had been friends when they both worked in the Department of Justice. John and I had agreed that a civil ceremony would be preferable, since both of us had been married before. But before we agreed on that, John considered asking Father John McLaughlin, the Jesuit priest who worked in the White House and later became one of President Nixon's diehard defenders, to marry us. Rehnquist was anxious to perform the ceremony but learned there was no precedent for a Supreme Court justice to do so. So we were married by a justice of the peace from Alexandria.

Throughout the day of the wedding, Bob Haldeman, John Ehrlichman and Ron Ziegler kept telephoning John, telling him there was a new "crisis" and that he must hurry to the White House at once. They were kidding. Two days later, they were not.

A few Watergate figures were among the guests. But mostly we just wanted family, close friends, schoolmates of John's, and the people we had worked with. Jack and Marge Caulfield were there. Jack was the former police officer who became an official in the Treasury Department and became involved in Watergate when he was chosen to offer executive clemency to keep James McCord from talking. Marnie Kleindienst was there, too. Her husband Richard was to become the first attorney general in history to plead guilty to a crime.

John's parents were able to come. We had not met before, and their first glimpse of their future daughter-in-law must have startled them. It was the day of the wedding, and they were planning to stay in the house, but since they were driving in from Pennsylvania, their time of arrival was uncertain. They drove up considerably earlier than I had expected and found me working in the garden in my blue jeans, with dirt and mud all over my hands and face.

John's roommate at Staunton Military Academy, Congressman Barry Goldwater, Jr., and his wife Susan were on the guest list, and so of course was my very dear friend Heidi. The other guests were all close friends, too, such as the Fieldings and Pete Kinsey, a dear friend who had worked with me at the marihuana commission and had later become a lawyer on John's White House staff.

I stayed alone in the house that night before the wedding. I made John stay with the Fieldings, and even insisted that he dress for the wedding in their house. On our wedding night, John's parents stayed in our town house while we ran off to a not exactly exotic honeymoon headquarters—a Marriott hotel.

Without my knowing anything about it, John did something needless, foolish, and, later, when he disclosed it, terribly embarrassing: he brought $4,850 in cash from a White House fund along on our honeymoon.

It was needless because he had enough money to pay for the wedding and the honeymoon, and because taking cash out of a fund and leaving your check in its place doesn't make any sense. Of course, he was going to pay it back—otherwise, why leave his check?

No one would ever have known of this transaction that gave John's enemies a weapon with which to attack him if he had not disclosed it himself when he decided to tell the full truth to the prosecutors. During the Ervin Committee hearings, and later when John testified in various trials, he was always taunted about this incident by lawyers who wanted the juries or the American people to believe that he was just a common thief. If that were so—or if people could be made to believe it were so—John would have little or no credibility.

I don't know why John took the money—except that he could not have had time to transfer his own money from the brokerage account he held in New York. He wanted to finish the patio, and pay for landscaping, my wedding dress, and the food, liquor, and flowers. We were going to Key Biscayne, Florida, for a two- or three-week honeymoon, so he spent almost $4,000, but the point is he had borrowed it.

I know it rankles John when lawyers make him recount the details of the $4,850 over and over again. He isn't proud of what he did. He does feel better about having owned up to it, however.

But on our first day as Mr. and Mrs. John Wesley Dean III we weren't thinking of anything but our own ecstasy. We had met, and begun a romance that quickly developed into love. We had drifted apart. John had had plenty of doubts, and plenty of time to resolve them. We had both had time to decide and to be sure that we wanted to go through life together. At last all the questions had faded away, all the decisions had been made. Once we had been less than completely honest with each other. Now we were convinced that our marriage would last forever if we were completely truthful with each other.

Sidney Charles Kane, 1945.

Irene Kelly Kane, 1941.

A gathering at the Kane home in Mar Vista, California. Left to right: Ronnie, a family friend, Mo and Mrs. Kane.

*Mo as a schoolgirl in 1959 at Notre Dame
Girls' Academy in Beverly Hills.*

Mo and Ronnie in 1961.

Christmas, 1972.

Official White House photograph, taken just before John made his decision to end the Watergate cover-up.

Mo and John with Mrs. Kane, 1972.

Clockwise, from left: Fred and Maria Fielding, Barry Goldwater, Jr., and John's parents congratulating the bride and groom.

October 13, 1972.

*John and his son, John Wesley Dean IV, Christmas, 1972. Taken by Mo, who
was then studying photography.*

*Mo as an American Airlines steward-
ess, 1966.*

November of 1962.

Mo and Michael Biner in Tijuana, Mexico, on their wedding day, September 3, 1967

In Las Vegas with Jacques Bergerac, October 1969.

Mo with Hugh O'Brian at the Sahara in Las Vegas.

Washington, 1971.

Heidi Rikan.

Mo with Susan Goldwater at Nathan's Restaurant, 1973.

John being sworn in at the Watergate hearings, June 25, 1973.

At the Watergate hearings. WIDE WORLD PHOTOS

Left to right: Mo, John, Cameron Keller and Gene Adcock at the Deans' after John's release from prison. ELLEN GRAHAM

Gucci, Mo and John. ELLEN GRAHAM

Looking back, I do not regard John's not telling me about Watergate as a failure to abide by this agreement. It was just one of the many elements of his work for the President, and neither of us wanted to talk all night about what he had been doing all day.

Who could blame us for being ecstatic? We had the most precious gift that can come to a woman and a man—love. We wished that morning that everyone could be as happy as we.

And on October 14, 1972, just three weeks before Richard Nixon's landslide reelection, we flew to Key Biscayne. Our future together looked bright. So did John's future in government, and as a lawyer in private practice after that.

We received hundreds of telegrams and messages wishing us well, some of which have a ring of irony to them now. One was from Hugh Scott of Pennsylvania, the Republican leader in the Senate. I read it to John on the plane:

"Congratulations to you and best wishes to your bride for many years of happiness. Hugh Scott, U.S. Senator."

Within a year, Hugh Scott would be telling the press that John was a consummate liar. He would insist that he had seen partial transcripts of taped White House conversations that proved the President was innocent and that John Dean had lied in testifying about meetings he had had with the President.

We were pleased by a lovely message from Senator and Mrs. Barry Goldwater that read:

"Congratulations and best wishes. May your lives be filled with much happiness. Peggy and Barry Goldwater."

But the message we prized above all—at the time—was one that went like this:

"Mrs. Nixon and I send you our heartfelt good wishes on your wedding. We hope that the joy you now share may grow with every passing year and that your life together may be as happy and rewarding as our own. Richard Nixon."

There was one other message, addressed only to me, and left on my mirror in the motel room before we left for Florida.

> *Good morning, Love*
> *I hope you had a good sleep—I know how tired you were—*
> *Smile—an owl loves ya—loves ya—yes, loves ya—*
> *P.S. I love you.*

The "signature" was a sketch of a man wearing owlish glasses. I had no difficulty recognizing him.

John and I were happier than either of us had ever been.

And we were blissfully unaware of the shattering events that lay just ahead, and that would abruptly alter the course of our lives—and so many others—forever.

This was a time to let my head sink into a pillow, and to squeeze John's hand as the jet winged out of the Washington cold and into the Florida sunshine.

This was a time for thoughts like Tennyson's:

> *I know not if I know what true love is,*
> *But if I know, then, if I love not him,*
> *I know there is none other I can love.*

6

A "Hot" Problem

The tempo of events accelerated dramatically almost from the moment we arrived at our $90-a-day villa at Key Biscayne. The villa was one of two that the government leased and in which certain high-ranking aides (Haldeman and Ehrlichman, mainly) stayed when the President was at his nearby Key Biscayne estate. Since John and I were there on a honeymoon rather than official business, we, of course, had to pay.

If the difference between a honeymoon and official business was only $90 a day, I remember thinking, it was well worth it.

No sooner had we settled in than the first sign of how crucial the Watergate situation was becoming made its appearance. Two men from the White House Communications Agency appeared at our door and announced that they were there to install a telephone.

I looked around the room.

There already was a telephone. The men had another one. I started to tell them they had made a mistake—that we already had a telephone—when John cut me off: "It's okay, dear. A special White House telephone."

Oh.

Well, great! I thought. The first day of our honeymoon and the White House isn't content with having one telephone on which to reach John—it has to have two. Of course, I realized that if some great emergency came up, the White House would want a direct line so there would be no delay in getting through. The germ of a thought began to take hold in my mind: maybe the White House *expects* a great emergency while we are down here.

Like what? I wondered.

John didn't often become very deeply involved in foreign policy, so it wasn't likely to be anything in that area. I assumed it must be some domestic matter or congressional problem for which legal counsel might be needed. Whatever it was, I hoped it could wait.

Our villa had a small, sun-bathed patio. So we got into our swimsuits, and sat in the sun while we had a cocktail and a chat. The sun was so warm and lovely. We were perfectly content. All the arrangements had been so efficiently and thoughtfully taken care of. For example, someone had arranged for us to use a car that was normally reserved for Julie Nixon Eisenhower, who was not at Key Biscayne at the time. It was a large Mercury Monterey with stereo, air conditioning, and automatic windows. The villa too was lovely—nicely furnished with brightly covered red, white, and blue chairs and sofas. It looked cheerful and inviting.

Yet I had the vague sense of something hanging over our heads. That extra telephone bothered me.

Soon both telephones started to ring. John would get up and dash in to answer both. At times he had a receiver pressed against each ear. It was really quite comical. I'm certain I would have been more annoyed than I was had not everything else been so perfect and had John and I been any less happy.

The next day—Sunday—matters went from bad to worse. Soon it made no sense for John to walk back out on the patio whenever he put one telephone down. It would begin to ring again immediately, or else the other one would. So he stayed inside on the telephone, and I soaked up the sun on the patio. At times I would wander down to the water alone, stick my toes in, and find the temperature of the water so wonderfully warm that I would plunge right in. What glorious days these were going to be—if John would ever get away from those horrible telephones!

By late Sunday afternoon, he was still picking up one telephone after the other. About 4 P.M., he picked up the telephone one more time. I was half dozing and didn't catch the drift of the conversation at all.

But soon I heard the sliding screen door pushed open and I thought: At last. It's all over now, or he wouldn't be leaving the phones.

But what really turned out to be "all over" was our honeymoon.

John let me down as gently as possible in the limited time available.

"Mo—that last call was from Larry Higby."

Then he paused, as if he were giving me time to let that information sink in. I had assumed many of the calls had been from Larry Higby and others.

"Something important?" I asked.

"Very."

"Anything wrong?"

"Something in Washington could be very troublesome. It's a problem related to the campaign, and it won't wait. It has to be taken care of right away."

"You don't mean Higby wants you to return?"

"I'm afraid so. But not for long. A few days and we can come right back here."

I could sense the tears rising in my eyes. Then, thank God, my pragmatic streak gained the upper hand. When John had paused after mentioning Higby's name, he was hoping I would figure out something for myself, and now I began figuring it out. Larry Higby was "Haldeman's Haldeman" —he was to Bob Haldeman what Haldeman himself was to

President Nixon—a completely loyal, dedicated assistant who would carry out orders swiftly and efficiently as soon as they were given to him. He did not *give* orders—he *relayed* them. His role was well understood by everyone in the White House. When he spoke, the effect was the same as if Haldeman or Nixon had spoken.

John did not have to explain further. Obviously, Haldeman or the President had a good and sufficient reason for wanting John to return. I said no more. I knew it was time to pack.

Understandably, my feelings were mixed. No woman is happy to have her honeymoon interrupted by the demands of her husband's work. She likes to think that on certain occasions she comes first and the job comes second. The honeymoon, wedding anniversaries, her birthday are among those "certain occasions."

But on the other hand, I could not help being very proud. Over the past several months, I could sense that John had become much more important to the President and others in the White House. Now it seemed to me he had become virtually indispensable. When we first met in late 1970, and during much of 1971 and early 1972 when we were living together, John was busy enough, heaven knows, and he worked brutally long hours. But it was nothing compared to the summer of 1972 (those early weeks when we saw each other) and the fall of that year (when we got back together again).

Without knowing the details, I thought I understood what was happening. The longer one knows John, the more one comes to rely on him. He's just that sort of person. His mind works like an automatic rifle—it's quick, sharp, decisive. His memory for detail has always been phenomenal, and I could sense that in the busy atmosphere of the White House, John must have been of great value in crucial meetings. Instead of having to look up something that had happened a year before, the President or Haldeman or Ehrlichman could simply ask John to recall the details. He has always had that ability. And John also has the ability to look ahead, to see beyond the immediate situation and tell you that if you decide on Plan A, then you had better be prepared for B, C, and D to happen. These qualities, I thought, had become increasingly important to the people in the White House and they were simply relying more and more on John.

Again I was right, in a general sense. Again I was unaware of specifics.

The Watergate break-in occurred on June 17, 1972, and the cover-up began immediately afterward. The dates coincided with John's enhanced importance at the White House, but I did not relate the two. I attributed the increasingly frenzied atmosphere to the nearness of the election, even though every poll predicted that President Nixon would win a landslide victory.

Also, on the afternoon that Higby called and during the weeks and months that followed, I was so happy to be married to John that nothing else mattered.

Anyway, I started to pack suitcases for both of us. When John packs for himself, he's likely to end up with only one sock, or with one black shoe and one brown one. While I gathered our things together, I had another occasion to marvel at the ever-efficient men from the White House Communications Agency. They magically appeared at the door again. They knew we were leaving, apparently as soon as we did, and maybe even sooner. They quietly removed the special White House telephone, and left.

Soon after, John and I were driven to the airport in Julie's car. We boarded a commercial jet headed for Washington. And that was that for our first honeymoon.

Even with all that was on his mind, John realized I needed to be consoled.

He said: "We'll come back just as soon as I take care of a hot problem."

I was beginning to wonder why everything in the White House these days seemed to be a "hot problem."

John then explained that the *Washington Post* had uncovered a Nixon campaign operation directed by a young lawyer I had never heard of. His name was Donald Segretti.

The *Post* was devoting columns and columns of space to interviews with people Segretti had tried to recruit for his campaign operation. Most of those interviewed detailed what Segretti had wanted them to do and explained why they had refused to become a part of it. These embarrassing revelations could be very harmful so close to election day.

The Segretti operation involved "dirty tricks," the *Post* was saying. Of course, the *Post* had never been enthusiastic about Mr. Nixon, and John and the other people in the White House felt that the Segretti stories were being wildly overplayed just because these were the final weeks before the election. While I agreed that the stories seemed to be overblown—in what campaign have there been no dirty tricks?—I was also somewhat startled by what seemed to me to be an overreaction in the White House. A few embarrassing revelations in newspaper articles surely wouldn't turn the whole campaign around. I still couldn't see that this situation necessitated bringing a man home from his honeymoon.

I had heard that President Nixon always gets very nervous before elections. He lost the 1960 presidential race by such a tiny margin, and he won in 1968 by a very few votes after being far ahead in the early polls. So I assumed that he was keyed up again, fearful that some last-minute disclosures could again turn what looked like a runaway victory into a very close election.

And I knew enough about the men around Nixon to realize that if *he* was nervous, *they* were nervous. That was the minimum requirement.

The Segretti stories ran for days on end, it seemed, and soon just about every reporter in Washington and in California—where Segretti lived—was trying to get more details. John was participating in sessions to decide how the press secretary, Ron Ziegler, should respond to reporters' questions at White House press briefings. I'm sure John was valuable—his judgment is always good—but again I was a bit perplexed. Why John?

But John did one other thing that, in retrospect, was more important—he met with Segretti, at John Ehrlichman's suggestion, and told him to go into hiding and not talk to anyone from the press.

I didn't understand then why John Ehrlichman couldn't have told Segretti that himself, but it became quite clear later on. Whenever there was a need to involve someone in the White House in something that was a little bit unsavory or that would be embarrassing if it were ever disclosed, everyone shielded the President. Then the higher your rank the more likely your role would be shielded, too. You would remain in the background while underlings took the risks.

John Ehrlichman did not want to talk to Segretti directly, because some day Segretti might be asked if he had ever talked with anyone in the White House. Segretti might have to answer. It was much better, from John Ehrlichman's standpoint, if Segretti's answer was, "Yes—John Dean" and not, "Yes—John Ehrlichman."

So it was indeed worthwhile to bring a man back from his honeymoon to help rehearse a press secretary—and to do the dirty work. There was nothing illegal about telling a man not to talk to the press—Segretti was not at that time the target of a criminal investigation—but Ehrlichman had followed the same pattern earlier in a case where a man was the subject of a criminal investigation. Shortly after the Watergate break-in, Ehrlichman decided that E.

73

Howard Hunt, who would soon be sought by investigators, should leave the country. But rather than tell Hunt himself, Ehrlichman ordered John to do it.

I'm not making excuses for John, since he doesn't make excuses for himself. He was a lawyer, and he knew that to order Hunt to flee was wrong, even if the order originated with the President of the United States. But in the White House power structure, every man wanted to win the approval of the man just ahead of him—and of the man on top. So—for too long a time—they all did what was "expected."

Looking back on this period, I know I am more angry now than I was then. At the time I did not realize how John was being "used"—willingly, of course. I was much prouder of his importance than I was disturbed by all the impositions being made on our lives.

The Segretti "dirty tricks" turned out to be somewhat more serious than the usual campaign "pranks" of disrupting an opponent's schedule, sending hecklers to his rallies, and so on. Segretti had arranged for the distribution of pamphlets during the Florida Democratic primary in March on Muskie letterheads charging Senators Hubert Humphrey and Henry Jackson with engaging in various sexual escapades. And there was another especially cruel one that said Representative Shirley Chisholm, who was also a presidential candidate in that primary, had been under treatment for mental illness. The object was to get the Democratic contenders so outraged with each other that they would never be able to unite behind one candidate for the campaign against President Nixon.

A few days after John and I returned from Florida the Segretti matter began to subside. The press had not learned what the White House had feared it might learn— who had hired Segretti and who had paid him. The Watergate prosecutors were not at all excited about Segretti, so it seemed that nothing would touch the White House, at least not until after the election.

What had made everyone so nervous was that Dwight Chapin, President Nixon's appointments secretary, had hired Segretti, and the President's personal attorney, Herbert Kalmbach, had paid him.

But by October 19, the situation seemed to be under control, and everyone could relax again, at least for a while.

So John and I returned to the villa at Key Biscayne to resume our honeymoon. This time we got four full glorious days and part of a fifth. There were telephone calls—but not so many as before.

By now I had caught on, and I wondered every minute when this second honeymoon would come to an abrupt end. I knew it would, and it did.

When John told me the morning of October 23 that Bob Haldeman had called to say that things were getting "a little sticky" again in Washington, I simply shrugged and started packing. Obviously our lives were going to be this way as long as John was in the White House.

7

Power: The Narcotic of the "Straight" World

The world of power in which John and I dwelt through 1971 and 1972 and part of 1973 is like no other. Power is an intoxicant. No—it's even worse. It seeps into your pores somehow, and soon you are giddy and want more power to achieve an even better feeling or at least to retain and prolong your present "high."

Its effects are generally more narcotic on the male than on the female. Whether that is because power is more readily accessible to men or whether the reason goes back to something inherent in the natures of the sexes is for someone more expert than I to say.

I do know that the side effects are observable in so many different ways even to or perhaps especially to a neophyte such as I was. To be admitted even to the fringes of the world of power for the first time is to bring a fresh and at first bewildered eye to a scene whose long-time participants are so jaded they are no longer aware of what they are caught up in.

It's strange the fascination and hold power has on all of its victims. Certainly they exceed that of money. Every new administration attracts to Washington dozens of men who willingly—almost anxiously—give up hundreds of thousands of dollars in income in order to be where the "action" is and to control part of that action themselves. Some, like Robert S. McNamara, who gave up the presidency of Ford Motor Company to come to Washington during the Kennedy years, never go back to the comparatively dull experience of making millions.

Perhaps because I am a woman or perhaps because I have a built-in immunity, I never became truly addicted to this narcotic of power that is stronger in Washington, D.C., than anywhere else in the world. It was intriguing to watch and observe, however, and everyone should have that opportunity.

Once you are personally exposed to the world of power and to the men and women who populate it, you either join it or rapidly and permanently lose your sense of awe. We all like to fantasize about our movie heroes and heroines, our athletic superstars, and, at least until recently, our high-ranking government officials. And we can do this as long as we observe their images through the filters of distance, and as long as there are more unknowns than knowns about them. But in life as on film, seeing close-ups can shatter all the illusions.

I don't mean to suggest that powerful figures in Washington are universally wicked, or even more wicked than people anywhere else. By and large they are decent, well intentioned, and hard-working. But they are on a stage all the time, trying to impress each other and the people back home. Most Americans see them from seats in the middle or back rows. When you stand alongside them on the stage, you can see the makeup, the wigs, the patched costumes, the wrinkles, the moles.

During the Nixon years, the White House became even more the focal point of the power world than it had been during previous administrations. President Nixon, instead of going to church on Sundays, brought church to the White House. President Nixon, instead of going out to a concert, brought the concert into the White House. And

White House parties became ever so much more a status symbol because the guest lists told so plainly who was "in" and who was "out". I am sure that is always the case to some degree, but most recent Presidents, including President Ford, have made a point of bringing some of their political "enemies" to the White House for social events and other activities, for a variety of reasons: to disarm them, to convert them, or maybe just to prove themselves magnanimous.

But probably because of the insecurity and paranoid tendencies of President Nixon, few "enemies" were ever invited to the White House, except by mistake. One reason for a White House "enemies list," with which John had a peripheral involvement, was to prevent real or imagined opponents of President Nixon or his programs from turning up on the premises. Some Republican senators who opposed a substantial number of the President's policies were not invited to the White House a single time during the six years of the Nixon Republican presidency.

My own experiences at the White House were few but memorable. Although I had lived in Washington with Heidi for six weeks back in 1969, I had never joined one of those White House tours that are musts for most visitors. The reason was not lack of interest. I just won't wait in line for anything. I don't like huge crowds, and I don't like too many people around. If I go to the supermarket and there are long lines at the checkout counters, I leave, even if there's no food in the house. If I'm just dying to see a certain movie, I'll die rather than wait in line for a seat or a ticket.

So my first visit to the White House was as a guest, not a tourist. It took place in late 1971 after I had been in Washington only a short time, and naturally I was awed by the historic mansion itself and by the powerful people inside it.

But even that first night I had vague inner suspicions

that the Washington power scene was not for me and never would be—the narcotic that gives so many a "high" just had no effect on me.

I naturally had no idea I would react this way, so when John invited me to my first White House party, I excitedly brought out the pale blue gown with silver threads that I had just bought for New Year's Eve. Heidi let me borrow her black sable coat. When John and I drove up to the White House in his burgundy Porsche with the black top, I felt every bit as grand as the senators and cabinet officers and corporation executives and their wives who stepped out of the big black Cadillac and Lincoln limousines.

I remember being momentarily concerned about checking Heidi's coat—I was afraid it might be stolen.

Get yourself together, girl, I told myself. This is no ordinary checkroom. This is the White House. And suddenly I felt safe.

The event that night was a concert by Beverly Sills, during which she split her dress accidentally and gave the evening its only bit of spice.

But before we were escorted upstairs for the concert, John and I milled around with lots of strangers. Everyone seemed on edge, seemed to be feeling out everyone else. Everyone looked around to see who else was there, and seemed worried that someone important would overlook him or her. It was work, not play, as so many Washington parties are, and there was no sense of having a relaxed, enjoyable evening.

I felt quite inadequate, but no more so than I usually do. The excitement of being in the White House for the first time sustained me, and I smiled at everyone, and pretended to have heard of all the people John introduced me to, even though I was still too new to the city to know who was who. Of course, no one was presented just as "Jim Smith" or "Dick Jones." It was always, "This is Jim Smith, who runs the Office of Management and Budget," or "This is Dick Jones, the congressman from Indiana." Everyone had a title, which he could not leave at home, even for one night.

Soon we were all ushered upstairs to the East Room by male and female military aides who showed us directly to our seats. I recall a maze of color—red jackets covered with gold braid, black pants and skirts, white shirts, white gloves and scarflike ties that doubled over—the prescribed dress for the aides.

The marble stairway that flares at the bottom is so beautiful and the entire mansion is so full of marvelous paintings, lovely draperies and carpets, china, silver, and various styles of furnishings that one cannot help being impressed and inspired by them and the sense of their history.

After everyone was seated, the President and the First Lady walked in. Everyone stood and applauded. I caught only a glimpse of them before the concert began, and I was excited of course—I had never seen either of them in person before. But it wasn't anything like our later encounter on Air Force One. This night, John and I were just part of a faceless, formless mob to them.

Beverly Sills was splendid, but I still felt uneasy and could hardly wait for the evening to end. I felt like a child in Sunday school—forced to sit still, remain silent, appear enraptured.

In the midst of an aria Beverly Sills split her dress in the back. No one would have been aware had she not told us, turned around to show us, and made a few engaging remarks. After a burst of applause, she continued with the program.

At last the concert was over, but the worst part of the evening was not. President Nixon made a few comments about the split dress, none of them particularly memorable, then brusquely urged the audience to hurry into the dining room for a reception. He seemed to regard the reception as just another duty—for him and for us. No warmth, no feeling of friendship or camaraderie! Let's get it over with—that was the mood.

Quickly, a short reception line formed, including President and Mrs. Nixon, Beverly Sills, and the singer's mother. Even though I felt as if I were on an assembly line, I did feel honored to be there. An aide instructed John to be on my left so he could introduce me, and we were whisked through the line. It was a thrill to see the President and the First Lady and to shake hands with them, but I had the uncomfortable feeling that they didn't really see me—or anyone. In the second or two allotted to me, I had time only to notice that Pat Nixon was taller and more slender than she appeared to be in photographs—also more attractive. The President looked much older to me in the glimpse I got of him. Both Richard and Pat Nixon were saying over and over, "Hello. How are you? Nice to see you" in a most robotlike manner.

Still, there was that feeling of exhilaration just seeing them. I thought of Mom and wished she could see all this and be with us. I also wished I had a photographic memory so I could tell her every detail of the evening.

The "reception" lasted fifteen or twenty minutes at most, and then the Nixons quickly disappeared. We found ourselves in a room where hors d'oeuvres and drinks were being served, and I had one drink—which I *really* needed.

It was so boring that even my feeling of excitement could no longer sustain me. The Nixons were lucky, I thought. When they became bored at their own parties, all they had to do was go upstairs.

"What do they do when they go upstairs this early?" I asked John.

"I don't know. Probably the President mixes himself a dry martini," he replied.

"Does the President drink?" I asked.

Said John: "He's been known to pop a few."

This was the only interesting conversation of the evening as far as I was concerned. I wanted to get out of there.

Suddenly it dawned on me that being there didn't mean a thing—not one thing. All of us were just a blur of faces to President and Mrs. Nixon, we meant nothing to each other, we weren't enjoying ourselves. None of us was really impressed with who else was there. We were too full of anxiety that *they* be impressed that *we* were there. The game wasn't worth the candle.

The counsel to the President and the counsel's date were among the first to leave. When John and I were standing outside the White House in the fresh night air, I realized even more clearly how stifling it had been inside. The atmosphere, not the temperature.

We drove straight home. John had a Scotch and soda, I had vodka with water, we listened to music, we talked. And I would not have traded those precious late evening hours for all the White House receptions of the next decade.

Of course, I telephoned Mom before and right after, and her delight and interest were the biggest dividends by far that were returned that evening.

"That's my daughter!" she squealed. "I always knew she'd make it to the White House." Then she burst into laughter.

After our experience at the Beverly Sills concert, John and I decided in favor of our "two-person parties" at home rather than any other White House functions to which we were invited—until one Sunday in the winter of 1973— shortly after President Nixon's second inauguration.

The event was a Sunday morning worship service in the East Room. John and I were probably included because our honeymoon had been interrupted twice and we had made no waves about it. Another probable reason was that John had been so helpful, from the White House point of view, on Watergate. The Nixon White House was always very attentive to passing out "perks"—perquisites.

A staff member who loyally accompanied the President to Chicago or Memphis instead of spending his wedding anniversary with his wife would be entitled to a "perk." So would one who missed his son's birthday celebration, or his daughter's wedding, in order to work out a sticky political situation for the President.

Such sacrifices were expected, but they did not go un noticed. In return for such evidence of loyalty and devotion to the President, a staff man might find himself given a new and more important assignment (which would require him to spend even less time with his family and more with his job). Or he would be invited to fly on Air Force One. Or he would be admitted to the select group entitled to use White House cars. Or he would be invited to a White House dinner party.

There were a thousand and one ways for the President and the men around him to acknowledge and reward devotion, and Watergate is more easily understood when this fact is taken into account.

The men at the second, third, and fourth echelons were ambitious and hotly competitive, and the competition was stimulated by the men at the top. Whenever someone did something very pleasing to the President, Haldeman, or Ehrlichman, even if it was something unethical or illegal, a "perk" followed. And everyone knew when anyone else was being rewarded and was "in" with the men at the top. When someone refused or, more likely, hesitated to do something for whatever reason—his own ethical standards, his conscience, or his better judgment—he qualified as a pain-in-the-neck and would increasingly be shunned and sidelined. A good example is Herb Klein, loser of several power struggles within the administration, most notably to Ron Ziegler and later to Chuck Colson. First Ziegler usurped Klein's role as the President's chief spokesman, and then Colson dominated the work of Klein's Office of Communications.

The word quickly filtered down if a member of the staff could not play "hard ball." Soon he would be looked upon by his peers as someone whose judgment and loyalty were suspect. Association with him might even taint others, so he would find himself eating alone in the White House mess. He might be moved to a smaller office, and his staff would be trimmed.

This is terribly difficult for most ambitious young men to endure. They fear that no one—not their wives, families, friends, the press, or the general public—will understand if they resign. And if they stay on, in disfavor, they know they will continue to lose various "perks" and most likely become the subject of rumors that they are no longer in favor at the White House. They are afraid there may be leaks to the press about them, suggesting that their resignations would be accepted.

And they worry that once out of the sphere of power under such unfavorable circumstances, they will continue to be plagued by whispers that they "couldn't cut it" in the big time. Otherwise, why are they job-hunting in the middle of an administration?

Thus the President's men—probably every President's men—try to gauge the mood at the top, and not simply keep pace with it, but get out in front of it. Why this went to greater lengths in the Nixon administration than in other ones probably has much to do with the various personalities involved, the President's personality above all others.

I do not write these words to excuse John Dean and the others. I just think they will lead to greater understanding of the atmosphere and the pressures that worked on all of these men.

So John's willingness—not to mention mine—to interrupt our honeymoon in order to try to stomp out a political fire was an example of the loyalty that was not allowed to go unrecognized at the White House. Hence the "perk"

—an invitation to the Sunday worship service. Frankly, I had no desire to go, but it meant something to John to be seen there, so we went.

Billy Graham was there in all his glory. He shared the religious duties, though not the limelight, with a rabbi from Los Angeles and a priest from I don't know where.

Chuck Colson, who was trying to leave the White House to go into private law practice, was leading a stocky, jowly man around as if he were the prize bull in a Mexican arena. Colson was slapping everyone's back, shaking hands with everyone, and introducing all to his "catch." He turned out to be quite a prospective catch indeed—Frank Fitzsimmons, president of the Teamsters Union. The Teamsters were about to retain Colson's new law firm for $100,000 a year, and Chuck wanted to make certain that everyone saw his potential client and that Fitzsimmons met all the important and powerful people Chuck already knew so well.

Of course, the occasion required a new dress for me; it was quite conservative for me, but it was appropriate for the occasion. Patty Colson complimented me on it and then told me what every woman dreads: another woman at the reception was wearing the identical dress!

My first reaction was that I wanted to go home.

This vanity about clothes is one I should not allow myself, but I do and there is no cure for it. John couldn't believe that I wanted to leave.

"Look. We're going to go through this line and say hello to the President of the United States," he said.

"Maybe you are," I replied. "But I'm not."

Then he got really stern:

"This is the silliest thing I ever heard of. You'll be sorry for the rest of your life if you rush off in a huff over something that doesn't matter at all."

Doesn't matter at all? Men!

As I began to walk through the receiving line, I went

into a semi-trance, saying no more than a statue, and displaying only slightly more physical dexterity. My neck was sufficiently pliable that I could nod to people as first one person and then another would say ". . . and this is Mrs. Dean." My eyes would barely meet the other person's, then they would turn to the next pair of eyes as I was being propelled along—so the assembly line would not jam.

I looked at John with eyes that tried to say: "Standing in line and shaking everybody's hand may be a big deal to you, but it's not a big deal to me." Hardly anyone is ever aware of whose hand he is shaking, anyway. It's like a cattle run. Everyone looks like everyone else. Everyone just moves along like a piece of machinery, going through a necessary bit of drudgery, everyone anxious for that moment when it will be possible to say: "Thank God, it's all over."

Looking blank and feeling annoyed by the people pressing in on me, moving me along, I recall reaching a point where the forward motion halted for a few seconds. In her surprisingly deep western twang, Pat Nixon was saying something about newlyweds. John was beaming, so I tried to turn on some sparkle myself.

Suddenly, I became vaguely aware that what never happens with a reception line was happening with this one. It had come to a complete halt! There was no one pressing in on me, moving me along.

I could see what had happened: among the powers reserved, apparently exclusively, to the President of the United States is the authority to halt a reception line. Everyone is astonished and White House aides become fidgety when he does it, but, of course, no one challenges his act.

President Nixon, his manner fatherly but his face stern, had grabbed John's arm and was conversing animatedly and earnestly with him.

I snapped out of my trance. Something serious was going on. The President's face was grim, and he was talking to John in a low, half-whispered tone. Frequently, he pounded his clenched right fist into his open left palm, emphasizing his points. Whatever they were discussing, it was evident John did not fully agree with the President, but whenever John said something, the President would come back more forcefully than ever.

A few times I thought I heard John say, "Well, I'll certainly look into it," or "I'll see what I can do, Mr. President." John looked nervous and uncomfortable, anxious to please this most powerful of all the world leaders, but fearful that he could not. How many more times he must have worn that same expression in the increasingly tumultuous months that followed for the Nixon White House!

While this conversation was taking place, I had plenty of time to observe, because no one was paying the slightest attention to me. The line had halted, Pat Nixon was talking to the people who were just behind me, casting occasional nervous glances at her husband, trying to send him a signal to get the line moving once again.

At length, the President received his cue. Again I heard the mumbled word "newlyweds," and I was whisked past the President.

"At last we can go," I thought. Wrong again.

At the end of every reception line, there is sort of a "nineteenth hole" at which beverages are available. Since this was Sunday morning, the offerings were limited to coffee and tea. John handed me a cup of coffee, took one himself, and began to "circulate." I kept an eye out for the woman in the same dress, but she never appeared, thank goodness.

I saw Julie Eisenhower and said hello to her. John introduced me to Mamie Eisenhower, who was very sweet and gracious. I could not suppress a chuckle when I noticed that Colson was still making the rounds with his potential prize catch in tow.

At last the time came to leave.

On the way home, John was in one of his moods—silent, withdrawn, worried.

"What did the President talk to you about?" I asked gingerly, hoping this was not one of those occasions when John would find it impossible to talk shop to me.

It was not.

The President, John said, was very upset about an incident that occurred during the Inaugural Parade. A totally unarmed man had broken through the lines somehow and tried to approach the limousine in which the President was riding. He was protesting the continuing war in Vietnam.

As always, the President was well guarded, and the Secret Service agents had no difficulty with the intruder.

"But the President is irate," John said. "He gave me orders to have the man prosecuted."

"Well," I replied, not knowing any better, "then I suppose you'll have to."

There was nothing to justify a prosecution, John told me. The incident was trivial. No one had attached great significance to it, not even the Secret Service.

Oh, there probably had been a routine investigation to see if the man was a persistent disrupter, and if he turned up for a future public appearance by the President, he would be closely watched.

"But a prosecution?" said John. "There is nothing that we can prosecute the man for."

I thought to myself: how tough it must be to work for a president—at least President Nixon. You want so much to please him, and you want to do exactly what he tells you to do.

But when you tell him—as John had tried to do—that what he wants is impossible, he just gets more emphatic and more insistent.

What do you do? I wondered.

It seemed to me there were only three options:

Tell the President there is no way to carry out his order and offer to resign.

Find some way to carry out the order, and do so.

Do nothing, and hope the incident will be forgotten.

John chose the final option this time.

And this time, it worked.

8

Cheers—and a Joyful Tear— for Richard Nixon

Those final months of the first Nixon administration, when the walls seemed to be crumbling in on every side, were so chaotic that there was no real pattern to my life. I was forever packing and unpacking, arriving and leaving, a yo-yo dangling at the end of a White House telephone line.

It was always Watergate that intruded.

I should explain my mood at this time, in late 1972—a mood shared by millions of Americans—but by no one with greater intensity than the concerned people around me, and especially those involved people around John.

I thought—we all thought—that the press was constantly after Richard Nixon's hide. When we listened to the television newscasts, we always felt we could detect a sinister arching of an eyebrow by Dan Rather, or a smirk on Walter Cronkite's face, whenever they broadcast the White House response to the Watergate development of the day. It was getting to the point where there was a Watergate development every day—especially in the *Washington Post,* which we all thought was full of contemptible lies.

Never (I hope and believe) totally naive, I did not blind myself to everything that had gone on and was going on.

The Watergate break-in, the surreptitious planting of bugs and tapes on telephones, Donald Segretti's cruel pamphlets—all this revolted me. But I was twenty-six at the time, wide-eyed about the world of politics and about how much was allowable. It was as if I was at ringside for my first prizefight: hitting below the belt would not send me off screaming "foul" at the referee, because I would not know that hitting below the belt was against the rules.

So to me and several other so-called Watergate wives, this was not simply a different kind of life, it was a new planet, peopled with strange creatures who were always reading or listening to and reacting to news. It was Powertown, and unless you were enormously brilliant or unabashedly presumptuous, you didn't stand up and shout to all these apparently wise and apparently well intentioned people: "Hey—what you're doing is wrong. Stop it. Speak out and admit it."

But by October of 1972, anyone with even a modest IQ could perceive the *illegal* aspects of the Watergate break-in. The five men who were caught on the premises of the Democratic National Committee, plus two alleged ringleaders, E. Howard Hunt, Jr., and G. Gordon Liddy, had all been charged and were facing trial.

They were zealous, people around me said, dedicated to the reelection of the president, and they went too far in their efforts to ensure his reelection.

Could anyone believe that the boyish-looking Jeb Stuart Magruder, who gave the appearance of fresh-faced openness and both physical and ethical cleanliness, would sully himself in something like this? No, he would be too concerned about his own future.

Could anyone imagine H. R. Haldeman and John Ehrlichman, coldly efficient though they sometimes were, puritanical as they were in their personal lives, stooping to criminality in their service to the President of the United States? At that time, not many people could, including me.

And to allow even the suspicion that President N . . .

No! Not even the press, the most powerful segments of which seemed to loathe him with a passion, had gone so far—then—as to suggest his involvement.

And to me the most unthinkable person to be part of a criminal conspiracy was John Wesley Dean III. No way— he was too good, too decent, too wise.

Whatever misgivings were beginning to stir within me were related to my perceptions of addiction to power. My husband and the men he worked with, including the President, talked more of "goals" than anything else—certainly more than Watergate, which, except for John, they didn't talk about at all when I was present. Once or twice this constant emphasis on "goals" caused me to wonder fleetingly how they could be *so certain* they were seeking the right goals—the goals best for the nation.

Late in October John sat me down for a serious discussion.

"Look, Mo, things are heating up," he told me. "It's close to the election now, and we can't let anything unravel at this late stage. So I may not be very good company for a couple of weeks." As it turned out, he *was* good company —but only on rare occasions.

Whenever John has to be away from me for any time, he first tries to arrange something to keep me busy. This time, he had spoken to Jeb Magruder and Bart Porter and others who were arranging the victory celebration to be held in the glittering Regency Ballroom of the Shoreham Hotel. They had need of volunteer help. Would I be interested?

Of course! To actually participate in the arrangements for a party celebrating the election of a President of the United States was an opportunity I did not expect to come my way more than once in my lifetime (how right I was). So with great enthusiasm I settled down to work while John spent most of his time trying to keep Watergate under control until after the election. What a relief it would be, I thought, to have President Nixon reelected and this bothersome Watergate matter off our hands. I fully expected that both events would transpire on or shortly after November 7, 1972.

Then, I thought, the President would be able to say, "Now here is what Watergate was all about, and it's not what the press and the Democrats were trying to make it into." I didn't know exactly what his explanation would be, but I knew it would be perfectly plausible.

President Nixon would be able to point out legitimate circumstances, I was sure, that had made the secrecy essential for the country's—not the party's—sake.

During this couple of weeks prior to the election, John and I rarely saw each other, although he did drop by the Shoreham once or twice to see how I was getting along. He was, as the White House tapes would later confirm, "putting out fires here, fires there," as prescribed by President Nixon. I was trying to light fires here, fires there, mainly under some fellow volunteers who seemed not to realize how little time was left before the Committee for the Re-election of the President's gala victory celebration.

I had not known Jeb Stuart Magruder, deputy chairman of the reelection committee very well until we worked together (with hundreds of others) on the victory gala.

Jeb was not actively involved except as an overseer, but there was something about him that made me vaguely ill at ease. On the surface, he was all smiles and good cheer —the chairman of the Junior Prom who wants to run for student body president next year. But he seemed even more affable and a great deal more cheerful when someone very important came by, someone who could mean a great deal to Jeb Magruder were he to pursue either a political or a business career.

Of all this Magruder seemed well aware. He was equally rank-conscious in the presence of other figures high in the administration or the business world. When someone would praise the floor plan or the decorations or the way arrangements had been programmed, Jeb would always respond with, "Oh, yes, yes, *we* thought it would work out best that way." Never did I hear him say: "Oh, Susan Smith and Artie Jones worked for weeks before they came up with that." The word "we" always included Jeb—or could have. "Susan Smith and Artie Jones," his subordinates, were not left out by use of the catchall "we," but they were not really given the credit they deserved, either.

Jeb was what I would call "slick." He was fully conscious at all times of his good looks, his good manners, his open, appealing personality. Yet there was something lacking. On stage, he was the suave, debonair, certain-to-succeed type, the crew captain from the Ivy League college whom every mother would hope her daughter would marry. But when the curtains were closed, and only when the curtains were closed, he was the taskmaster, the instant critic, the perfectionist offended by the imperfection of others. I suppose you could say Jeb was the perfect bureaucrat: if you did something poorly or just adequately, he would criticize your work in generalities and ask you to do it again. If you did a fabulous job on something, Jeb would add a touch or two and then take all the praise that was forthcoming. I saw more of this in him later.

There is a tendency to lump all of the middle- or lower-echelon Watergate guilty in one broad category: overambitious young men without principles. Categorization is not that simple. John and others were ambitious, overly ambitious, but they were generally not so insecure that they could not stand to have underlings given credit for anything. Jeb was.

Although I worked on the floor plans for various rooms at the Shoreham victory party, I was really what you'd call a "gopher"—go for this and go for that. But the fact that I was married to a high-ranking assistant to the President gave me a little bit of extra status. I thought of this when some of the higher-ranking people seemed to take extra pains to be nice to me. After all, I would muse, they can't be sure who John Dean will be in the next administration, so they want to be extra nice to his wife.

I didn't know who John Dean would be, either, but I knew it would be someone very, very important. The White House was relying on him a great deal. John worked closely with Haldeman and Ehrlichman, though all three remained clearly aware of who among them was lowest on the White House totem pole. Because Haldeman and Ehrlichman obviously respected John's judgment and ability, they wanted him around when Watergate matters arose; to help keep things under control.

And then there was John Mitchell, the former attorney general and Nixon campaign director. I never really got to know Mr. Mitchell well, but everyone said that John Dean was a Mitchell protégé. So it was easy for me to conclude that whichever power faction prevailed in the White House—the Haldeman-Ehrlichman combination, which seemed clearly in control, or the Mitchell faction, which was then definitely on the outside looking in but could stage a comeback, John Dean stood well with both.

At last *the big day* was here. The Nixon men and women, myself included, were relaxed, happy, confident. Some who had been through previous Nixon campaigns admitted that the atmosphere had always been quite different before. This time there would be none of that edginess, fingernail biting, and sweating it out in 1972. Around the Shoreham, we couldn't believe beforehand that the margin would be quite as big as it was, but to the great relief of those who had suffered through tension-filled election nights of the past, everyone knew it would be big enough.

One of the main concerns of the election celebration was which button a person was entitled to. This was *crucial*. The button you wore told security men at the various rooms whether you were entitled to be admitted. The brass enameled buttons of various designs were real status symbols: about all the lowest one would do was to get you into the hotel. The next highest would get you into the large ballroom. Others would enable you to attend a succession of VIP parties. At one you might see a few low-ranking White House aides and perhaps a congressman or two; at another, there would be a few senators, maybe a governor, and some officials of the reelection committee and the Republican National Committee. Still another would be sure to attract cabinet secretaries and major contributors, and the best party of all would be one that might be visited by the President and that was likely to include his closest friends, such as Bebe Rebozo, and his most powerful political allies.

"Don't fight for the best one," John had advised me. "We'll get in anyway." I was glad. I don't like to fight for things, and I'm really not at all good at it. Besides, so many of the volunteers and other workers were disappointed with the buttons they were getting that I thought perhaps someone would be really delighted to get mine.

It seemed to be a sort of "caste system" that was in operation, but everyone thought it was necessary. Thousands more people than could be accommodated wanted to be in the rooms where the celebrities gathered, and it wasn't simply a matter of rubbing elbows with those celebrities. Everyone wanted to be seen by others, and to tell others who could not get in at all that "as I was saying to Henry Kissinger last night" or "John Connally told me over a drink that he'll probably turn Republican within a year." All that is so big and so important in Washington, particularly to businessmen (who want to tell the board chairman —unless they are the board chairman), to lobbyists (who think—correctly—that the firms they represent will be duly impressed by their ability to penetrate the corridors of power), by lawyers (especially those with corporate clients), and by politicians (who at that time had detected no taint in being associated with Richard Nixon, and were convinced in any event by the precincts that were reporting in that here was a powerful man whose power would increase in quantum leaps with the new mandate).

On election morning John and I drove to the Alexandria City Hall, where we voted. Straight Republican, of course. It never occurred to me to do otherwise, considering the element we were living in. Also, being a relative newcomer to Virginia, I had virtually no knowledge of the candidates for the other offices, anyway.

From City Hall, we drove to the White House. John hopped out, and I continued in the Porsche to the Shoreham, but I planned to stay there for only a short time. Everything seemed in perfect order and there was very little to be done. Besides, it was going to take me a long time to get ready for this one!

It was truly a happy day for all these people I had come to know. Thinking back, it seems to me it was the last happy day for most.

The gown I wore was a red, full-length knit with a high collar and long sleeves. I also wore small gold earrings with diamonds and rubies, which sound grander than they are, and we tooled right up to the door of the Shoreham in our little Porsche. Once again it seemed that we were about the only ones not driving or being driven in a huge black limousine, but I thought that was good—it made us seem less stuffy. We had been given valet parking privileges, however, a fact that for an instant seemed to startle the doorman. His expression seemed to ask: "But where's your Cadillac? Or Lincoln?" But the parking credentials were valid enough, and a young valet took our car.

It was about eight o'clock, and hundreds of people were milling around. We went right to the rooms where there was less congestion. In the first one, I remember listening to the Young Americans singing group, then we went from room to room, all of them filling up with people and all with television sets just beginning to blare the good tidings—the earliest returns were Nixon all the way.

At last we wound up in the VIP room, the top of the Shoreham totem pole. Attorney General Richard Kleindienst, jovial and wisecracking as always, seemed to be having a great time. Clark MacGregor, who had succeeded John Mitchell as campaign director, wore a perpetual smile and accepted congratulations from all sides. (The next day, he resigned as head of the Committee for the Re-election of the President, with a suddenness that startled everyone. It seemed that he could not wait to get away. The abrupt, almost rude departure cast the first pall over the reelection joyousness. But not the last.)

Jeb Magruder and his wife Gail were there. People were saying they were really struck by how well Jeb looked. Now we know there was a reason. Right after the Watergate break-in and the arrests, Jeb became nervous and uptight and lost an alarming amount of weight. Most people, I was told, assumed that he was simply fearful of being fired because, being in charge of the committee for a time, he had hired Gordon Liddy, and because one of the men arrested at the Watergate was James McCord, the top security man for the Nixon reelection committee, who was answerable to Jeb.

Now on election night, he looked *really* great. Jeb probably thought, like all of us, that the reelection landslide meant that the questions of Watergate would be buried under the deluge of Nixon votes. And if not buried, at least kept under control. During his uptight, weight-losing period, Jeb had been lying to grand juries and to prosecutors, but now that was all in the past, the President was being reelected, and surely there was small reason to worry about Watergate. Even the prosecutors seemed convinced that the conspiracy went no higher than the men already indicted, and Attorney General Kleindienst had stated during the campaign that no one higher up was involved.

Other figures who were to become much better known were in the VIP suite that night. Among them were Carol and Herbert (Bart) Porter, a bright and personable young couple. Bart was particularly easy to talk to—full of jokes and wisecracks, obviously well informed on a variety of subjects. He, too, had been lying to the grand jury and the prosecutors, but to a much lesser degree than Magruder, because it was only to support Magruder's testimony. Since his involvement was so slight, he probably wasn't worried, and that night he was having a ball.

Chuck and Patty Colson came by. I remember meeting J. Clement Stone, the Chicago businessman who had contributed more than $1 million to the campaign. Maurice Stans, proud of having directed the effort that raised more than $60 million, the largest amount ever collected for a political campaign, was positively beaming as the favorable results flowed in and everyone congratulated him for his role in the victory. Others we saw were General Alexander Haig, handsome and cool, but for whom many rough months were ahead, Daniel Hofgren, Peter Flanigan, and so many others who are now just a blur to me.

I learned later that Flanigan had gone to the main ballroom to gloat about the returns with some reporters who had been anything but admiring of the Nixon administration. Some had written harsh articles about the close ties between big business and the Nixon White House, articles that particularly incensed Flanigan, since he was the White House liaison to the business community.

After baiting the reporters briefly, Flanigan asked them if they were up on the latest returns, and asked why, if the Nixon administration had been so evil, it was being returned to office by probably the largest vote margin in history.

Flanigan concluded with a memorable answer to his own question: "The reason is that this has been a very moral administration."

There was one "special suite" that we still had not visited—one in which only close friends and aides and contributors were permitted. John confessed to me that he didn't particularly want to go up.

I felt so relieved. I didn't want to go up, either. That feeling that seems to descend on me at White House functions and big political gatherings was closing in. I looked around the room we were in—the men periodically huddling around television sets, cheering loudly when new returns favorable to Nixon came in, the women standing around and chatting, looking each other up and down to see who had the most expensive jewelry.

Again, there was only one place I wanted to be: home.

"Uh-uh," said John. "But we can't high-tail it out of here until after the President arrives and finishes his speech."

About eleven o'clock, President Nixon and the First Lady did arrive, creating a mob scene that I would not have plunged into for all the diamonds and rubies in the hotel that night. Every inch of the ballroom where he was to speak was taken up by cameras, lights, and, mainly, wall-to-wall people.

We heard the President's speech on television in a room with just a few people. On the screen, Richard Nixon's face looked happier than I remembered having seen it before.

And small wonder. Here was this man who had tasted such bitter political defeats in the past, who knew he had legions of detractors and people who simply hated him— here he was, despite all the press had written, despite the "political obituaries" that had been broadcast in years past—here he was on the night of one of the greatest electoral triumphs in the history of presidential elections.

My eyes were just a little moist when I looked at him and at Pat, savoring this golden moment after so many promised ones that had turned to ashes.

John W. Dean III stood beside me, grinning broadly.

None of us could know how soon this latest and most glittering moment for Richard Nixon would also turn to ashes, nor who would light the flames.

9

Serious Business—
with a Tape Recorder

The growing shadow across the Nixon administration was not lifted magically after the votes were counted. The President was no more successful in saying, "Out, damned shadow" than Lady Macbeth had been in ordering: "Out, damned spot." In fact, the shadow darkened—almost immediately.

The last precincts had not even reported (but who needed to wait for them in a landslide election?) when John had another "Segretti matter" to attend to. It was the day after the election, and it seemed to me the President and all his supporters should just revel in the glory of their victory. For a few days, at least.

But there was very little reveling. Now, John told me, there were only a little more than four years for the Nixon men to make their mark in history.

For the first—and last—time, the President had his mandate. He could not again seek reelection. He wanted to mold the country in accordance with his own philosophy and ideology. After so many rebuffs and disappointments through the years, Richard Nixon was now at the zenith of his powers. Now he need not soften this stand or that position to appease a faction whose support he needed. Now it would be full speed ahead on a Nixon program that would impress the country not just for the rest of the decade but through the century and beyond.

Fine, I thought. But why not take a few days off first?

As events would have it, little Mo Dean, to whom R and R is essential, *would* get a few days off, even if no one else in the nation's capital would. Donald Segretti was again the reason for my being on an airplane. Fortunately for me, Segretti had made his way to southern California, and John had orders to meet with him there. John told me *Segretti* means "secret" in Italian. Very appropriate.

This trip was fine with me. I'd get to see Mom and Ronnie and Jayne and maybe even my old roommate, Pat Hornung. John and I caught a morning flight for Los Angeles. I was very pleased to be headed for "home" again. John was subdued and reflective during the flight, and I wondered: Will it be like this for four more years? The back-breaking hours? The never-ending telephone calls? The sudden changes in plans? The impossibility of living a personal life for more than the few hours here and there when the White House somehow would leave us alone?

John talked of leaving government. He had a number of good offers. But then he would quickly talk of an ambassadorship to a small country, maybe in a couple of years. Small and warm, I hoped—and far away, where the White House could not dog our every step.

There were, however, some positive aspects to our present life: there certainly weren't many dull moments, and—even more important—I was terribly proud of John, and happy to know that he was doing what he wanted to be doing.

When our plane landed at Los Angeles International Airport, we went straight to Mother's house, where Ronnie and Jayne were waiting for us. I was so happy—not just to be with the people who were dearest in all the world to me, but also to see how fond of each other Ronnie and John had become. I thought back to that night when Ronnie would not even say goodbye to me when I was leaving Los Angeles to be with John in Washington. Now the two of them acted as if they were lifelong buddies.

The next day we had to get away early. John's mission was to get to Palm Springs, where Segretti was, by the fastest means possible. We rushed to the Santa Monica Airport where the U.S. Customs Service, at John's request, had made a government helicopter available to us. Today— after all that has gone on, and after all the revelations about questionable government spending, including that on President Nixon's houses—I would have to ask myself whether it was proper for us to use government property in this manner.

But at that time, such a thought never occurred to me. In the first place, I still naively believed that the White House would not do anything that was improper. Second, I regarded the Segretti problem not as primarily political but as a genuine concern of the government. Therefore, it certainly was a legitimate function of the counsel to the President to try to solve it. And, of course, the White House could order Customs or any other agency to provide transportation and other assistance.

Flying in a helicopter was a little scary, but exciting. There were just the three of us—the pilot, John, and myself. I sat in the co-pilot's seat and looked through the all-glass bubble as the earth seemed to pull away from us, rather than we from it. When we attained the proper altitude and started moving horizontally, I got over my fright and loved watching the freeway traffic, the ocean, the palm trees, and finally the desert land below.

Once we landed at Palm Springs, I could sense that John was again tense and impatient. We rented a car and drove to a lovely cottage that was located on a golf course at the El Dorado Country Club. It was owned by friends of Herb Kalmbach, but whether Herb knew John was to meet Segretti there or not I really don't know, though I doubt it.

Herb Kalmbach is a big, bashful, by-gosh-and-by-golly sort who would do anything for anybody. He would also believe that anybody would do anything for him, if he ever asked, which he probably never would. His assumption always is that other people are decently motivated and are doing the proper thing, perhaps because that is the way he is. Of all the figures of Watergate, Herb Kalmbach is to me one of the most tragic. To anyone who does not know him, it must seem beyond belief that a man who was the head of a business organization and a law firm could have been so naive as to commit crimes without even realizing that he was doing so.

But to people who know Herb Kalmbach well, it is almost impossible to believe any other version. If someone Herb knows and believes in asks him to do something, he will assume the request is proper or else it would not have been made. And if the request comes from someone who does not wish to reveal some of the facts, Herb will not pry. He will assume that there is good and sufficient reason for his having been told only what he was told, and he will set forth to complete the assignment. Even after his bitter experience and his prison sentence, I fear Herb may still be this way. I just hope he does not again encounter "friends" so willing to gamble with his future.

I don't believe Herb had any idea that John was there to meet Segretti. Not that he would have objected, in any event. John probably just called Kalmbach, told him he was on his way to the West Coast on an important White House mission, would need accommodations in Palm Springs, and asked him if he could take care of it. Of course, he could, and gladly did.

Once again in the lap of luxury, I couldn't wait to get into my swimsuit and to soak up some sun. John did nothing to discourage me, since my presence inside the cottage while he met with Segretti was neither required nor desired.

So I lay by the pool, dozed a little, read some, and took a brief dip. Then I sunbathed a while longer and after two hours was reminded by my reddening arms and legs that I had had enough sun for the moment.

I returned to the cottage and went into the kitchen. I could hear the sound of voices coming from the far end of the cottage—voices but not words. I called out to ask John if anyone would care for some lemonade, and he said yes. So I filled a pitcher and carried it and some glasses to where John and a tape recorder and a youthful-looking Segretti were engaged in what was obviously very serious business.

I couldn't believe I was gazing on the fearsome ogre of the 1972 Nixon campaign, Donald Segretti.

I really don't know what I expected. Probably Michael Corleone, or at least Ernest Borgnine in one of his most unendearing roles. It is strange what a steady diet of newspaper headlines—the constant repetition of a name in a negative context—can do to one's imagination.

My mental picture of Donald Segretti was so far from the actual individual that I almost burst into laughter. I had been expecting Genghis Khan, and here was Huckleberry Finn. It would have been very rude to laugh, and of course there was nothing funny about his appearance. The humor lay in the gulf between conception and reality. I still sometimes had difficulty keeping the lead players of the huge Watergate cast straight, let alone the extras. And Segretti was something of an extra.

He looked so very young, as if he had just gotten out of high school. His face was covered with freckles, he had a warm smile, and he was extremely courteous. If a director were casting a Watergate movie, the last person he would choose for the role of Donald Segretti would be Donald Segretti.

Palm Springs is sort of an oasis on the Mojave Desert, and Segretti had actually been living out in the desert for weeks in a successful effort to elude the press. He had been sleeping in a sleeping bag, eating canned food he'd brought with him, slipping into the town now and again for fresh supplies, and then resuming his lonely, fugitive's life. I felt very sorry for him.

At John's suggestion he also had ridden across the country in trains to avoid the possibility of being spotted at an airport. Don agreed that the press would assume that no one of any importance or news interest would ever be riding on a train. He was correct about the press, too. No one ever spotted him.

Now he was sipping lemonade at the El Dorado Country Club. It was a deliciously ironic situation, I thought. The hated press had been thoroughly frustrated by him, and I was getting so I could enjoy the tiniest victory by "our side" over the press. We weren't scoring many, although I was sure that the press attitude toward us (I was now beginning to think of myself as a member of the beleaguered team) would soften now that the election was over.

After Segretti left, I asked John to tell me what had been going on.

"Well," he said, "for two hours I've been interviewing this fellow, and having him put everything on tape." He explained that it was important for the White House to know everything Segretti had done during the campaign.

That made good sense. The White House could not respond intelligently to press reports about Segretti's "dirty tricks" unless it had all the facts. But it seemed to me odd that there was so much concern about getting the facts *now*—now that the election was over.

John also said something about a "possible legal problem," and I pressed him no further. Lawyers are forever seeing a "possible legal problem" in everything. What I could not know, of course, was that a criminal investigation would get under way in Florida, where Segretti's campaign tricks had had their longest run. A grand jury would indict

Segretti and others later on, but at this stage I had little curiosity about Segretti and the details of his "legal problem." For one thing, his boyish appearance had disarmed me. He looked and acted like someone who might get into some innocent mischief now and again, but "criminal" was not a word that one would connect with Donald Segretti.

While I showered and dressed for dinner, John made a few telephone calls. How great it would be now, I thought. John had completed his assignment, and we could enjoy the sun for a day or two—an enticing prospect for me at any time, but particularly when the alternative is Washington, D.C., in mid-November.

By now I should have learned that whenever I get my head in the clouds, it rains. Bubbling with happiness, ready for a relaxing and loving evening with just the two of us, and hoping our stay could be stretched through the weekend (John couldn't have gotten back to the office before Friday now, anyway), I confronted my husband with a friendly ultimatum: he would not be allowed to receive or make any more telephone calls until he had taken me to dinner.

I smiled as I said it. But John seemed to have barely heard me. His face wore that strained, worried expression that was beginning to be his normal look, and his eyes were on the floor more than on me when he began to talk.

"Dinner? Oh, sure—dinner," he mumbled, as if trying to grasp the meaning of the word. "Uh . . . right." (Well, I thought, thank goodness that's settled.)

Then John looked at me, and his shoulders sort of half shrugged, half drooped. I knew the signal. He had something unpleasant to tell me.

"Mo, we can't stay on beyond tonight. Todd Hullen (Ehrlichman's aide) called from Florida. I have to go back —right away."

I sank slowly into a chair. What a dummy you are, I said to myself. When will you learn to stop planning ahead

more than ten minutes? You get your heart set on something without ever thinking that it simply isn't going to
work out—and it never does work out.

"I'm sorry," John said. "Can't be helped."

And, of course, it couldn't.

The next morning we drove to the airport, where a
small plane was waiting for us. Like the helicopter, it was
owned by the U.S. Customs Service. This time there were
just four of us aboard—the pilot, co-pilot, John, and I.
We flew to Los Angeles, where we boarded a commercial
jet for Miami. The President, Haldeman, Ehrlichman, and
others were at Key Biscayne, John said, and one or more
of them would want to listen to the Segretti tape.

Understandable. But why the rush?

Well, I thought, this is the way the White House does
things. With so much to be done, this probably is the only
way. Win an election one day, jump right back to work
the next. From such a procedure it would follow logically
that if you tape an interview with a man one day, you play
the tape for someone the next. This thought consoled me.
So did the fact that we were flying to Florida, which in
November is generally warmer and sunnier than Washington, D.C.

By the time we had spanned the continent, losing three
hours in the process, it was early evening in Miami. We
were met at the plane and driven to Key Biscayne, and to
a small house right at the edge of the presidential compound. Even though it was dark, I was able to get an idea
of what the compound is like. It is overgrown with plants,
terribly humid, practically surrounded by water. President
Nixon's home is large, of course, and it was heavily
guarded.

Military aides assigned to the compound were tussling
with a less than cosmic problem: where to find a place for the
Deans to put up that night. Apparently there was a short-
age of hotel rooms. The military aides were calling around

the Miami area to see if there was a vacant hotel room somewhere for us. I felt slightly embarrassed. With all the great concerns they had, they certainly must have been annoyed at having to try to make a hotel reservation. But orders are orders, and that was among their orders.

In the little house where we were waiting, there were government-issue desks in every room, and a television set was on in one of them. A couple of Secret Service men were asleep on some beds in the main room. They were wearing only their shorts. No one seemed to mind my presence (the men in shorts weren't even aware of it, of course). So I stayed. I wondered why the government could not provide a nearby hotel room or something better than this for off-duty Secret Service men. This place looked like a fire station. When I mentioned the fact to John, he agreed, but he also told me that the house was a very expensive one, and the government was paying dearly to lease it. Anything on Key Biscayne comes dearly.

Finally, we were told that a room had been found for us at the Doral Hotel in Miami Beach. By this time I was so tired I would have slept on an extra cot in the Secret Service headquarters. But I was glad it wouldn't be necessary.

Two military aides drove us to the hotel, a huge, gaudy place that I hated instantly. When John telephoned Lance Cooper, a friend from his Staunton Military Academy days, Lance told us to check out of the hotel immediately and he would find something better for us. We jumped at the offer.

Lance was as good as his word. He installed us in some lovely rooms at the Palm Bay Club, a beautiful tennis and swimming club in Miami. And once again, almost as soon as we arrived, so did the men from the White House Communications Agency. Silently, quickly, efficiently, they installed a telephone connected directly to the Florida White House switchboard, smiled, said goodbye, and left. I thought: Keep in touch with these fellows, Mo. They may be able to give you an advance tip on when you're going to have to leave here. I knew the minute the decision was made, they'd be back to remove the telephone.

As soon as the phones were in they began ringing. John took several calls, and then he told me to get some sun and enjoy myself: he had to go to Key Biscayne for a meeting. I assumed the meeting would be about Segretti and the taped interview from the day before at Palm Springs. Later I learned that John played the tape for Bob Haldeman and John Ehrlichman, who were so entranced with what they were hearing that when the President summoned Haldeman—which he did several times—Haldeman told him he would just have to wait "until we get through with John."

John returned to the Palm Bay Club in time to join Lance and his date, and me, for dinner there. But there was more excitement than that in store.

A commercial airliner had been hijacked, and the hijacker apparently had ordered the pilot to circle over the presidential compound. Everyone seemed tense and worried, but no one was in a panic. The acting director of the FBI, L. Patrick Gray, was in constant contact with his agents at various airports where the plane might land, and with the compound, which was naturally anxious to stay abreast of developments. In the end, the plane landed at a military base, and before it could take off again, Pat Gray ordered his agents to shoot out the tires. John talked to Gray several times that evening, but did not presume to offer him any advice on what to do.

Before we went to sleep, John told me he had some good news and some bad news.

The bad news first: we had to return to Washington the following day—Sunday, November 12. Brrrr.

Then the good news: we had been invited to fly back on Air Force One with the President and Mrs. Nixon!

I squealed with delight. If I could fly on the plane of the

President of the United States, I didn't care if it was headed for Point Barrow, Alaska.

That night I hardly slept a wink.

Was I excited?

Yes. I was excited.

To fly with the President of the United States and the First Family in the presidential plane! It was a long way from Mar Vista for Sidney Charles Kane and Irene Kelly's little girl Mo, and she had to pinch herself a time or two to make sure she wasn't dreaming. The very special aura of the American presidency had not acquired any real tarnish at that time, remember. Richard Nixon was held in just as much awe by me and millions of other Americans as any President in our history.

I couldn't wait for the flight home.

Most of all, I couldn't wait to get on the telephone at 100 Quay Street, dial Mom's number and ask:

"How do you think your daughter flew back from Florida today? Guess who was on the same plane?"

I could just see Irene Kelly Kane. She'd know right away.

And she'd be so happy she'd have one of the most joyous cries of her life.

10
The First Family

Now who would be the first of the presidential party to arrive at planeside?

The Deans, of course.

I wanted this very special event to last as long as possible. I planned to savor every second of it. John even perked up a little bit. This was not a first for him, but he took something of a paternal delight in my excitement.

Of one fact I became instantly convinced: *this* is the way to travel.

First, a car and driver were sent to pick us up. The driver would not allow us to so much as pick up a bag. He loaded all of our luggage in the car, and off we went to Homestead Air Force Base, where the big silver-blue jet— with "The United States of America" displayed in bold black letters, "The Spirit of '76" painted on the nose, and the presidential seal imprinted on the side—looked like a giant, majestic bird with its wings outstretched, ready to take flight. To me, that plane is always a thrilling sight. It represents our country, our President. I get a tingle in my spine just looking at it. Imagine how I felt about boarding it and actually flying in it!

At Homestead, were we ever given royal treatment! Again, we were not allowed to touch our luggage. Attendants met the car and whisked the bags away. No waiting in long checking lines. No struggling through endless airport corridors. Instead, we were escorted directly into the VIP lounge, where wives of men stationed at the base were serving hors d'oeuvres they had prepared for the President's guests.

And, of course, there was a bar. John ordered a Coke. From the expression on his face, I gathered that I had better order a Coke, too. While we sipped our drinks and chatted with some of the women, a polite young attendant came up to us and said: "You may board the aircraft now if you would like to."

I was dying to see the interior, so we hurried to the ramp leading to the aft door. Here we encountered the only bit of red tape there was, and the fuss was minimal. A man stood there with a manifest containing the names of all passengers scheduled to fly back to Washington with the President. We gave him our names, he put check marks alongside them on the manifest, and that was all there was to it.

Inside the aft door was an ordinary-looking galley, larger but not much different from those on commercial aircraft. Alongside and in front of the galley was the press section. During the Nixon years, only a small number of pool reporters actually flew on the presidential plane. Those not in the pool followed or flew ahead in a plane chartered for the press.

And on Air Force One the seats designated for the pool reporters were definitely "in the back of the bus." The reporters rarely saw the President, except for catching a glimpse of him as he boarded and alighted. They were not allowed in the forward section, and the President never came back to chat with them.

I understand that on one flight, Theodore H. White, the author who was writing another of his "Making of the President" books, was allowed to step into the forward section to pick up some "atmosphere" for one of his chapters. He was in and out within sixty seconds.

All of the seats were first class—that is, wide and with plenty of leg room, like those in the first-class sections of commercial airliners. On the armrests separating the seats were dishes full of candy, chewing gum, and cigarettes, the latter in special packages labeled "The Spirit of '76." As a former stewardess, I was alarmed. "Everything will fall over when the plane takes off," I told John. "These things should all be tied down in some way."

He grinned. Then he suggested that the United States Air Force knew as much as an ex-"stew" about how to fly the President's plane.

We knew right where to sit. There were name cards for every passenger.

The captain of the aircraft, Colonel Ralph J. Albertazzi, came back to exchange greetings. He was warm and jovial. "Welcome aboard," he said. "First trip?" I said yes. "Like to go through the aircraft?" Would we! He assigned a steward to show us through.

The plane was just incredible. We walked through a door to the staff working area, where there were an electric typewriter, a copying machine, and a long work table with chairs on both sides. From a passageway we entered the President's sitting room on the right, and the First Lady's sitting room on the left. Both looked comfortable and homey. There was a bathroom, which I looked into and, like a woman, noticed that it had a large makeup mirror that could be pulled down.

Just ahead was the family room, where the entire First Family could sit and enjoy the flight. Beyond, on the right side, was the presidential galley, well stocked with food and liquors. Beyond that was an unbelievable communications center, with more buttons and knobs than I've ever seen in my life.

"We can reach any post in the world like that," the steward said, snapping his fingers. There were teletype machines clicking away, and finally, up front, I was re-

lieved to see that they had left room for a cabin for the
pilot and co-pilot.

As a stewardess I had seen many planes, but none like
this. It was almost too comfortable. I couldn't imagine why
President Nixon had ordered a new plane, and I asked
myself why on earth he would even *want* a new plane.
Imagine! Push one button and reach someone in Balti-
more. Push another and get a response from Tokyo. And
the basic soft colors were so lovely, the chairs so comfortable. The carpeting was of moderate but adequate quality.
But for the new plane there would be very expensive, light
blue shag carpeting. Surely the President didn't need a
whole new airplane just to get quality carpeting, I thought.

At one point, Captain Albertazzi told John that the
President really wanted a new 747, which would cost
several millions more than the 707s then in use. But the
President had been persuaded to settle for another 707
when he was informed that 747s were too large to land on
most airfields, including several to which the President
frequently traveled and would want to travel.

It is not that I object to comfort and luxury for the
President of the United States, whoever he is. Foreign
leaders, even of some democracies, enjoy much more. The
President simply is not an average citizen with average
burdens to bear. He is on duty twenty-four hours a day—
at least he must be accessible twenty-four hours a day—
and a luxury aircraft and other perquisites are deserved
tokens of respect. What I do object to is *excess* for anyone
who is supported by taxpayers' money.

When we returned to the passenger section, I noticed
that a few others had boarded the aircraft. The first person
I recognized was Rose Mary Woods, the President's personal secretary. She was cheerful and very relaxed, enjoying
drinks with a woman friend. John introduced me to Rose,
and she said some very kind things.

I liked her instantly. Basically, I like everyone, but Rose

was special. She was in her mid-fifties, and she wore a dress and jacket, certainly conservative in dress, as befits someone working for Richard Nixon, I thought.

I wondered to myself why Rose Mary Woods never married. She is not an unattractive woman and she is intelligent and personable. My assumption is that she has always been in love with Richard Nixon.

I don't mean in any physical sense. Rose has just been so completely wrapped up in him and his career to the point that her own life and interests were always subordinated. I cannot think of any reason other than love that would cause a woman to devote virtually her entire life to Richard Nixon, or to any man not her husband. Rose worked ten- to fifteen-hour days during much of her career. She had no time to become involved with other men, or to fall in love with someone else. It's sad. But on the other hand, it is what she chose to do.

Noticing how conservatively Rose was dressed, I became conscious of my own attire and wondered how it would go over with the presidential entourage. I hoped I wouldn't attract looks of disapproval or embarrass John. I wore black gabardine slacks that day, a white blouse, and a black crew-neck sweater. Color certainly was out. I also wore Mother's $20 gold piece on a chain. I wasn't aware of anyone looking askance at me, so I stopped thinking about clothes.

Seated behind Rose and her friend were Manolo Sanchez, the President's valet, and his wife, who worked for the First Family as a maid. John chatted with them briefly while I sat—all smiles and full of anticipation—with my eyes focused on the door that led to the First Family's quarters. I was still having a difficult time believing that I was actually where I was.

Now we were airborne. It seemed to happen quite suddenly.

John explained: "The President boards last, and the minute he's on board, we take off."

My God, I gasped. The President of the United States is just a few feet from where I am sitting!

Then—suddenly—he was even closer than that.

As I stared at the door, it flew open and there he was. Except in one or two reception lines, which really don't count because you are propelled through them so rapidly, I had never seen Richard Nixon this close up before. He looked like countless photographs I had seen, but somehow more impressive in person. He did not look as tall as I had expected, but he was slouching somewhat, as always, and that may account for the other inch or two I expected.

Wait till I tell Mother about this! I thought to myself. And I just sat and stared.

President Nixon was wearing his "uniform": blue suit, white shirt, blue tie, black shoes, the American flag lapel pin. As I say—he looked impressive. I suppose any President does the first time you see him right in front of you— merely from the fact of being President. But the longer I looked at him, the more I became aware of his pale, almost pasty-looking complexion, which seemed so unusual after several days in Florida. I wondered if he had powder on, but couldn't imagine why he would.

I liked and admired President Nixon. I was all for him. If I had had any personal reservations about him, they would have been very quickly dispelled by one very good and, to me, sufficient reason: my husband was absolutely devoted to him. I know John W. Dean III will go down in history as the man who brought about Richard Nixon's downfall, and I believe that to be true. Even so, John thought then and thinks now that there was much that was great—truly great—about Richard Nixon. He believed in him, and in his policies. Of course, John was ambitious, and expected that his loyalty would be rewarded. But he could not have given such loyal service to a man he did not admire, to a President he thought was leading the country in the wrong direction.

I was able to continue to stare at and think about the President because he was greeting others and not looking directly at me. But after a minute or two he approached John and me.

It was then that I fell to pieces. I was in a panic.

What should I do? Stand up? Remain seated? Genuflect? Curtsy? Oh—why didn't I work all this out beforehand? Now it was too late. Whatever I would do now would be sure to be wrong. I would disgrace myself and humiliate John!

I had no choice. I just froze.

Then the President put his hand out to me. Thank goodness I had the presence of mind to shake it rather than kiss it. With my latent Catholicism stirring within, the thought of kissing his hand did cross my mind—fleetingly. I would have died of embarrassment if I had.

Mercifully, the President quickly turned his attentions to John, who had started to rise to his feet.

"No, no, no—be seated," the President insisted. Then, to both of us: "I'm sorry to cut your honeymoon short."

We both pretended it didn't matter at all.

Then the President addressed me again.

"Are you sure you're glad you married this guy? We're going to keep him very busy."

Somehow I was able to activate my apparently paralyzed tongue.

"I hope not *too* busy."

"*Very* busy," the President replied.

Then he spoke a few more words to John. I didn't listen to what they were, because I was struck by the fact that the President's voice in casual conversation is identical to his speech-making voice. I was aware less of his words than of the deep, strong, resonant tones and the formal quality of his speech. It was almost as if he were reading from an invisible text, even when saying "Hello, how are you?" or "How are things going?" It's strange.

Small talk is not President Nixon's strong suit, as is well known. He always avoided it when he could. In fact, he rarely came back to the passenger section on these flights. Later, everyone said I should be flattered, because it was obvious that the only reason he came back was to see me.

Soon, he turned to say a word to Manolo Sanchez and then to his doctor, Walter Tkach. Then, possibly by pre-arrangement, the door opened again and Bob Haldeman, a severe and unsmiling expression on his face, signaled—I could say practically ordered—the President to return to his quarters. The President did so immediately.

As he was leaving, President Nixon gave John a rather strong slap on the cheek. It was entirely a friendly gesture, even though the President probably used a little more muscle than was needed or than he intended. This incident returned to my mind years later when the President was embattled. At an airport, he was greeted by a large number of spectators, including an Air Force sergeant holding a small child. After greeting the sergeant and the child, the President slapped the man on the cheek, arousing questions in the press about his mental and emotional stability. I am sure the two incidents were identical in intent and spirit—and the one involving John occurred at a time when not many people were questioning Richard Nixon's stability.

Despite his facial expression when he came to the door, Haldeman (anyone would have known instantly who he was by his crew cut) could not have been nicer to us on the flight. He came by to see us later, and I liked him very much. He struck me as very personable, very thoughtful, and very real. He was so apologetic for having to call us back to Washington a second time. I was aware of Haldeman's fearsome reputation, but in all honesty I must say he was completely disarming on the flight from Florida.

John Ehrlichman also was on the plane, but he did not come into the passenger section at all.

Ron Ziegler did, however. John said the reason was that Ron wanted to take a look at me, but from what he was saying to us and others, I think it more likely that he wanted all of us to give him the credit for the fact that the President had come back to the passenger section. He kept making it clear, over and over, that it was he who had convinced the President to make that rare little visit.

Nevertheless, I thought that Ziegler was amusing. He had an endless store of funny comments. But he was also insufferably egotistical and arrogant. Nothing that happened later altered these opinions of mine about Ziegler. But I must say that when I saw more of John Ehrlichman, I realized that for egotism and arrogance, Ziegler had more than his equal in the White House.

Julie Nixon Eisenhower also came back from the family quarters to visit. At first, she spent several minutes talking to Rose Woods, and then she casually said hello to John, who introduced her to me. My gosh! She's so much prettier and so much taller than I had thought, I said to myself. And, of course, I was not in the least surprised at how conservatively *she* was dressed.

Julie wore a navy blue dress and a sweater—certainly not high fashion. She struck me as being a friendly person, somewhat like her father, but with more warmth and polish. She is much more at ease than he in social situations. Yet even during our brief chat, I could tell she has the same political attitudes as Richard Nixon, and the same all-else-is-excluded approach to politics. She talked as if she were on a campaign. With all that, I still found her sweet and nice, and I thought she looked much younger than her age. Her features are lovely. She is the type of woman who will become even prettier as she ages.

There was only one bad "vibe" between us as far as I

was concerned, and that was that she could not avoid conveying the impression that it was almost part of her "job" to come back, a "good idea" for her to do so—something she ought to do as opposed to something she really wanted to do.

Tricia Nixon Cox was also aboard, but she did not come back at all. I'd rather have it that way. If anyone wished to see us or anyone else, fine. But if anyone felt duty-bound, I'd prefer they forget it.

The First Lady herself provided me with my most startling encounter of the entire flight. Again, I had seen her before only in those mechanical Washington reception lines, where no one looks into anyone's eyes, no one remembers anyone's name, and everyone can hardly wait until it's all over.

But Pat Nixon in a less formal situation is not the same Pat Nixon. Tall, slender and pretty, she stepped through the door, wearing a silky, high-necked, mint-green dress. She struck me even on first glance as being so human—sincerely friendly, genuinely fond of people, very vulnerable, and—at that moment—supremely happy. Here was a woman who was not uptight, not aloof, not on guard against displaying any of her very human emotions. Unlike Julie, the First Lady gave no impression that she was out campaigning. She was visiting people she cared for, because she wanted to see them, and they wanted to see her.

After chatting easily with several people, Mrs. Nixon made her way to Rose Mary Woods.

There were three White House dogs in our section of the plane—King Timahoe and two smaller dogs. For most of the trip, they just slept, stirring themselves only when someone arrived to feed them something. King Timahoe, when he wasn't sleeping or eating, just sat and stared.

But the dogs apparently know a real person when they see one. All three of them were up and in the aisle now that Pat Nixon had arrived, and in a flash the dignified

First Lady was on her knees, patting and playing with the dogs, laughing gaily, having a marvelous time. At first I could hardly believe what was happening, but it went on for several minutes. Pat Nixon wasn't worrying about what anyone might think—she was having a good time with her pets. The dogs romped around and even on her, and she loved it. She displayed no inhibitions whatever.

Gee, I thought to myself, she's the only human in the entire family.

I must say that it had never occurred to me that my first real one-on-one encounter with the First Lady would take place with her down on her hands and knees.

After several minutes, she stood up, straightened her dress, brushed back her hair, and said a cheery hello to Manolo and his wife. Then she turned to John and me, smiled sweetly, greeted us, and then she disappeared up front.

I thought she was just *great*.

While I was living and loving these cherished experiences, I failed to notice a mood change in John. After all the visitations, I ordered a vodka and tonic, but again all John had was a Coke. He seemed unusually quiet, but then he always seemed quiet and even inhibited among the other members of the White House staff. He was so young to be in the midst of so many famous and powerful people.

Too soon, we arrived at Andrews Air Force Base in Maryland, and from my window seat I could see dozens of big black limousines lined up to drive most of us to our homes. There was a driver assigned to us. John identified our bags, and again we weren't allowed to carry any of them. While the luggage was being collected, I stood and watched while the President and his family boarded a helicopter. It lifted off very quickly. John and I piled into the limousine and were driven to our front door.

All of this luxury left me with no guilt feelings. I loved

it. I've always had a great talent for being able to wallow in luxury.

On the way home, John was even more moody and aloof. I got the message. When he wants some private moments to think and worry, I know enough to not intrude. We held hands, said nothing.

It occurred to me that we had not discussed why he was being called back to Washington. In all the excitement I really hadn't given the matter much thought.

But now I knew without asking. One matter was looming larger and larger in John's official life, absorbing more and more of his time and attention, plunging him into more and more frequent periods of worrying and brooding.

I did not ask for details, but I knew why we had had to return again.

The reason was Watergate.

11

Non-Fun and Games on the Washington Social Scene

John to Camp David and New York
Home for dinner

Why did I make such an entry on my calendar for
November 15, 1972?

Simply because that was the most noteworthy occurrence
of that day as far as I was concerned. It seemed innocuous
enough at the time I jotted it down. Several months later,
government prosecutors and Senate Watergate Committee
staff investigators, trying to determine if the incredible
story John Dean was telling them had even a kernel of
truth to it, found the notation intriguing. It supported
what John had been telling them as to what he had done
on that date. One investigator was suspicious, though—
he thought I might have penned it in *after* John had
begun to talk to the prosecutors.

But that was not the case. Nor was it true that I made
the note that day with the thought that in the future John
would need corroboration as to his whereabouts on *any*
given day. I am only glad my little kitchen calendar came
to be regarded as corroborative evidence.

Like many women, I make notations on a calendar as a substitute for keeping a diary. It serves to remind me of social engagements coming up, the dates on which I worked for the reelection committee or whatever, when John last took me shopping, when to start (or stop) my birth control pills, who was over on what night for cocktails or dinner.

Some other sample entries from November 1972 clearly illustrate that this was not the most lustrous period of my life. John was so deeply involved in Watergate-related matters that we did very little socially. November 14, for instance: "Shopping. Stayed home in evening." For Saturday, November 18, "Party at Taptich's 8:30 P.M." is scratched out, and there is the notation: "Stayed home." On Sunday, November 19, we were invited to a party for Isaiah Jackson, given by Mr. and Mrs. Donald Rumsfeld, but that, too, is crossed out. At the bottom of the square, there is again the notation: "Stayed home."

John told me where he had been on November 15, but not *why* he had been there.

I thought about it for a while. It was part of a developing pattern of mystery—no, more than mystery, paranoia that was gripping the White House. More and more, John and the people he was talking with on the telephone were dealing in code names and initials. His occasional references to "spaghetti" I soon realized were references to Segretti. There were allusions to "The Pipe" (John Mitchell) and "The Brush" (the then crew-cut H. R. Haldeman). Often, just the initials would be used: "CC" for Colson, "JE" for Ehrlichman; and "the P" of course meant the President.

Whom were they trying to shut out? Me? I wondered. The press? Or did they suspect that the telephones were bugged or tapped?

The answer, I finally decided, was that they were trying

to shut out everyone—and that they did fear their telephone conversations might be intercepted.

Being left out bothered me, as I'm sure it bothered other "Watergate wives." But John conveyed to me, subtly, the sense that what was being dealt with here was so *volatile,* the stakes so high that the possibility of disclosure was a risk that simply could not be taken. I soon understood that matters of vital importance to the future of our country and to the effectiveness of the administration were being dealt with—by only a few trusted aides of the President. An analogy that stuck in my mind—John may have suggested it to me—was of men wearing asbestos gloves and carrying explosive atomic materials from place to place. The only pathway was a narrow ledge on a steep canyon wall. Some day the materials would all be safely transported, but meanwhile there obviously could not be too much caution.

That elusive "some day" bothered me. I had assumed that after the election the concern over Watergate matters would diminish, not increase.

But there had been no public explanation about Watergate, and the obsession with secrecy was greater than it had ever been. I had very real misgivings, but they always gave way to my total confidence in John and to my belief in President Nixon and the hard-working, able, top people in his administration.

So when John told me where he had been on November 15, I realized all that travel was necessary because whatever the problem was, it was too explosive to be dealt with by telephone.

Suddenly, a tinge of fright ran through me.

I decided that I didn't want to know the details, and John was obviously tired and didn't want to talk.

"Hectic day," I remember him saying. He also told me that he had seen Haldeman and Ehrlichman at Camp

David, and then had flown to New York to see John Mitchell. I also recall his saying that he had sat with Maurice Stans on the flight from Washington to New York.

Whew! In those days, that constituted about as powerful a group as any that could be assembled outside the presence of the President.

There was no suspicion surrounding these men at that time, and whenever I had met any of them, I had found them brilliant and—above all—devoted. Ehrlichman's arrogance turned me off to him personally, but it in no way affected my belief that he was a thoroughly capable and entirely honorable aide to the President. The other three were all that and more—for they were courteous, pleasant people to be around.

What I did not learn about that day until much later—when I was typing John's statement for the Senate Watergate Committee, in fact—was that John had carried a cassette containing a tape-recorded conversation both to Camp David and New York. The conversation was between Chuck Colson and Howard Hunt, with Hunt demanding more money and other help for himself and the others arrested during or soon after the Watergate break-in. In the conversation there was the hint that if the demands were not met, the five men arrested in the Democratic headquarters in the Watergate, and Hunt and Gordon Liddy, might no longer remain silent about the involvement of others.

Haldeman and Ehrlichman, who deny to this day that John or anyone else ever played such a tape for them, always tried to pretend that such matters did not involve the White House directly, but only the Committee for the Re-election of the President, which Mitchell had headed. So they told John to fly to New York and play the tape for Mitchell, which he did—as Mitchell admits.

Looking back, I don't know what I would have done if

I had known the full details of what went on that day. I like to think I would have said. "John! This amounts to blackmail. You can't have anything to do with it!"

But it's useless to speculate, simply because the entire truth would not have been laid out before me or any other Watergate wife at that time. The cover-up had gone too far, and yet the men involved in it still thought it could succeed. In their minds, the power of the presidency was still so enormous that with one more little step here and maybe another little step there, the lid would be clamped on tightly and the problem that was consuming them all would cease to exist.

But on November 15 they did not realize how much distance they had already traveled, taking those "little steps." Only someone on the outside, someone not involved, someone with an objective point of view, could have perceived reality for them at that point.

John was exhausted, but there was no way I could insist that he do less during his working hours. And by now it was certainly clear to me that wherever we were, if there was an emergency at the White House, John would respond to it.

One thing I could do right then, however, was to try to help him get some relaxation between the ever-encroaching times of crisis.

I was becoming aware of something that would be far more evident and worrisome to me later on—John was drinking more than usual. He never got drunk—he never does, no matter how much he drinks. His speech is never slurred, and, in fact, the only way I became aware of the extra drinks was that I tried to keep up with him. Ordinarily, we would have two drinks at night. Suddenly, John was asking for a third. I would join him. Then it was a fourth. I would join him again—and pay for it the next morning. Obviously, that couldn't last. I dropped out. And since John's behavior was always normal and rational, I let him go on with the extra drinks without me. It was the tension he was under, I told myself.

Good medicine for tension was at hand. John's parents had invited us to join them for the Thanksgiving weekend at their home in Greenville, Pennsylvania. That sounded marvelous to me: a small town, everyone enjoying Thanksgiving dinner, no need to playact, no real concern about the power structure.

We flew to Greenville, had a wonderful home-cooked dinner—and once again I sank into a state of relaxed bliss, knowing we would be out of the pressure cooker for four full days.

Some things, I just never learn.

As I should have expected, the telephone rang on Friday morning. It was an urgent call, of course. It was for John, of course. And he had to return to Washington immediately—of course.

This time it was not the White House, but John Mitchell who had located John through the White House switchboard. About what? Mitchell didn't say. He had just asked John to return, and when a man like Mitchell, who was always the gentlest and most considerate of the major administration figures, made such a request, there had to be a real emergency.

I could see that despite John's parents' obvious disappointment, the Deans were glowing with pride at how important their son was. Imagine, a man like John Mitchell—the former attorney general, the President's key advisor—calling *their* son to return to Washington for a meeting. I began to beam a bit, too. *My* husband, their son, was indeed someone to be proud of.

John had no trouble making flight arrangements on the Friday after Thanksgiving, a day when most normal people stay put with their loved ones. He promised he would return the next day, in time for the big party his parents had planned in our honor at the Greenville Country Club Saturday night.

And he was as good as his word, flying in again on Saturday with a worried look on his face—a look that disappeared when he saw how delighted the three of us were to have him back. John also knew how much pleasure his parents would derive from the Saturday night party, introducing their son—*President Nixon's counsel*—and his wife to all their friends and neighbors. This was a night they would always cherish, and John was not going to spoil it by being in a dour mood.

I barely got to ask him the question, "How'd things go?"

"Rough. It was a complicated meeting. Haldeman and Ehrlichman were down from Camp David. But let's start thinking about the party."

Whatever the explanation could have been, to me the meeting became just one more mysterious bead on a lengthening string, and I took John's suggestion and started concentrating on the party—which, as we expected, turned out to be a delightful and joyous event.

Back in Washington, D.C., through December I busied myself with Christmas shopping and cooking and entertaining, the last in a small way. We were still canceling a number of invitations to dinners and cocktail parties— John either worked too late to get to them, or he knew in advance he would be exhausted and therefore would ask me to make excuses.

One dinner party we did attend, however, was at the home of Kenneth Parkinson, a lawyer for the Committee for the Re-election of the President, who would one day sit in a courtroom alongside John Mitchell, H. R. Haldeman, John Ehrlichman, and Robert Mardian, accused of involvement in the Watergate scandals. He would be the only one of the five to be acquitted.

But in December 1972, Kenneth Wells Parkinson, a

sandy-haired, mild-appearing, soft-spoken, moderately affluent lawyer who lived in Westmoreland Hills, Maryland,
and his wife Pam were two pleasant human beings who
seemed genuinely concerned with other people's problems
and with putting everyone at ease.

It was a lovely evening, with good feelings all the way
around. The only note even slightly off-key was the one
that kept rattling around in my head: Why were we
there? John and I were quite a bit younger than the Par-
kinsons, and we didn't know them at all well.

On the way home, I remarked about this to John, who
smiled and said: "Ken probably thinks it won't hurt him
to have some friends who work at the White House."

Of course, I thought. That was it. The old Washington
power game not only never comes to an end—there isn't
even a timeout. But I was just beginning to get wise. From
that evening on, I think that every time we went out, I
would subconsciously ask myself: Now why are *they* giving
the party? Why are *we* invited? How come the Joneses
have been invited and the Smiths have been left out?

You hate yourself for thinking such thoughts, but you
think them anyway. And if you're like me, you treasure
more and more the "two-person parties" and the evenings
with just Peter Kinsey, the Fieldings, or Heidi and Mor-
gan, or Barry and Susie, the evenings when you don't have
to wonder why anyone is there—you know: it's because
they are your *friends.*

I guess I'm funny in a way—I can't really relax under
any other social circumstances. That's why I was most often
relieved, not miffed—when John asked me to cancel engagements we had accepted. Eyeing everyone suspiciously
is not my idea of a pleasant social evening.

We canceled more parties than we attended during that
month, and finally it was Christmas Day. For us the high-
light was the visit to our town house of John's son by his
first wife, Karla. Johnny and his dad are crazy about each

other, even though they sometimes go for long periods without being able to get together. Johnny was four in 1972, and I often reflect on what a blessing it was that he was no older. He was just the right age to be interested in the fact that his father worked for the President, but not so overwhelmed that he peppered his father with questions about the Nixons, the White House, Air Force One, the helicopters, and so on. Thus they were able to get to other subjects rather quickly, and that was good medicine for John. He and Johnny spent most of their time dealing with important matters like toy trucks and trains, tricycles and roller skates. It was good therapy for the father, and Johnny's merry eyes and squeals of delight made it rather clear that he, too, was enjoying himself to the fullest.

Karla had done a marvelous job with Johnny. He is a bright, well-behaved, cheerful little fellow, and with so much notoriety swirling around his father for so long, he has adjusted well. Karla and John have maintained a friendly, understanding relationship.

As 1972 drew to an end, things seemed to ease up slightly for John at the White House. Perhaps it was just the holiday season, a time when even to men driven by power the importance of family reasserts itself. Somewhat to my surprise—because the pace had been so hectic for so long—John suggested one day that we spend the tag end of December and the first few days of January in Palm Springs, California.

The President and his family would be in Florida, and Haldeman had arranged for a back-up Air Force One flight to carry some of the staff and their families to California—including the Deans!

As I have made clear all along, I am always willing to trade a wet and often cold and raw climate for one that features sunshine and balmy breezes. We left Washington the day after Christmas.

This time the President and his family were not aboard,

but plenty of interesting people were. Most of them had their children along, and I thought how good it was to see these men—for once—not flying without their wives, not bustling around with worried scowls on their faces, not acting as if their failure to be attentive to business for even five minutes might sink the Republic.

The Haldemans were among the passengers—foremost among the passengers, in fact, since, with the President not aboard, his chief of staff was the highest-ranking member of the administration present. The Ehrlichmans were also on the flight with some of their handsome children, and so were the Zieglers, the Kleins, the Higbys and the Kehrlis.

For once, these powerful, driven men were not operating in that tight little world of their own, where they talked only to each other and where I doubt if they even thought very often of their wives or the world in which these women lived.

On this winter vacation flight to the West Coast, they were so much more human than I had ever seen them before. Haldeman and Ehrlichman in particular seemed to enjoy their children and this opportunity to witness once again what marvelous jobs their wives had been doing in bringing them up. But I wondered how often—or, indeed, if—they gave any thought to all that the mothers had done while they attended to business and political matters that somehow are always so much more important than raising the next generation.

Jo Haldeman and Jeanne Ehrlichman are both very attractive and intelligent women. I never got to know either of them well, but in our brief encounters I liked and admired both of them.

We didn't see a lot of the Zieglers on the trip. Their children were much younger, and I imagine the parents had to keep an eye on them all the time. Of course, we already knew the Higbys well, and Herb Klein—well, everyone has always liked Herb Klein. President Nixon once said of Herb, as revealed on a White House tape, that his head just wasn't "screwed on right," but everyone else seemed to find it so. Long before December 1972, Klein had fallen from grace in the White House, and everyone knew it. He was often the subject of snide remarks by Haldeman, Ehrlichman, and Ziegler, and there was something slightly pitiful about this earnest, decent man whose major failing seemed to be that he would not play what the White House called "hard ball." Herb was fully aware that he no longer belonged to the inner circle, but he stayed on at the White House because he felt that he could do some good for Richard Nixon, not because the President could do some good for him. Herb Klein was rare—and precious. And unappreciated.

We landed at an Air Force base near Palm Springs, and to my amazement (I should have been getting used to it by then) the White House had thoughtfully provided a fleet of limousines to pick us up. There was no mention—no thought, even—of the fact that the taxpayers had paid for our flight and now would pay for our transportation from the airport to where we would stay—an hour's drive away. It just seemed perfectly proper that people in responsible posts in the government should be treated in this fashion. Had this happened later, after all the criticisms of the "imperial presidency" had begun to sink in on me, I would have had some second thoughts. In 1972, we did not look upon our President or ourselves as "imperial." We simply radiated delight at the various perquisites, assumed they were no more than we deserved, and enjoyed them to the fullest.

In addition to free air and ground transportation, there was yet another "perk"—free housing. After several days at the El Dorado we joined the Higbys and the Kehrlis in a four-bedroom house with a swimming pool, that was on sale for $95,000. I remember the price so well because John and I briefly considered buying it.

The home was owned by Jack Mulcahey, of whom I had never heard, but I was told he also had a large estate in Ireland. Someone described him as a friend and supporter of the President, who, on a presidential trip to Ireland, had given extravagant gifts to some of the White House staff. If any thought was given to the propriety of White House staff members' staying, rent free, in a home owned by a man who conceivably could want favors from the government, that thought was never expressed in my presence.

Nor did it occur to me. John and I were always staying in the homes of friends, and having friends stay with us, and I had not acquired the habit of thinking of ourselves and the Higbys and Kehrlis as people with influence. To me, we were still all just friendly young couples, frequent givers and recipients of hospitality.

I assume the other couples on the trip stayed in other houses provided by affluent friends of the President, but I didn't wonder about it. I honestly thought some people just do nice things for other people without consciously thinking of asking for or getting anything in return.

Without trying to justify what went on and what has always gone on, I do believe that people in government sometimes accept such gestures without thinking any more about it than ordinary people involved in identical situations. It just isn't human nature for everyone who joins a government payroll to begin immediately to forget his past life pattern and to question the motives of everyone who does him a favor. At least, it hasn't been human nature. In the post-Watergate era, perhaps it will be.

So it wasn't my conscience that was bothering me when I begged John to take me to a hotel. Rather, it was the idea of staying in the same house with people I did not feel terribly close to. I like my privacy, and am willing to surrender it only when people I know well and love dearly invite us to stay with them, or come to stay with us.

We had known the Higbys fairly well for several months, and I liked them, but we weren't intimate friends. The Kehrlis were people I had known only a short time, and I feel terribly shy and ill at ease around strangers. I didn't want to spend twenty-four hours a day feeling ill at ease, and it would have been worth it to me to pay for a hotel room just so John and I could be alone.

John said no. It would be rude. We would needlessly offend people he had to work closely with. Higby was a top aide to Haldeman, and Kehrli was also a very important member of Haldeman's staff who later became the White House staff secretary.

When John stubbornly refused to move to a hotel, I exploded. It was one of the worst arguments we had had since I insisted that we either get married or forget about each other.

This arrangement wasn't living—it was playacting. We were on stage, being careful not to miss a cue, watching our words and actions and even our costumes to make certain they did not offend someone, because that someone might be in a position to take it out on us later. I wondered then—and now I wonder even more—what it must have been like to work in the White House, being on edge every moment, trusting no one, fearing that dreadful moment when the word would finally come from on high that you were no longer in favor, you were no longer trusted, your loyalty was suspect, you were on the down side of the hill. Yet men subject themselves to this sort of uncertainty and torment and unreality for four years or eight years and in some cases even longer.

My patience is one of my failings, and probably one of my saving graces as well. But on this occasion, it deserted me. I could not see why anyone would be offended if we moved out—they probably would have enjoyed the added privacy too.

But John, during that time in California, wasn't willing to offend anyone—except his wife. So we stayed. I should have known. Wives and family always play second fiddle to power. Why should this occasion have been any different?

Like a good soldier (all Washington wives must be good soldiers), I took my expected defeat with as much good grace as I could muster. That did not preclude my sulking, spending most of my time reading and sleeping, and snapping churlishly whenever John came around to urge me to join the "fun." After a while, he gave up on me (I didn't care) and spent most of his time playing tennis with Haldeman, Ziegler, and Higby. Don't ask me what *their* wives were doing. Sulking, too, perhaps.

While playing golf at the El Dorado Country Club with Herb Kalmbach, John encountered one of the President's richest and most important supporters, Leonard Firestone. He is, of course, the fantastically wealthy owner of the automobile tire manufacturing company that bears his family name. For years, Leonard Firestone had entertained Richard Nixon and his family at his palatial home in Palm Springs, and of course all the President's men fully realized the importance of not offending *this* key supporter.

Firestone graciously invited the Kalmbachs and the Deans to join him and Mrs. Firestone for tea, and, of course, they were happy to accept. But John W. Dean III ran into a problem: his wife, still in a snit, had disappeared, and he could not locate her. I had gone shopping, bought myself more than my budget allowed, and was not the least apologetic about my purchases or about missing the tea at the Firestones, which John had attended alone.

John was a bit nicer to me after that, and I even emerged from my seclusion long enough to soak up some sun. But I never felt really happy. After John apologized to me, I realized that he wasn't really relaxed and happy either and that he needed rest and recreation a lot more than I did.

I felt selfish for having taken out on him what really was less his fault than the fault of the kind of life we were caught up in.

By the time New Year's Eve arrived, no one was in the mood for an uproarious celebration. For one thing, we didn't feel completely at home with each other—far from it. For another, White House people in social situations cannot afford to shed their images—how they want others to think of them. I often wondered how these people acted when they had their guard down. Haldeman and Ehrlichman were devout Christian Scientists and of course never drank or smoked, but surely they weren't *always* "at attention." I wondered if when no one was looking, one or both of them might sneak up and slap their wives on the behind, or if one or both might lounge around the house in pajamas on a Sunday morning, playing with the dog, or even playing a practical joke on one of their children. And I wondered what Bruce Kehrli might be like when he was in his own home, alone with his wife, protected from disapproving glances.

In any event, I didn't have to wonder what New Year's Eve would be like with the Higbys and the Kehrlis. They —and we—would all be on best behavior, not doing or saying anything that might conceivably provoke displeasure and send a talebearer with New Year's Day tidings to Haldeman or Ehrlichman. It wasn't quite that bad—but it was a dull evening.

So our behavior that New Year's Eve at a popular restaurant called Ethel's Hideaway was extremely decorous— a few drinks, properly spaced; polite talk, a nice dinner, and bemused, slightly disapproving observations of the other "revelers" at Ethel's Hideaway. Came midnight, we allowed ourselves a mild toast to 1973 (the way that year turned out for most of us, we should have filled our glasses fuller, with something a lot stronger). Then, for perhaps two minutes, we really took leave of our dignity and tooted horns. Embarrassed by our own raucous behavior, we put down our horns, made no attempt to stifle yawns, and before the New Year was five minutes old, we headed for home and bed. As far as I could tell, no one had taken offense at anything anyone else had done or said, so the evening had to be chalked up as a roaring success. For me, there was an added joy: John said we would be going home on January 2.

It is difficult for me to describe my feeling about this vacation without reflecting on personalities rather than circumstances. The Higbys and the Kehrlis were and are fine people, and were and are my friends. But we were all prisoners, thrust together in intimate situations that probably none of us would have chosen, but that came about because—as I have said before—the power game knows no intermissions.

New Year's Day passed uneventfully—sitting in the sun, more tennis, some watching of the college football bowl games on television. But there was exciting news that made me more anxious than ever for the trip home the following day.

The President's brand new Air Force One—in which he had not even flown—would fly us back to Washington!

Although I couldn't imagine a plane more luxurious than the old Air Force One, I knew this one just had to be, since everyone said the President was so excited about it and so anxious to fly in it. But he couldn't—at least, not just yet. And I could! That was such delicious irony.

Whenever a new aircraft joins the presidential fleet, it must have a minimum of fifty hours in the air before the President is allowed to travel in it. A wise safety precaution, I thought. But then I began to worry: Are we being used as human guinea pigs? Does anyone know if the thing will get off the ground—and stay off until it makes its designated landing?

When I told John what I was thinking, he chuckled and

reassured me. The plane needed only one more flight to complete the required fifty hours. In other words, it had already flown about forty-five hours—with no problems whatsoever.

In that case, I told John, I would submerge my urge to rush to the telephone to call American Airlines for a reservation.

The last test flight was even more uneventful than I could have wished. Following the drive to the airport, again courtesy of the taxpayers, we boarded, oohed and aahed at the newness of everything, remembered not to drop cigarette ashes on the beautiful light blue carpeting (the seats were covered with protective sheets), and five hours later we landed at Andrews Air Force Base.

If I had worried about such things, I would have felt all right about the legitimacy of this return flight. The plane had to go somewhere during its fifty hours of test flying, and it might just as well go with people on board and take them where they wanted to go.

There was plenty of liquor on the flight, just about the same amount at the end as at the beginning. No one really drank much on those flights—we all had to maintain our images of sobriety in front of each other. Rose Woods—on my first Air Force One flight from Miami—was the only person I ever remember seeing take more than one or two drinks.

At the end of the flight, there they were again—the big black White House limousines, each driver seeking out his passengers, locating their luggage, and then delivering them to their front door.

It's the *only* way to travel.

"Feeling better?" John asked me. "About things?"

As a matter of fact I was. I couldn't deny that I enjoyed the comforts and the attention and the excitement of flying in the President's plane.

Well, John said while we were being driven home, there

was more excitement coming up—the second inauguration of Richard M. Nixon as President of the United States. Would I like to work with the Inaugural Committee? It would be fun—and something I could tell our grandchildren about. And I would be in on the takeoff of what John said—and at the time sincerely believed—would be one of the most exciting and successful presidential administrations in the nation's history.

"Of course," I squealed. "I'd love it."

"I'll talk to Jeb in the morning," John said. "He's the man in charge."

Just then the limousine stopped in front of 100 Quay Street in Alexandria, and the driver brought our luggage in while I delightedly sank into a chair and kicked off my shoes.

"Mo," said John, looking at me and suddenly turning serious, ". . . about the second administration, the excitement and all—there are going to be some rough stretches of road along the way, too, some pretty big bumps. You should know that."

Oh, John, I thought. What a worrier. What a foolish worrier.

12

The Selling of the Presidential Inauguration

January 1973. Long before "the fall," and long before anyone really expected there to be a "fall." The weather—mild. Spirits—rising. The pace—slower. The atmosphere —not nearly so charged.

John was looking better. He was even getting home earlier. Chuck Colson was more cheerful than I had ever seen him, inviting his White House colleagues to come out to his wooded estate in McLean, Virginia, and to help themselves to the plentiful supply of firewood. Ken Clawson, who was very close to Colson and who seemed determined to fill his vacancy in the post of White House tough guy or hatchet man once Colson had left, was delightedly hosting Sunday brunches at his home. The social scene—which did not exactly glitter at any time during the Nixon years—began at least to sparkle a little bit here and there. With the second inauguration coming up, many people who didn't ordinarily give dinner parties were doing so. In little more than a week, John and I were invited to two receptions at Washington's exclusive F Street Club, where I had never been before.

All of this activity was highly visible, and it seemed to pervade the entire city. From all parts of the country, wealthy businessmen and their wives, heavily laden with jewels and furs, were descending on Washington, hungering for invitations to the best parties, and absolutely ravenous for someone, anyone, in high office to pay attention to the fact that they were there. In cases where contributions to the campaign had been generous, this was no problem.

Among the parties we attended was one of the strangest ever during our years in Washington—because it was so informal.

The host was G. Bradford Cook, a very wealthy and high-ranking member of the staff of the Securities and Exchange Commission. Cook, as much as anyone I met in Washington, appeared to be a man who had come to stay. He and his wife had bought an enormous six-bedroom home in Spring Valley, the exclusive tree-lined area in northwest Washington where both Presidents Johnson and Nixon lived while they were vice president.

Cook, ordinarily not the ebullient type, was positively joyous this cold January night. Just why is now known. He was about to become chairman of the SEC, succeeding William Casey, who was a guest at the party that night. Another guest was Maurice Stans, who was riding high at that time because he had been so successful in raising funds —$60 million—for the campaign. Obviously Stans was a man of great influence with the President, and John noticed how attentive Cook was being to Stans. When I asked why, John explained that Stans would have a voice in who would become the new chairman of the SEC.

The scene featuring the pampered guest and the overly solicitous host sticks in my mind because it so plainly illustrates one of the most disillusioning aspects of life in Washington, D.C. In little more than a year, Stans would be on trial in the notorious Vesco case, and one of the key witnesses against him would be Bradford Cook. A lesser witness would be John Dean. The scene shifts that fast—

from what appear to be unlimited horizons to a precipice so sharp that even those who seem surest of foot cannot avoid falling from it.

Cook was so anxious to make his mark on the Washington scene—and so sure that cocktail parties featuring prominent guests were one way to do it—that his new house had not even been furnished by the night of the party. There may have been other reasons for holding the party under those circumstances. For one thing, there was a band, and without furniture, there certainly was plenty of room for dancing. I must say that the idea that someone would give a party in Washington without everything in perfect order appealed to me. The informality was a touch of Beverly Hills.

While John and I danced, I noticed the Colsons drift by, and Clark and Barbara MacGregor, the Kleindiensts, Ron Ziegler, Dean Birch, and others. The world was beginning to crumble around many of us at that very moment, but we were unaware. The least aware seemed to be Stans and Cook. Brad Cook's need for the lovely house in Spring Valley was to vanish along with his brilliant future and his reputation. It was to be the pattern of the lives of almost half the people at the party that night, our own included.

All that glitters is not all that goes on in Washington. While people stumbled over each other trying to get to parties, often missing the entire event because they could not make their way through the traffic-clogged streets of the inauguration-obsessed capital, cash was being stuffed into envelopes and surreptitiously delivered to lawyers and/or wives of the seven Watergate defendants, whose trials were under way and were attracting little attention.

The scene in Washington that January almost defies description. Power was evident everywhere. President Nixon had ordered the Christmas bombing in North Vietnam, and despite some outcry, there was no significant challenge to this or any other action he took. To me, still an ingénue in politics, Washington at that time was unlike any city I had ever been in before—including the Washington of the first Nixon administration. Always before, there had seemed to be a number of powerful forces battling one another—the Congress versus the White House, the press against the President, the Democrats fighting the Republicans. Now it seemed that the few voices that were raised against the President were too puny to be effectively heard. Not that I minded. It just seemed so different that it was— in a way I can't explain—frightening.

The feeling was not often expressed, but it was there. President Nixon had won every state except Massachusetts, and the District of Columbia. Obviously, the people of the country approved of him and the way he and his men (there weren't many women of power) were running the country. You could almost sense that people who had been strong critics of Nixon were now asking themselves if there were not some things they had missed. Perhaps this man and his policies, after all the years of bitter struggle against both, were really what the country wanted and needed.

During those heady days leading up to the inauguration, only a handful of people were fully aware of the scandals that were gnawing away at the administration.

Looking back, I wish that I had known about one element of those scandals—the payment of money to the Watergate defendants. By January 1973, it was too late for me to have done a whole lot of good, even if I had known and had acted as I believe I would have. But I might have helped some.

This aspect of the cover-up—when I first learned of it and since—is something I really cannot imagine intelligent men allowing themselves to become involved in. In the first place, there is no end to it. When people demand money in exchange for silence, or in exchange for anything, no amount will ever satisfy them. They will go on and on until the well runs dry. Surely everyone knows this. Why wouldn't the President's men?

Besides, if John had confided this part of Watergate to me, I am sure I would have said what I have said on so many other occasions: that the truth always emerges. How could anyone believe that men like James McCord and Howard Hunt would simply traipse off to jail, accept the fact that their lives had been ruined, and never reveal to anyone what they knew about the involvement of men whose reputations were still intact? It isn't human nature —except for very unusual people, like Gordon Liddy. I also hope I would have pointed out to John that it was terribly wrong.

I think I could have convinced him. He tended to that line of thought, anyway, as he later proved. He knew the following March that the best thing for the administration to do was to air all the facts and take its losses—because the whole history of Watergate was that things kept getting progressively worse.

The men involved in Watergate needed someone to point out reality to them. When power swallows you whole, it swallows your ability to think that what you are doing is a *crime,* particularly if you are in the White House, working for the President. You have a higher calling, a cause. You can explain all this to your wife, and she'll probably believe all you say. But if you go further and add that "in order to serve this higher cause—the President's cause—we're passing out hundred dollar bills to six or seven burglars," even your wife will probably say: "Are you crazy? That's against the law!" But no wife had that opportunity. She was not told.

During the days preceding the second inauguration, I had work to do. John had talked with Jeb Magruder, who still had all of his regained aplomb, and who was the head of the Inaugural Committee. Jeb introduced me to Mike

Duval, who was chief of one of the many divisions into which the committee had been divided. Mike's division was in charge of having special inaugural coins and medals struck, all with likenesses of the two men around whom all the hoopla revolved—Richard M. Nixon and Spiro T. Agnew. Mike said he needed help with the medals.

I was underpaid and overworked, but it didn't matter. Neither did the fact that we worked in old, uncomfortable buildings on a deteriorating military post. It was thrilling to have any role at all in such a historic event. Every other night or so I would telephone Mother, and, as always, she was the most thrilled of all.

The design of the medals had been decided upon, but it was necessary to get bids, so I was assigned to contact manufacturers and to arrange meetings at which they could submit prices. I remember that we found three firms that were anxious to bid. Everything went well.

But my other role on the committee turned out to be lost motion. Everyone wanted to raise as much money as possible from the inauguration, which struck me as rather odd and tasteless. The tickets to the various receptions ranged in price from $15 to $25 per person, and everything else had its price tag—the coins, the medals, souvenir books, and so on. I could understand that the committee should not sustain a loss, but the emphasis on all sides was not on breaking even, but on making a profit—and the larger the profit, the better. Why? The campaign was over, and the surplus was several million dollars. Why bleed the people more to see their own President inaugurated?

Among the ideas bandied about for getting more dollars into the till was one that landed in my lap. Someone thought it would be great—and very profitable—to sell a special Nixon inaugural wine. The idea was to buy a certain quantity of wine from one of the domestic producers, apply special inaugural labels to the bottles, and sell the wine for what the market would bear. It fell to me to contact vineyards all over the West Coast and in upstate New York, to outline the project, and to get the wheels turning.

Well, despite some misgivings about the commercial aura of the inauguration in general (I was really bothered by the thought that only the affluent could attend most of the events), I wanted this wine project to succeed—because it was my assignment. Besides, purchase of the special wine was in the category of options. Those who could afford it could buy it if they wanted to. For those who could not, it certainly was less a calamity than being frozen out of inaugural festivities (other than the public swearing-in ceremony, the President's speech, and the parade) for lack of money to buy a ticket.

Several wineries were interested in bottling the special inaugural wine, including Gallo and Paul Masson. I sent a steady stream of memos to Jeb Magruder and to the honorary chairman of the inauguration, J. Willard Marriott, who, as a devout, teetotaling Mormon, probably had a dim view of the project from the beginning. All of the communications back and forth went through Mike Duval, of course, and he, after I had worked somewhat feverishly for several days, told me "everyone thinks it's a great idea," but that there was too little time. Perhaps that was so, but I always suspected that Mr. Marriott's lack of enthusiasm doomed the project. He was willing to sell alcohol at his motels and restaurants but took a dim view of associating it with the President of the United States.

Until Inauguration Day itself, I was busy attending meeting after meeting, and seeing that orders for the medals were fulfilled.

Jeb Magruder had fulfilled his role effectively, and everything went smoothly on Inauguration Day.

At last the big day arrived. I was determined to enjoy it, and not miss a single second if I could help it. The majesty of it all was overwhelming: the President and the First Family all looking so happy, so distinguished, so clean, so *good.* And Vice President and Mrs. Agnew—the same. Chief Justice of the Supreme Court Warren Burger, white-haired, handsome, seemed to have been specially molded for the post he held—he looked exactly the way a chief justice ought to look. And then there were all the cabinet secretaries, the prominent senators and congressmen, governors from all over. I kept reminding myself that I was really and truly there, and that I should make the most of it—it might not happen to me again.

John went to his office in the morning, and the plan was for me to join him there, so we could then go to the Capitol together for the late morning swearing-in and the Inaugural Address, for which he had reserved seats in a special section. But John—surprisingly—decided not to go to the Capitol ceremonies. I was disappointed, and wanted to know why.

"I have work to do, Mo."

"Can't it wait?"

"No, it can't."

There was a finality to his last remark that I had come to recognize. I never argued with him to persuade him to change his mind when he said something that positively. I knew that he had a very special job, and that as long as he held it, there would be many situations like this.

And as always in such circumstances, John had thoughtfully arranged for me to be taken care of. Chuck and Patty Colson would swing by the Executive Office Building in a White House car, and the three of us would ride to the Capitol together, and sit together for the ceremonies.

It was a happy occasion. Inauguration Day is somewhat like New Year's Day. You feel the slate is wiped clean. There is a fresh beginning. Even people who oppose the President who is being inaugurated (in Richard Nixon's case, the District of Columbia was filled with them) seem inclined to give him the benefit of every doubt, and to want him to succeed. And so it was when Richard Nixon raised his right arm that day and swore to "preserve, protect and defend the Constitution of the United States of America—so help me God." I looked at the Democratic senators who had been so opposed to the President—Humphrey, Muskie, Kennedy—and wondered why the defeated Democratic candidate, Senator George McGovern, had not the grace to attend. Then there were Mike Mansfield, Robert Byrd, Hugh Scott, Robert Griffin, the majority and minority leaders in the Senate. My dear friend, Senator Barry Goldwater, whom I had come to know when I was dating Barry, Jr., could not disguise his pleasure at being present for another inauguration of a Republican as President. Barry and Peggy Goldwater had invited us to have dinner with them the following week, and I was looking forward to it. Although Barry Goldwater's political philosophy is highly controversial, there can be no dispute about his warmth and decency and his sense of humor, which make him very pleasant company. I'm crazy about him.

After the ceremonies, the Colsons and I boarded a specially chartered bus that took us back to the White House where we could watch the Inaugural Parade as it crawled along Pennsylvania Avenue from the Capitol to the White House. We bumped into Jeb and Gail Magruder and chatted with them during the brief ride.

Back at the White House, I felt (1) exhilarated, (2) exhausted, and (3) exempt from further activities until a VIP reception in the Executive Office Building. I rested briefly in John's office, and from there, we went together to the reception.

The first familiar face that I spotted told me—if I had had any doubts—that this was *the* reception of the entire inauguration. The face belonged to Charles G. (Bebe) Rebozo, President Nixon's closest friend, who was squiring a very pretty woman. If this was the reception Rebozo had chosen to attend, then obviously it was the one for the people closest to the President, and those in the highest positions in the government or in the party.

No doubt about it. Next I saw Nancy Reagan and Governor Ronald Reagan of California, his hair a trifle orange-ish, his smile and manner so familiar to me, and to anyone who has lived in or near Hollywood. Herb Kalmbach had come east for the occasion, and he was the only one who didn't seem to be enjoying himself to the fullest. He seemed preoccupied and somewhat uptight, which is not characteristic of him. I was to learn much later that Herb, who had given up the task of raising money for the Watergate defendants the previous September, had been summoned to a meeting in the midst of the inaugural festivities, and had been asked to raise even more money. He had left the meeting, held in John Mitchell's office and attended by John among others, in a dejected mood.

That happy inauguration time was not a happy time for Herb. He had been forcibly reminded that despite all the surface indications that all was well and that the future looked bright, payoffs were still being made to the Watergate burglars—nearly five months after he had belatedly sensed the wrongness of that particular operation and had bowed out of it. No wonder Herb's basset hound eyes looked particularly doleful that night.

The array of arriving and departing celebrities almost made me dizzy. Happy Rockefeller was there with Governor Nelson Rockefeller of New York, Vice President and Mrs. Agnew, more senators, more congressmen, and more governors came into view, and soon I began to sense that old familiar feeling inside that demands: let's get out of here. It's a feeling that I am about to suffocate, and it always hits me, sooner or later, at a large formal gathering.

With all the parties that we had gone to since Christmas, John and I were ginger ale-ing it, so we stopped in at only one of several cocktail parties that were going on (one given by Jack Gleason, a fund-raiser who was later indicted) and then to my great relief—we made our way home.

We had happily given our tickets for one of the several inaugural balls to Lance Cooper, John's old and dear friend who had come up from Miami in the hope of getting in on some of the exciting activities. Our tickets were to the ball held at the Smithsonian, and we agreed to pick up Lance and a woman friend there after we were certain the President had been at the Smithsonian and had departed for one of the other galas.

That agreement was a mistake. Washington traffic is always bad. That night, it was horrendous. There must have been a thousand huge black limousines, including those from the White House, the State Department and Pentagon, the diplomatic corps, the congressional leadership—plus several privately owned "limos" and every one that was available for rental. There were hundreds of Mercedes, and ordinary Chevrolets, Buicks, Fords, and Chryslers were mixed in, and the result was inevitable: chaos. By some miracle, we made it to the Smithsonian, even though our military driver provided by the Inaugural Committee did not know Washington. We plucked Lance and his friend from the huge mob in front, and spirited them away.

Lance was like a little boy at Christmas—filled with excitement and enthusiasm. It was his first presidential inauguration, and he was thrilled in all respects save one— he had not seen the President. Neither had thousands of others.

I was tempted to suggest to Lance that he could have had the same experience he'd just had at a sale in Macy's basement, but I couldn't be so cruel.

Besides, Lance and so many just like him were proud— proud to be Americans, proud to be in their nation's capital, proud to have any role whatever, even that of a jostling and jostled spectator, in the inauguration of their President.

I—and so many like me—lived in a cocoon during those giddy days, a cocoon reinforced by the pageantry of the inauguration, by the sight of powerful men, by the monuments and statues, by the history around us—the history committed to books, and the history being made as we watched.

Anyone who has never felt this throb of patriotism, this love of country, this near-ecstasy over what a great and powerful and just nation America is will not understand why, on January 20, 1973, it was beyond my capacity to associate criminality with the President of the United States, or with the men who served him.

Five weeks later, it would be less difficult.

13

"Oh, What a Tangled Web We Weave..."

The President is just like most bosses—only more so. When he is around, everyone is around, impressing the Number 1 man with his brilliance, energy, and loyalty. And essentiality.

But when he is away, the activity level sinks perceptibly. In part, this is because he takes some of the activity with him—including some of the top personnel. But it is also because White House people—and they are merely mortal like the rest of us—let down while the boss is out of town and not around to notice.

President Nixon always used superior judgment, I believed, in deciding when to go to San Clemente or Key Biscayne. The visits to his two sun country estates so often coincided with the dreariest times of the year in Washington.

I was not in the least surprised, therefore, to read in the newspaper that the President would spend the first two or three weeks of February—a time of constant drizzle in Washington—at San Clemente. This meant that a lot of feet would go up on a lot of desks at the White House. There would be fewer meetings for John to attend, fewer memos to read or write, and not nearly so many telephone calls. Presto! An ideal time for a vacation. John agreed. He had lots of time coming, and he sagely observed that the White House counsel had to move quickly when a vacation opportunity arose, because it could be the last one for a long time. For us, it turned out to be the last one, period.

Since the President, Haldeman, and Ehrlichman were in California, we decided that the best place for us would be Florida. The two White House villas were available, we had friends in the area, and—best of all—we'd be by ourselves, away from the White House people and away from the White House compulsiveness to work.

Once again, I dropped into ecstasy without a backward glance.

And once again what always happened happened once again.

This time it was Ehrlichman who called.

It was a Friday afternoon and I was home packing for the two of us when John telephoned with that old familiar: "Mo, I'm afraid we'll have to change our plans."

I think what made me angriest was that I never seemed to catch on. No matter how many times our plans were disrupted like this, when we would make new ones some days or weeks later, it would never occur to me that we would again be unable to carry them out. It's my lifelong habit of living always in the present—never in the past, and never in the future—that is at fault. Except when I am forced to do so, I never look back and I never look very far ahead.

While calling myself a fool and worse under my breath, I managed a small question for John.

"What is it this time?"

He told me it was not so bad as it sounded—something I had also heard before.

"We'll still get to Florida. The only difference is we'll go to California first. You'll get to see your mom."

Well—that really pleased me, of course. I really had no complaint coming. Things would work out well. But I still wanted so much to make plans once—just once—and have them fulfilled.

"We're all packed," I sighed. "What time does the plane leave?"

We flew west that evening with Richard Moore, the fatherly, white-haired friend and advisor to President Nixon who always seemed so much older than everybody at the White House, but who really was slightly younger than the President. Dick Moore came across to most of the country as a fool when he testified before the Senate Watergate Committee, because he became flustered and said he couldn't remember telling the committee staff something only a short time after he had told it to them. When he was asked which story he stood by—the one he had told earlier or the one he was telling now on national television—he said: "I'll stick to my story, whatever it was."

But Dick Moore was not a fool—just a warm, friendly human being whose counsel was valued by several of the men at the White House—certainly by John. I was pleased to know he would be with us for the flight to San Diego. Dick's wife and their little boy were along, too, because, like the Deans, the Moores also had been planning a vacation. They were all packed and set to go by train to southern Virginia, but Moore had received a call from John, at Ehrlichman's request.

This time it was no secret what Ehrlichman had in mind.

The United States Senate, by a vote of 77 to 0, had agreed that there should be a Senate investigation of the Watergate matter. Wouldn't that Watergate situation *ever* go away? From where I sat, which may have been near the edge but which was certainly within the Nixon circle,

Watergate had been a creation of the press and the Democrats, a desperate inflation of a minor slip-up that—if it
could have been blown up enough—might have kept
President Nixon from being reelected. I accepted it for
that. Because it kept intruding itself on our plans, I also
regarded Watergate as something of a personal vexation:
it kept John away from me, it took him away from me even
on our first and second honeymoons, and it soured his
mood and made him drink too much at night.

I fully expected Watergate to disappear from the front
pages, from the television screen, and from my life once
the President had been reelected. It had not turned out
that way.

True—after the election, there was much less about
Watergate in the newspapers and on the newscasts. So I
assumed it was fading away and would be forgotten. I have
reason to believe that the people in the White House,
including some of the very top people, felt the same way.

But here it was February 1973, and Watergate still had
not vanished. To realize how insulated we all were, you
really had to be one of us. My husband and I, and our
White House associates, certainly had what I have heard
referred to as a "siege" mentality. We felt that the enemies
of a great and good President, the press and the Democrats
in particular, were unwilling to let a minor incident die
because it was their most effective weapon with which to
get at the President.

And now the Senate was going to have an investigation
of Watergate. This fact obviously disturbed John, who told
me that he might have to testify, and that others in the
White House might also be called upon to testify. His attitude was not that he or they had anything really bad to
hide, but that once you are witness in front of a group of
politicians with their own axes to grind, you can become
very uncomfortable and flustered, and come off looking
guilty whether you are or not.

Months earlier there had been talk of a Watergate investigation by a House committee, but John and Bill Timmons, the White House congressional liaison, and Gerald Ford, the House Minority Leader, had been effective in turning that off. I could tell John was keenly disappointed that the Senate investigation had not been similarly extinguished.

There obviously was concern at San Clemente over the coming Senate hearings. That was why Ehrlichman had called for John and Dick Moore to come out. He and Haldeman and the President wanted to discuss just what the White House posture toward the committee ought to be: Should White House staff members be allowed to testify? Or should executive privilege be claimed to prevent them from doing so? If staff members were permitted to testify, who should be exempted? John, for instance, because he was the White House counsel? And what about Ehrlichman and Haldeman, whose relationship with the President was *so* confidential? What about people like Chuck Colson, who had knowledge of Watergate and would be sought as witnesses, but who were no longer on the White House staff? Could executive privilege be claimed for them?

Well, a good legal mind was needed, and that is why John Dean was told to drop all his personal plans and fly west. Dick Moore was needed out there, John later told me, for public relations input.

Rooms for both the Moores and us had been reserved at the La Costa Resort Hotel near San Clemente. This was no Holiday Inn, needless to say. It was something on the order of a health spa, in fact, with steam rooms, saunas, swimming pools, tennis courts, and a golf course. The rooms weren't all that plush, but there was an art gallery that I enjoyed. And with all the other facilities, it was a great place to stay.

Again, looking back, I wonder how necessary it was for the health of the Republic, or the health of the Republic's servants, to stay at such a resort. I have no idea what it cost, but it must have been plenty. I do remember that John ordered a hamburger for each of us from room service, and the bill came to $10. Miserable food, too. I shudder to think what the other meals and the room itself cost.

The taxpayers, of course, were also footing the bill for Haldeman, Ehrlichman, Moore, and John (we paid for my air fare and meals), Larry Higby, and Todd Hullen. There may have been others from Washington as well. I know that Haldeman and Ehrlichman and Higby and Hullen got in a lot of tennis. "Ehrlichman likes the physical facilities here," John told me by way of explanation—although I didn't need one. He also said that since Haldeman and Ehrlichman wanted to play tennis, they might as well stay at a place that had courts.

On Saturday, February 10, the day after our arrival, John was away for several hours of meetings. I wandered around the lobby of the hotel, spending a great deal of time at the art exhibit and at an exhibit of sculpture nearby. One of the managers of the hotel took note of my interest and also of the fact that I was alone, and very kindly invited me to have coffee with him, which I did. He told me the history of the hotel, and a great deal about the works of art that were on exhibit. It helped to have someone to talk to.

When John finally was through with his meetings—"all about the Senate committee," he told me—we had dinner and decided that on the following day, Sunday, since there would be more meetings lasting who knows how long, it would be best for me to go to Los Angeles to be with my mother. John thought he would not have to be at La Costa for more than another day, anyway, so if I were to spend any time at all with Mom, I had better head for her home on Sunday. John thought we would probably be free to fly to Florida on Monday.

Again the White House and the taxpayers were gen-

erous. On Sunday, a special White House car and driver
were provided to drive me from La Costa to my mother's
home in Los Angeles. It struck me at the time as something
very nice, and no more, really, than I deserved.

I had a wonderful day with Mother and with my brother
and his family. John, also chauffeured in a White House
limousine, was able to join us late that evening, so it was
a wonderful family reunion—even if it lasted only a day.

We were both really anxious to get on to Florida—to be
by ourselves, and to begin the few days of relaxation that
we had looked forward to. It was clear that John now
needed the rest more than ever. Whatever had happened
at the La Costa meetings (some of the sessions were held at
San Clemente), it was obvious that John was upset. When
we were finally alone that night, I asked: "Dear, what is
it?"

"I'm just a little unhappy about Dick Moore. He's got
a hell of a tough assignment that I shouldn't talk about."

"From the President?" I asked.

"No. Ehrlichman. Maybe it will all work out."

Not until I typed a draft of John's Watergate Committee
testimony later did I learn what Moore's "tough assignment" was. He was told by Ehrlichman to go to New
York to persuade John Mitchell to raise more money for
the seven Watergate defendants. The men had all pleaded
guilty or been convicted, and the White House did not
wish to risk the possibility that one or more of them might
talk just as the Senate Watergate Committee was preparing
its hearings. John had mentioned to Haldeman and Ehrlichman that some of the defendants were requesting more
money, and that there was no more money. So Ehrlichman
told Moore to ask Mitchell to raise it.

As in times past, John was not in a talkative mood.
Again, I did not press him. The medicine he needed most
at that time, I thought, was to escape from all this White
House business—if there was any escape.

Early on Monday morning, we caught a commercial flight to Miami. It was a happy, relaxed flight for both of us. John was able to put La Costa and San Clemente out of his mind, at least temporarily. He was fully aware of the fact that if he did not put those things aside at least for a few days, he might suffer a breakdown. This was a real possibility. John was a terribly burdened and very troubled man.

We had made advance arrangements to stay in one of the White House villas at Key Biscayne. Of course, the White House phones would be reinstalled, but no matter where we went, there would be special White House telephones. Since we were on vacation, we had to pay for the villa, but we would have had to pay almost as much for less comfort and privacy somewhere else. It made sense to go there. Or so we thought.

Once in the villa, the telephone calls began immediately. This time I was prepared for them and made no complaint —why complain because the sun sets, the grass is green and the ocean is salty? Higby, Dick Moore, and Wally Johnson, all of whom were playing major roles for the White House in regard to the Senate committee, were the ones who called most often. But in between, John and I had nearly two glorious days alone, and by then I had caught on to the fact that two days of relative privacy and togetherness were about the most I could expect.

Wednesday was St. Valentine's Day. John and I sat in the sun, dozed, had lunch, walked on the beach: a perfect day for lovers. Then, toward evening, a baldish, rosy-cheeked Irishman named Paul O'Brien appeared at the villa. John greeted him warmly.

I had heard of Paul O'Brien. He was a lawyer for the Nixon reelection committee, whom John has since said was the one man, other than Dick Moore, in whom he was able to confide. O'Brien was apologetic about the intrusion, which wasn't really an intrusion at all since it had been prearranged for him to fly down to visit John.

The question, of course, was why.

Here we were, officially on vacation, trying our best to relax in the sun for a few days, and yet something was so urgent that John agreed to have our vacation interrupted by a lawyer for the reelection committee. It had occurred to me some time ago that John ought to put his foot down, and I would have told him to do so on this occasion, but my instincts advised against it. There was something so *intent* about John during this period. He was obviously anguished, worried, uptight.

And looking into that increasingly drawn face, seeing that desolate expression in those otherwise tender, loving eyes, I knew this: I could not add to John's problems. If I could lighten his load in any way, I desperately wanted to do so. This was a man under such strain that he might not have been able to tolerate the additional burden of a demanding wife, even if her demands were just.

When John said that Paul O'Brien was coming down "for some talks that just won't wait," I did not nag, pout, or complain. In all honesty, it took a bit of doing to hold myself in, but I believe all I said was:

"Oh. Will he be staying long?"

"I don't think so," John replied.

We did not discuss the matter further until O'Brien arrived.

By now, the men of Richard Nixon's administration were so paranoid that they did not even trust each other. For a long time after the Watergate break-in there had been a certain pulling together by all the Nixon people. This feeling had lasted because there was such confidence that the little step taken here and the little step taken there would relegate Watergate to the obscurity we all thought it so richly deserved.

But now Paul O'Brien was paying his emergency visit to

John *because John Mitchell could not be certain that what he was hearing from Dick Moore about the La Costa meetings was actually the truth.* He wanted John Dean's version—independently—and had sent O'Brien to get it.

To anyone who knew the full facts, it would have been clear that the finger-pointing stage of Watergate was nearing. Mitchell didn't really distrust Moore—he just didn't trust Ehrlichman. Mitchell probably was fearful that Ehrlichman had given Moore instructions after the La Costa meetings that none of the other participants had agreed to. In any event, he wanted to check. Mitchell trusted O'Brien, and he knew that John had confidence in O'Brien, too. The incident was a harbinger of things to come. Everyone was still confident that Watergate would fade away, but several of the men were beginning to protect their own flanks—just in case.

I can truthfully say that John was not yet thinking about protecting his flanks—he did not see the O'Brien visit for what it was: evidence of a widening schism between Mitchell on one side and Haldeman and Ehrlichman on the other. The schism had existed before. Now it was growing. Mitchell had begun to sense that if there had to be a Watergate scapegoat some day, he plainly was the nominee of Haldeman and Ehrlichman.

On Valentine's Day 1973, I did not realize all this. Nor did John; he was so deep in the forest he could not see the trees. Soon he would see them.

If I seem to render myself blameless, it is both unintentional and contrary to the facts. I could and should have done much more than I did.

I performed the way a basically timid, nonassertive person generally performs. I permitted myself to be sidelined, so to speak. I suppose it all boils down to a lack of confidence. I was in over my head. It never occurred to me that the President of the United States, my husband, or the principal aides to the President of the United States would ever do anything illegal. That is point Number 1. Had such a thought entered my head, I like to think I would have demanded to know everything. Instead, assuming what had happened was on the up and up but complicated and political, I assumed the role of a shy and helpful woman—helpful by not becoming a pest and demanding that someone explain everything to me.

By no means am I a women's liberationist, but I hope that members of my sex can benefit from my experience, and from the experiences of the other Watergate wives. I think we now constitute the prime argument *against* women accepting the role of complete outsider. Men shut us out because we accept their notion that what they are involved in is complicated, sensitive, and beyond our grasp. Even now, I don't deny that much of that theory is valid. What I emphatically deny is that a woman should therefore be relegated to the home and the children and the cooking and the sewing. A woman always has an unobstructed view of fundamentals—of right and wrong. She also has an ingrained skepticism about men, based on years of experience and observation, beginning from her first date, that have taught her that men are not really very different from each other, and that no man, whatever his title or station, has many godlike qualities. It has always astonished me that men can become so caught up with other men, attributing to them greatness and even infallibility, which—as most women know—it has not been God's design, as yet, to bestow upon mere mortals, male or female.

I think one of the reasons for man's infatuation with man is that at some juncture the self-interests of several men begin to meld. A group of men strikes out for some sort of power situation—a congressional or Senate seat, a governorship, the presidency. One among them is a candidate, so all of them in that particular coterie acquire a vested interest in the degree of his erudition, his goodness, his greatness. The better he is, the better they are. The better he fares, the better they fare. Thus they are inclined to think that his decision here, his words of wisdom there, are really a lot better than they actually are. Senator Howard Baker, whom I thought was on stage and overly sanctimonious during most of the Watergate hearings, nonetheless may also have made the wisest statement of all by a senator—when he told Bart Porter that the greatest service a man can render to his President is to speak his own mind and his own conscience. I'm afraid that not many men do, and that not many Presidents would tolerate it if they did.

But on that first evening in Key Biscayne, John and Paul O'Brien seemed not to want to plunge immediately into confidential discussions. O'Brien seemed reluctant to send me off into isolation too abruptly, so the three of us went to dinner together and had an evening that was free of much serious talk.

I liked Paul O'Brien. At the end of the evening, John insisted that Paul stay in the other bedroom in our villa, so the two of them could begin their discussions early the next day. When I joined John in asking Paul to stay with us, he seemed reassured about my acceptance of his "intruder" role and agreed to stay.

The next day we all slept late. As soon as our breakfast was finished, I knew the time had arrived for me to disappear. I told Paul and John I had been looking forward to several hours of sunbathing and reading, that I could only do this alone, and that they were to go about their business without any thought or worry about me. They both smiled understandingly. And then they took off together for a walk down the beach, while I concentrated on ridding myself of my Washington pallor before I had to return to Washington.

It was mid-afternoon when the two men returned from their walk. O'Brien seemed troubled, picked up the telephone, and called John Mitchell. John and I discreetly left the villa, for neither of us thought we should be listening to even a word of Paul's end of the conversation. After a fairly long time, O'Brien came out on the patio where we were sunning and said that Mitchell wanted to talk to John.

"What was that about?" I asked when John had come back outside.

"About minority counsel for the Senate committee," he said. Then he mentioned a number of names that he had discussed with Mitchell, none of which meant anything to me. Nor did it seem at all odd to me that the former attorney general and the White House counsel were discussing possible nominees for Republican counsel of a *Senate* committee. Why should anyone outside the Senate have any concern with the appointment of a counsel to a Senate committee? The thought occurs to me now. It did not at the time. I was not alone in thinking, then, that the White House was involved—rightfully involved—in everything that went on.

Soon after the telephone conversation with Mitchell, Paul O'Brien packed his things, thanked us for our hospitality, and left to catch a plane to Washington. John and I looked at each other, smiled and sighed happily. We had what was left of Thursday, all day Friday and Saturday, and most of Sunday all to ourselves—barring the unexpected, of course.

And this time, the unexpected did *not* occur. Except, in one sense: we did *not* receive any urgent calls to fly north or west.

But there was one unpleasant incident that simply reinforced my already strong views about John Ehrlichman.

The volume of telephone calls had dropped off to almost zero. Therefore it was a little surprising when the phone did ring rather demandingly late that evening. John answered, and when he put the receiver down, his eyes were blazing.

"Who was it? What's wrong now?" I pleaded.

"Higby," John snapped. "He thinks we'd better get the hell out of here. He said he thinks Ehrlichman will raise hell if he finds you and me in the villa he wants to use."

"Why?" I cried.

"Just out of the villa, not out of Florida. We're going to stay in Florida through the weekend no matter what. But Ehrlichman is coming in tomorrow with his family. He wants to use both villas because he's got some of the kids along."

Oh! That John Ehrlichman! That arrogant, thoughtless creature. I never could stand him, and now this. He and his family could easily have stayed in one villa (there weren't that many children), or he and Jeanne and some of the children could have stayed in the single villa while the others put up at one of the nearby hotels. Or it wouldn't have hurt the kids to sleep in sleeping bags on the floor for one or two or even three nights. Had they asked, John and I would even have been happy to have let the kids stay in our extra bedroom now that Paul O'Brien was gone.

But no. Higby was saying that he thought we had better get out. And there was no confusion in either of our minds as to how right Higby was in his assessment of the situation.

John was only "madder than hell." I was outraged. I was all for staying put—at first. So what if Ehrlichman could pull "rank"—this wasn't the military. Let him come in and try, just try, to get us out.

It's funny to look back on the situation now. John and I were both denouncing and daring Ehrlichman, our words coming at a fast clip, our voices agitated.

Then, like an old phonograph record on a wind-up machine that is grinding down, our voices became slower and slower, and lower and lower. Reality was setting in. First, there was the fact of rank, which was very real indeed, military or no. But even more important was the realization that if we insisted on staying on, we'd have really a great time, wouldn't we, with the Ehrlichmans right next door? I could see John Ehrlichman, who was then very fat and very imperious, lumbering around on his patio, saying something like: "This is all very well, Dean, but it's something I won't forget."

It was that thought, in fact, that helped convince us to move—the fact that Ehrlichman would have other ways of getting back at us, as well as the fact that it would not be a very merry time for anybody if we decided to stay on.

At last John and I stopped talking and started packing. We moved to a hotel in the Coconut Grove section of Miami, but that didn't work out well, either. The hotel was full of press people, who were now beginning to trail White House personnel everywhere, sensing—accurately— that things were beginning to unravel.

John's passion for anonymity had stood him in good stead for all his years in the White House, but this, too, was beginning to come to an end. Reporters recognized and approached him in the lobby, in the restaurant, in the bar. He mentioned this annoying fact to a good friend and supporter of the President, Bob Gallagher, whom we knew and who had come over to the hotel to visit with us. Bob had a home in Miami with ample space, and he insisted that we check out of the hotel and stay with him.

All this bouncing around wasn't doing a thing for my peace of mind, nor for John's, but we gladly took this latest suggestion. Otherwise, we couldn't swim, we couldn't sun ourselves, we couldn't eat, we couldn't go in for a drink without attracting one to half a dozen reporters, all of whom felt it was their duty to strike up a conversation with us on the off chance that they would learn something about what was going on in the White House, at San Clemente, at Key Biscayne.

I wasn't used to reporters then, and neither was John. I think now I have a better sense of why they have to be as aggressive as they are—not that I really like it that way. But then, on my first real exposure, I thought it was appalling that two people on vacation couldn't move without being pursued by the press. I didn't fully appreciate that if you decide to become a public figure, you sacrifice a certain amount of privacy. The reason I didn't realize this was that I had not decided to become a public figure.

John, of course, was on the public payroll, and that made him fair game.

From Washington to La Costa to Los Angeles to Key Biscayne to a hotel in Coconut Grove and now to Bob Gallagher's home—all in nine days. This was our vacation, our opportunity to be alone, to relax and regenerate ourselves, John especially, for the really tough days ahead.

As I sat on the edge of the bed in Bob Gallagher's home and thought over the whirlwind events of the past several days, I felt like crying.

But as I looked up at John's somber face, staring intently at me as if he felt like crying, too, the whole situation began to seem so ridiculous.

I burst out laughing.

John—delighted—broke into laughter too.

Laughter was our salvation, then and many times later.

14
A Cancer
That Killed a President

JOHN DEAN—BRIGHT, SHARP, COMPLETELY LOYAL

(Washington Post, March 14, 1973)

When we bade farewell to Florida on Sunday, February 18, the strangest feeling overwhelmed me. I had tried to cling to those few and precious days, to make them last forever, as if I sensed that a chapter in my life would be closing if they ended.

This is not to suggest that I had any conscious realization of the days of shock, fright, and despair that lay just ahead. God in his mercy spared me that.

And, of course, I had taken leave of Florida many times before, and would many times again. But this parting was special. As I gazed out over the water, watched the palm trees wave in the fresh sea breeze, I wanted to linger. For a long, long time. A peacefulness settled over me, and something inside told me not to go—that once I left this haven, I would be in another world, not beautiful, but ugly, not secure, but full of perils and turbulence.

One shakes off such feelings with some embarrassment, because idylls do end, realities must be faced, time does not stand still. And one is inclined to discount—at the time—the possible validity of any premonition, any forewarning.

I think most often that the feelings that sometimes come over us on such occasions are the products of wishful thinking, of wanting playtime never to yield to worries and work time.

Only in retrospect do I wonder: Was somebody trying to tell me something?

No matter, the fact is that those precious days in Florida were the calm prelude to the stormiest days of my never really tranquil life, days so bewildering that I was driven to wonder about what kind of a country I lived in, whether my own life and my husband's life were in danger, whether the next knock on the door would be from an American version of a storm trooper. This seems so melodramatic now. It was very real then.

The last ten days of February telescope in my mind. John was alternately excited, nervous—then quiet, reflective. He never wanted to go out. The best day he had during that period—and a great day for me, too—was when his son Johnny spent all day with us on Sunday, February 25. On all the other days, John had stayed at the office until eight, nine, or ten at night. When he finally did come home, I could get a Scotch in his hand, but never his dinner down him, before the telephone started to ring and never stopped.

Again, John was drinking heavily at night. Again, it affected him not at all as far as speech, awareness, and mannerisms were concerned. When I asked him if he thought it was wise to drink three or four or five Scotches in an evening, he would say: "Mo—I have to. If I don't, I can't sleep."

It was true, but it was also something I was not going to put up with for very long. If the strains and tensions of John's job were such that he was unable to sleep at night without virtually drinking himself into oblivion, then the job had become a monster. Life was too short. If things continued like this for very much longer, I would be at the breaking point whether or not John would be, and I rather imagined we'd be there together. Being counsel to the President, flying on Air Force One, being chauffeured in big black limousines—all this was fine. But it was not worth two wrecked lives, and the way we were going, that seemed to be the price that was being exacted.

I was sure we were heading pell-mell for a crisis. Then, with a suddenness I didn't understand at all, John took hold of himself. It was the Monday after that completely diverting Sunday with Johnny. John came home from the office at a reasonable hour, the telephone rang only once or twice, we had only one drink before dinner, and then we had a very quiet, peaceful meal.

Something had changed, obviously. Somehow I knew that John would tell me what. In his relaxed mood (which is his normal mood, the White House years excepted) he always confides in me, fully—when "state secrets" are not at issue.

There was an air of the fatalist about him that night. Strangely, I thought, he had insisted that wills be prepared for both of us, and this had been done several days before. Now, subdued and thoughtful, though obviously anticipating something, John sat me down and told me that he would be meeting with the President in private the following morning. From what he told me, I gathered that he felt more at ease than he had for several weeks past because he believed that by meeting face to face with the President, he could get a presidential focus on Watergate that the situation had not previously had, and that he could initiate steps toward its resolution. I think he believed that the President had not been getting full or entirely correct information after it was filtered through Haldeman or Ehrlichman, and that for this reason, the President underestimated how serious the problem was.

I think, and thought, that at this point—late February, 1973—when the counsel to the President was meeting pri-

vately with the President for the first time since September
15, 1972, that John believed he at last had an opportunity
to convey the real dimensions of Watergate to the President. And I think he still had enough confidence in the
powers of the office and the integrity of Richard Nixon to
believe that somehow—perhaps with a wave of a magic
wand—the matter could at last be resolved and put completely to rest. Of course, John overrated the presidency
and the President, and underrated what he understood
better than either—the power of the law.

Since John felt better about things, so did I. By nature
I am the eternal optimist. Even a slight suggestion than an
ugly problem can be solved cheers me more than it should,
and my escapist tendencies enable me to put the problem
out of my mind—at least for a time.

Afterwards, John said the meeting had gone well, but he
did not seem as pleased with its results as he had been with
the prospect of its being held. The discussions had centered
on the Ervin Committee, he said, and the President had
decided that no one from the White House staff would
appear to testify in person.

Today, I can see how this decision was interpreted by
almost everyone except those of us who were directly
affected: it appeared to the news media, the Congress and,
most important, the public that the administration had
something to hide. My own view was colored by my relief
that John would not have to testify. Considering the job
that John held, we were still relatively private people, not
widely known in Washington, and certainly not known
at all to the public. I wanted it kept that way, and I know
John did, too. Besides, I had heard him talking on the
telephone about the "circus" the committee would conduct. The temptation to perform is irresistible to a poli-
tician once the network television cameras are trained on
him. The thought that all those Democratic senators and
maybe even one or two Republicans would be trying to

embarrass John while the whole country watched was very distressing to me. Not that I lacked confidence in John's ability to hold his own. It just seemed like an unpleasant experience to have to go through.

I imagine the relief was even greater in the Haldeman and Ehrlichman households, because all along it had been thought that John, as the counsel to the President, could claim lawyer-client privilege and thereby be excused from testifying anywhere. But now that the President had ruled out testimony by any of his staff, that just made it all the more certain that John would escape the ordeal of being grilled on national television.

Or so we thought.

In some ways, this decision by the President was one of the worst he ever made. As soon as it became public, many people who until that time had full confidence in President Nixon began to wonder. *Why* did he not want his staff to testify? In addition to giving the appearance of there being something to hide, the decision had an air of elitism about it. Any citizen called to appear before a committee of Congress would have to do so, either voluntarily or under subpoena. Why should the people who worked for the President be exempt?

It was clear from the adverse reaction to this decision that millions of Americans were, for the first time, beginning to wonder about their President. I was not yet among them.

I have often read about how insulated the President was from the real world. He was—a thousand times more than any of us. But we were sheltered to a major degree, too. John did little else but work, so he was with the same people all day long. At night, he would again be talking—by telephone—with the same people. The few friends we saw were either White House people themselves, White House–oriented, or too polite to offer harsh criticisms of

the President to the President's counsel—or to the wife of
the President's counsel, for that matter.

So I wondered a little bit about the cold reception given
to the President's decision. I accepted the view that I had
heard so often from my husband and others: that the Ervin
Committee was simply out to embarrass the President and
the administration, that Congress had no right to pry into
the confidential meetings of the President with his closest
aides, and that the President had the right to invoke executive privilege to keep the office of the presidency safe from
congressional "fishing expeditions." Why couldn't all those
people "out there" understand this?

As a matter of fact, the people understood only too well.
They may not have been able to define "executive privilege," but they were able to sense that their President was
not behaving the way a person with nothing to hide should
behave. They were far ahead of me, I must say. The ex-
planations made by the President sounded perfectly plausible to me. I blamed the bias of the press for the fact that
they did not strike the public in the same manner. We
were all great at deluding ourselves about the press. Years
before, the President and everyone around him had written
off the press as the enemy, and thereafter paid little attention to what it said. Well, they paid attention, but did
not believe. Little wonder that the President and the people around him were among the last to realize how seriously the country was taking Watergate. I honestly do not
think that reality struck the President fully until the time
came when he was forced to resign.

The meetings between John and the President continued. There were many, many meetings and telephone
calls in March 1973. John and I did not talk about all of
them, but he did tell me that President Nixon wanted to
deal with him alone on Watergate, not with Haldeman and
Ehrlichman present. I gathered from what little John did

say that the meetings most often revolved about the Ervin Committee hearings. Occasionally, he would tell me something else—something he had said, or something the President had said—but the impression left in my mind was of much talk about the Ervin Committee and how to deal with it. My eyes glaze over when terms like "executive privilege," "immunity," and "subpoena power" come up—or at least they used to.

So I gauged my husband and his activities more by his mood and disposition than by his words. I still had no inclination—not the slightest—to suspect that anything remotely resembling criminal activity was taking place at the White House. John's mood was fine when his talks with the President first began; I believe he really felt that this apparently interminable Watergate situation would be brought under control at last.

But the calmer, more at ease John Dean soon gave way to the nervous, uptight, deeply troubled John Dean of before. Obviously, things were not going as he had expected them to when he first resumed his private meetings with the President.

In addition, something that John had always before avoided successfully—publicity—was now a daily fact of our lives. The Senate Judiciary Committee was holding hearings on the nomination of Pat Gray to be director of the FBI. Gray had been acting director ever since J. Edgar Hoover's death in May 1972—just six weeks before the Watergate break-in. So it was under Gray that the FBI Watergate investigation had been conducted, and he was being asked about nothing else at the confirmation hearings. He kept bringing John into his answers, so every night on television I would hear the commentators mention John's name, and every morning there would be newspaper accounts, with John's name moving from the body of the stories up into the headlines—which seemed to be getting larger and larger.

What Gray was telling the committee about John was true—that John had read the FBI reports of the Watergate investigation. Although Gray insisted that this was proper —because John was the representative of the President of the United States, and the President was in charge of the Justice Department of which the FBI was a part—the senators were incredulous. Since the Watergate matter involved some members of the Committee for the Re-election of the President, some of John's associates, why would the FBI be laying out its investigation in front of the President's counsel? Some Democratic senators made what seemed to me at the time to be a rather ugly insinuation—that Gray had been revealing the details of his investigation to the very people under investigation.

This infuriated me. The very idea—to suggest that John and the President were "the very people under investigation." Would these people never accept the fact that Gordon Liddy, Howard Hunt, and James McCord were far removed from Richard Nixon and John Dean?

As Gray was questioned day after day about his relationships with John and others at the White House during the Watergate investigation, I grew more and more nervous. Some of the reports I heard and read suggested that Gray had been wrong to turn over any of this "raw" material to John. This was the first time that it entered my head that John might have inadvertently done something illegal. I didn't know that it was illegal for him to have received the reports, and I did not see how it could be. The President of the United States, as Gray had testified, was in charge of the executive branch, including the Justice Department and the FBI, and if he designated a subordinate to follow a case for him, he had a perfect right to do so—it seemed to me. But I worried about it.

John soothed me when I brought this matter up with him. At one of their meetings, John said, the President had told him that he was entitled to look at the FBI reports because he was conducting an investigation for the President. I remembered then the President's press conference statement of the previous August—he said that John Dean had completed an investigation and found that no one employed at the White House was involved in Watergate.

"But you didn't conduct an investigation," I reminded him.

"I know. But the President said I did."

John wasn't comfortable with that response, and neither was I, but it was soon forgotten in the face of a daily torrent of more urgent concerns. Crises were becoming a routine for us.

The Senate Judiciary Committee decided to "invite" John to testify during the Gray hearings. President Nixon immediately let it be known that he would order John not to appear. "No President could ever agree to allow the counsel to the President to go down and testify before a committee," he said.

John's picture was on all the front pages and on all the television news programs now. The *Washington Post* ran a rather flattering profile on John that, under the circumstances, we both would have preferred to do without.

After predicting that John would reject the invitation to testify, the article said John was "fastidiously correct in manner, almost totally uninformative to outsiders, and completely loyal to his employer."

It continued: "These qualities, along with a deep admiration for President Nixon and a reputation as a bright, sharp and pragmatic operator, have combined to bring Dean increased White House influence and, especially in recent months, fuller meaning to his title of counsel to the President."

After noting the President's "growing reliance on the 34-year-old aide," the article observed that "friends and former associates who agree about Dean's intensity and charm are divided over whether he is capable of some of the gravest deeds suggested during the grilling of . . . Gray, whose confirmation could be delayed for months if Dean maintains his refusal to testify."

Well! Thanks for the kind words, *Washington Post,* but how dare you leave open the question of whether John is capable of "the gravest deeds"! The article made me furious. I had never before in my life heard anyone suggest that John could intentionally do something that was really wrong, and the thought certainly had never occurred to me.

But as March wore on, I was becoming more and more baffled and distressed. Even I had my private moments now of wondering why the White House was playing this "stonewall" game. Why not play things straight and end the furor? As bad as I thought it would be for John to have to go before the committee and testify, I was beginning to wonder if all the clamor and the headlines and the harsh statements being hurled back and forth were not even worse for the administration—and for John.

With John's name and picture so much in the news, Mom and Ron began calling almost every night to make sure John and I were really okay, as we kept assuring them we were. A lot of my old Beverly Hills friends, I'm sure, thought that all the publicity was wonderful. In Beverly Hills, it matters not what anybody writes about you. Having your name in print is what counts. As Sam Goldwyn used to say, "I don't care what you say about me, just so you spell my name right."

Mom, who had come to love John so much she wouldn't believe anything bad about him, solved the developing situation in her own inimitable way: she just adamantly refused to believe anything that was said on the air or in print if it reflected poorly on John. Ronnie was more deeply concerned, fearing that the situation was more serious than we were letting on in our telephone conversations. But John reassured him that things would work out, that the situation actually was not so grim as the one being presented in the media.

On St. Patrick's Day, a Saturday, I had been in the pressure cooker long enough. We had an invitation to a dinner party at the Kleindiensts, and I told John I simply had to get out of the house for one evening, get him away from the telephones, and get us both away from Ervin committees, judiciary committees, Pat Grays, executive privileges, and whatever.

John sensed my need, but made no promises until after he had been to the office and had met with the President. He found the President in such a chipper mood—wearing a green shamrock, chatting about various matters—that I assume John figured maybe he could afford to loosen up a bit, too. After all, if the President could be that confident and jovial, maybe everything was not as bleak as John had thought it was.

Dick Kleindienst may not sound like the ideal person to be with when one is trying to get away from problems like the Gray hearings. After all, Dick was attorney general then, and really in the eye of the hurricane that was building up all around. But I knew this much about Dick Kleindienst even without knowing him very well: he is the kind of person who knows how to shed his problems for social occasions.

I was right. Dick Kleindienst was witty and cheerful during cocktails, and determined to have a good time. He was playing gin rummy with another guest when we arrived, but stopped and greeted us warmly, and I knew I had done the right thing for both John and me in insisting that we come.

Marnie Kleindienst is a very level-headed, intelligent woman. I helped her fix the salad for the dinner, and her husband cooked the steaks. Don Santarelli, who worked with John in the Justice Department, was among the guests at the small dinner party. Another of the guests was a lawyer who is a partner of John Connally. Everyone was in a very good mood when we sat down at the table.

For me, the mood didn't last. The warm glow I had for the attorney general faded slightly. I was seated to his left, so we talked. When I told him something about the work I had done for the Commission on Marihuana and Drug Abuse, he looked at me with the most startled expression. "You worked?"

I couldn't have surprised him more if I had told him I once played fullback for the Chicago Bears. He was absolutely dumbfounded that an attractive young woman could register any achievement unrelated to the kitchen, bedroom, or nursery.

I found Kleindienst's unsubtle putdown of women so crass that it stirred even me to the defense of my sex. Our discussion became rather heated. He obviously had very fixed notions about the limited role that a woman could and should fulfill.

I was beginning to get a little paranoid about the kind of luck I was having. Here we had gone to dinner to get away from such matters as the Pat Gray hearings, succeeded in doing that all right—and then I had wound up in an argument about the worth of women. The situation was so ridiculous that on the way home I thought about it to myself and then suddenly burst out laughing. I don't remember if John asked me what was so funny. We were getting into the period when each of us was so pleased to hear the other laugh occasionally that we really didn't care what it was about.

I didn't like what was happening to my life, what was happening to our lives. My love for John was stronger than ever. It had to have been strong for me to have continued to put up with all the long hours, the never-ending telephone calls, the abrupt changes in all our personal plans,

John's periodic moodiness, the tension. Now there was still another dimension—loss of privacy. It started with the Gray hearings and would soon escalate.

The Gray hearings continued, and one day Senator Robert Byrd read to Pat Gray an account of an FBI interview with John Dean. According to the account, shortly after the Watergate arrests an agent had asked John if Howard Hunt had an office in the White House. John's reply supposedly was that he would have to check and find out.

Then Senator Byrd read from other reports that stated clearly that John had been present when Hunt's safe was opened right after the arrests. If that account were true, then obviously John knew that Hunt had an office in the White House and had been in it.

After laying out these reports (and not taking into account that the FBI version of its interview with John could have been in error), Senator Byrd looked right at Gray and said:

"Mr. Dean lied to the agent, didn't he?"

Gray tried to avoid the question. But Byrd repeated it several times: "Mr. Dean lied to the agent, didn't he?"

At last Gray said: "Yes."

Of course, it was the most dramatic moment of the hearing, and John really made the big, black banner headlines that day. He was terribly upset at being branded a liar by a government official at a Senate hearing. He thought about me, he thought about Johnny, he thought about his parents, he thought about our friends, and he thought a lot about his reputation. As soon as he could, John called Gray, explained that the FBI agent had asked him if he could inspect Hunt's office, and that he had replied that he would have to check and find out. He asked Gray to explain that the following day. Gray refused.

The sensational statement, and the other sensational revelations at the hearings, had made John a "hot" item for the press, a fact that soon assured us a permanent, 24-hour delegation of reporters and cameramen in front of our town house at 100 Quay Street. If we started off anywhere in our Porsche, they would pursue us. If I left to buy groceries, some of them would follow me. One time a correspondent even helped me carry a large bag of groceries from the car to the kitchen. John more often than not would enter and leave the house via the back door. Once John, who took great pride in his driving, managed to elude several cars of pursuing newsmen, and on another occasion when we escaped, the scene was hilarious: two reporters dashed to their car so they could follow us, each tried to enter through the same door at the same moment. They collided—at the hips—and we laughed merrily as we drove away.

I realized these people had their work to do, and I did not resent them as individuals. What really bothered me was that now, in addition to everything else, we had lost the little bit of private life we had managed to preserve. I would continue on this way, for John's sake, but not forever. If he realized I was losing heart, it was not from anything I said. The last thing in the world I wanted to do was add to my husband's burdens, which clearly were weighing more heavily on him with each passing day.

On Monday, March 19, Chuck and Patty Colson were giving a big reception—so big they were holding it at Blair House, the mansion across from the White House where visiting kings and other heads of state headquarter when they visit Washington. Blair House is also where President Truman lived when the White House was being repaired and remodeled. The decorator within me and the historian within John urged us to go, but John's historian was not nearly so influential at that time as John's conscience—which was beginning to tell him things—very important things—that he must do.

Despite my suggestion that we just drop in long enough

to take one whirl through the main rooms at Blair House, and then leave, John refused to consider going at all. "There are lots and lots of things running through my mind," he said. "I've just got to give full time to sorting things out."

"Can I help?"

"Maybe later. Right now, this is something I got myself into and something I have to get myself out of."

Meanwhile, he made clear to me, he was in no mood to be pumping arms at a social event, no matter where it was being held. "All I want to do, Mo—is think, think, think. You can go if you wish. I just have to be home tonight." What a silly thought. John knew big receptions frightened me to death even when he was with me. Alone I would be absolutely petrified. On the evening of March 19, Mr. and Mrs. Dean were at home, having one of their two-person parties, with one of the guests a moody, quiet sort who acted as if he might enjoy a one-person party more.

Mrs. Dean turned in very early that night, and no doubt slept more soundly than Mr. Dean, who was at the brink of making a major decision affecting not just John Wesley Dean III, not just his wife Maureen, not just Richard M. Nixon, President of the United States, but affecting the course of United States history for who knows how many years to come. That John Dean temporarily backed away from this major decision does not alter the fact that he made it—and later implemented it. There is a little of the historian in me—just enough to tell me that in the decades and generations to come, that decision by John Dean will come to be regarded as one that saved the nation from a President and an administration that could have wrecked it. Absolutely wrecked it.

Such a perception may seem apocalyptic to some. It is anything but. What John Dean did, he should have done sooner, without any question. He should never have become involved in a cover-up, in blackmail, and most important, he should have recognized his activities for what they were—crimes—and not acts of loyalty to the President of the United States. But what was stirring John Dean the night of March 19, 1973, will some day be appreciated for what it was—a recognition that powerful men were appropriating the country for their own uses, that he was a part of the misappropriation, and that even if no one would listen to a 34-year-old, second-echelon presidential assistant, much less believe him, he was going to say what had to be said, first to the President. If that did not reverse the administration's direction—he was confident that it would—he would have to consider a next step.

It is so strange to look back at that night, to think of the dimensions of John's considerations, to think of the impact those thoughts would have on millions and millions of people, and to realize that I—the only witness—was so completely oblivious to it. It's important to me that people know why: the integrity of the President of the United States was still beyond question to me; the integrity of my husband was even further beyond question. And John, now realizing fully that he held the continuance of a presidential administration in his very hands, could not risk inadvertent disclosure of the facts, particularly since he still thought the administration could be saved.

There was one other point that mattered very much to John—he did not wish to risk involving me in what he now knew could be the biggest government scandal in the history of the United States. He had kept Fred Fielding, Pete Kinsey, and others in his office far away from it; he was determined to keep his wife even further isolated. However remote the possibility that I could ever be tagged as an accessory or be accused of concealing the commission of a felony, John wanted to take absolutely no chances. Things were quite bad enough as they were.

Throughout this nightmare—his and the country's—John was protective: of his wife, his staff, and, unfortunately, as it turned out, of his President.

On March 20, John left for the White House with a look of grim determination on his face. He told me that he did not know if he would be meeting with the President that day, but that if he did not, he would request a meeting for March 21. "There are some things I just have to tell him," he said.

Of course, I knew it was Watergate. What else? What else had dominated our lives for so many months? I was glad. Now, I thought, this whole nightmare was going to come to an end. At last these dreadful shadows of suspicion would be removed from John, from the President, from all those not responsible.

"Why hasn't the President insisted that whoever else is tangled up in this come forward and take his medicine?" I had once asked John. "Why is he allowing himself to take such a terrible beating over it?"

Replied my husband: "I don't know."

I knew that some kind of a watershed was being reached. John was not the sort to idly ask for a meeting with the President. He was very reserved in his work at the White House, fully aware of his place in the pecking order, not anxious to overstep—ever—and certainly not anxious to build an empire of his own. If he felt he had to see the President, then something was coming to a head.

That evening, Peter Kinsey dropped over for a drink, and John came home just a little before seven-thirty—by way of Fred Fielding's house and our back door to avoid the press out front. John kissed me, said he had had an interesting visit with Dick Moore (whom he had told of his plans to tell the President everything he knew about the cover-up). Our living room was on a different level from our dining room and kitchen, so I told John to sit down in the living room in a comfortable chair and chat with Pete while I fixed him his drink. John's mood was good—as if at least part of the heavy load had been removed from his mind. He decided to help me fix the drink. I poured some Scotch and water over ice cubes, and we were about to join Pete when the telephone rang—hardly a unique event once John was in the house. John asked Pete to answer and find out who it was—he didn't especially want to take calls unless they were urgent.

Pete, a slender, generally disheveled, boyish-looking fellow who is such a dear friend, picked up the telephone and said "Hello."

Pete's complexion is always pale. Suddenly it turned a ghostly white.

"Oh, yes, uh . . . yes, he's here, just came in as a matter of fact," Pete stammered, then limply let his arm and the telephone sink into a soft pillow.

"You'll want to take this call," he said, and John started down the steps.

"Who is it?" John called out.

"The President," Pete replied.

Then he sprawled out on the sofa in a mock faint.

John took the receiver out of Pete's hand, and I—excited as always when the President of the United States was dealing with my husband—handed John his drink over the stairway railing. Pete, ever the diplomat, came upstairs and joined me in the kitchen so John could talk with complete freedom.

It was not a long conversation, and shortly after it was over, Pete left.

John and I talked a lot that night.

The statement that really stayed with me was this:

"I'm going to end the cover-up by telling the President the cover-up is impossible to continue and for him to get out in front of it."

I thought I understood. *Someone* was involved in covering up the Watergate matter. But it wasn't the President.

And it wasn't John. Thank goodness John would now tell the President the best way to get the facts out, and at last this dreadful matter would go away.

The President would meet with him at 10 A.M., John said. "I told him I wanted to talk about the Watergate situation because I don't think he realizes how serious the damn thing is. Wish me luck."

We turned in early, and John was up and out of the house early the next morning. I'm sure he wanted to gather some memos or take some notes or in some way prepare for what he obviously considered to be a very important meeting.

March 21, 1973. A historic date. It was a Wednesday. I went about my business—cleaning up the house, picking up some groceries. I carefully avoided calling John in the morning, remembering his meeting with the President would begin at 10 A.M. and probably go on for an hour or two.

Sometime between twelve and one o'clock, John called me. I asked him about the meeting, and he said it went fine. He sounded so depressed as he said it, but John is always very cool, very unexcitable. Some rather "delicate" matters had been discussed, he said, and he didn't think we should talk about them—maybe not for some time. But things had gone along "fairly well."

We had been invited to a big dinner being given by the recording industry. Did he want to go?

"No. Why don't we just stay home?"

The dinner did not sound very appealing to me, either. I was glad to be staying home, even if our guardians from the press should turn up, forcing us to draw all the shades, close all the draperies.

John was very tender that night. We felt especially close and loving. I didn't pump him about the meeting—he had said it was "delicate" and that I might not learn about it for some time.

As the whole world would later learn, the March 21 meeting was one that will never be forgotten as long as there is a United States.

John Dean had told Richard Nixon that there was a "cancer on the presidency" and that it had to be removed or it would kill the President.

In response Richard Nixon told John Dean and others that it would be no problem to raise an additional $1 million to buy the continued silence of some convicted burglars.

The cancer was not removed, then or later.

It did "kill" the President.

15

There Is
No Shangri-La

EHRLICHMAN: Exactly right. You see, you're the one who . . .
said . . . "send that man to Camp David . . . and have him
take as much time as necessary and let's get it all down."
That's when he was uncovered.
NIXON: I suppose that really isn't true . . . Well, that's what we
have to say.

(From a White House tape of April 19, 1973)

John W. Dean III was "that man" who was sent to Camp
David by the President in March 1973.

I was oblivious to all the backstage maneuverings that
preceded that trip. Thinking back to the night before the
trip whose historical significance would have mystified me
had someone told me of it at the time, I can plainly see
John arriving at home on the night of March 22, 1973. He
came through the back door—reporters, cameramen, and
television crews were still swarming at the front door,
hoping to obtain a glimpse of John and a few words from
him. He was determined to give them neither.

Now that the name John Dean is so well known, it is
difficult to recall that during his White House years John
was as anonymous as a top aide to the President can possibly be. His anonymity suited President Nixon and Bob

Haldeman. It also suited John—and me; fundamentally we are—or were—very private people. While wishing we still were, I understand that we will not be again.

The press had been intensely interested in John from the moment that L. Patrick Gray III had told the Senate Judiciary Committee that John had received FBI reports during the Watergate investigation. Before that, John's major national exposure had come when President Nixon told a press conference that his counsel, John Dean, had conducted an investigation and determined that no one in the White House, "presently employed," had played a role in the Watergate burglary.

Gray's statement—that the counsel to the President had lied to an FBI agent—was a sensation, and the press, in varying numbers, was encamped on our front doorstep from that moment on.

Maybe because I love intrigue, I didn't really mind at first. We were compelled to keep the shades of our town house drawn all the time, and I couldn't even leave the house. But I loved to peek out and watch all the cameramen and reporters. Occasionally I would see faces that I recognized from television news programs.

But John didn't find it exciting at all, which is why he chose to enter his own home through the back door that night. Fred and Maria Fielding lived just a block away, so John came home with Fred (the deputy counsel to the President), and when John entered his own home, the press did not even know he was there. And he was not about to peek out and risk being seen.

I sensed that so many, many strange things were taking place. I couldn't begin to understand them all. That night when I played peekaboo with the photographers I had no understanding or even suspicion that my husband was reaching a decision that would topple the Nixon presidency. Should I feel hurt that my husband would not confide in me at such a critical moment, not just in the life of the nation, but in our own lives as well? Probably.

But John was gently and subtly preparing me for the hard fall that was to come, and it was such a hard fall! He was giving me a small dose at a time—not the entire contents of the medicine bottle in one swallow. In retrospect, I think he was wise.

Since the Gray statement, John was almost constantly in a deep, blue mood, nervous and irritable, unable to get home at a decent hour, and unable to keep off the phone for more than ten or fifteen minutes at a stretch when he finally did come home.

When the press "stakeouts" began, John disconnected the doorbell. He's good at mechanical things. Our telephone number was unlisted. The press could not get to John at the White House, so reporters had no choice except to hope to catch him going to or coming from his home. That wasn't a very promising possibility, either.

When John burst through the door that night, I made certain that there was a drink ready for him. We chatted with neighbor friends who also came in through the back door. What was most important to me, knowing the stress John was under, was to get him to relax and enjoy himself if only for a couple of hours.

It worked fairly well that night, although John still seemed distracted—and so burdened, in an indefinable way. How I wanted to help! And how helpless I felt.

One course I quickly ruled out: I was not about to nag him into telling me everything that was on his mind. Of course, I wanted to know. But even more, I wanted John to have some time when his mind did not have to focus on the problems he was compelled to wrestle with for ten or twelve or fourteen hours a day.

We had dinner and went to bed. Upstairs, I peeked through the shades again, and, as I expected, the cameras were still there. I felt sorry for the people who had to stand around all night in the cold while John and I were in our warm, comfortable bed.

We prayed together as we always do, and I, at least, fell asleep. John probably fretted most of the night, and lay awake and thought for hours. He had been doing just that, it seemed to me, for months. I sensed that he was slowly letting me know the details. I could not have rushed him if I wanted to, and I did not want to. But my intuition told me that John had some very bad news indeed to impart.

On the morning of March 23, John slept late. He lazily inquired about the size of the press corps outside, and decided not to go to the office. The telephone never stopped ringing, but John accepted only a few calls.

In early afternoon, the White House operator was on the line. I was trying to screen John's calls, so naturally I asked:

"Who's calling?"

There was a brief and dead silence.

Then the operator said, a bit petulantly, as if I'd had my nerve even to ask:

"The President."

My heart seemed to stop beating. Needless to say, John accepted that call.

What happened next is a bit vague in my mind. I'm sure I just beamed proudly on my husband while he conversed with the President of the United States. It was a short conversation, at the conclusion of which John turned to me and said: "Well, how would you like to go to Camp David?"

That put me on Cloud Nine.

Of course, there was the excitement of going to the presidential retreat, which so few citizens of the United States— who really own it—are ever privileged to do. But even more than that, I was positively ecstatic at the thought of getting away with John. We could be *alone*. We could talk to each other. We could love each other. We could spend hours and hours *with* each other. Certainly, I knew there would be work for John—there always was. Nor was I foolish enough to believe that the telephone calls would stop. But we would at least be away from the house that had become a sort of prison, away from the press, away from John's office—*away*. I hadn't been so happy in weeks.

John explained the situation: the President had specified that both of us should go to Camp David and relax. John had protested at first, reminding the President that the First Lady and Tricia were at Camp David, and that Tricia was ill. I wondered how he knew all that, but John always seemed to know so many things. The President had told John not to concern himself about Mrs. Nixon and their daughter—to go anyway. I have ever since been curious about what happened to them. We left within about an hour for Camp David, stayed for several days, and we never saw either Pat Nixon or Tricia. It would not have occurred to me at the time that the President might have told them to leave so John and I could have the place to ourselves. But now that I know the importance the President attached to having John go to Camp David, I can easily believe that he ordered his wife and sick daughter to vacate the premises and to leave the retreat entirely to us.

In any event, after the telephone call from the President, and after John told me to get ready, I was terror-stricken. What, I asked myself, does a woman wear to Camp David? I had no idea.

Fortunately, there was no time to decide. A White House limousine picked us up about an hour after the President's call, and somehow or other I got my act together and I was ready when John said, a bit irritably, I thought, "Now, dear, *now*. We have to leave."

I sank into the back seat, close to John. Somehow or other, we had managed to escape the press. I can't remember how. What I do recall is squeezing John's arm and saying, somewhat inanely: "I can't believe we're going to Camp David!"

John Wesley Dean III was totally unresponsive. He was a million miles away from me. Really, that ride was like two strangers sharing a taxicab—maybe worse. John looked at the newspaper and hardly spoke to me at all.

Obviously, there was something heavy on his mind. But I did not know *how* heavy his burden really was.

I didn't let it bother me too much. After being virtual prisoners in our home, now we would have several days together in an isolated, rustic setting. Together. Alone. Maybe after some walks in the woods, and some delicious dinners with the great wines I had heard were served at Camp David, John would be able to sort things out, confide in me, and stop brooding.

Since John paid so little attention to me during the hour's ride, I watched the scenery, the road, and the driver. Near the end of the trip, the driver was—of all things— having trouble locating Camp David. The main road had been closed, and he had to take a different route. We came to a fork, and I could tell he did not know whether to go right or left. Feeling slightly mischievous and a lot more perky than my gloomy husband, I commanded: "Turn right."

I had no idea where that would lead us. And the driver followed my order. The road took us right to Camp David. That was such fun. I smiled sweetly and was about to aim an elbow at John's ribs. But fortunately I saw his eyes first. They were glazed and unseeing. And he did not crack a smile.

You can't believe Camp David unless you see it. I suppose that when a man gets there he feels like a king, because when I arrived I felt like a queen. Camp David does nothing to fortify one's belief in the democratic process, nor does it set one to reflecting on the plight of the common man. More accurately, it lulls one into the belief that perhaps creature comforts are meant for the few, and if you are one of those few, then it's perfectly all right.

We arrived at a checkpoint at the main gate. The guards know who is coming, so there's no red tape. You know the guards are there, that they are efficient, and that as long as they are there, you are safe. You also know that the very fact that you are there indicates you are important. Or someone special. It's a heady feeling. You can almost picture yourself issuing orders to the rest of the country: send the bombers north; impound a billion dollars; do as I say and whatever I say, I'm the king of the mountain.

Beginning with the high, barbed-wire fence, I took in everything. The lodges and the cabins—the rustic, unfinished look of the place, the "log cabin" construction, and the somewhat strange "southern" feel to the place. John likened it to a boys' camp. But neither boy campers nor girl campers ever had their every wish and whim fulfilled almost before they could even express them. We did.

A young Navy ensign greeted us on arrival, with information about where everything was—the swimming pools and bowling alleys, the bicycles and golf carts, the Laurel Lodge with its huge dining room, the movie theater with a projectionist available twenty-four hours a day, the President's quarters. It was as if the Grand Hotel—the grandest of Grand Hotels—was being operated exclusively for us. When we were in one of the lodges, all we had to do to order a cocktail, or lunch or dinner, or wine, or anything at all was to pick up the telephone. Immediately a steward would materialize in front of us, and almost anything we ordered would be there about thirty seconds later. The stewards, virtually all Filipino, were amazingly quick and courteous. They seemed to have a perfect sense of timing. When dining, just as we'd finished our soup course, they would come in with the salad. The stewards anticipated our needs and were there without being summoned.

I wondered: What does such a palace atmosphere do to the men and women who are the temporary kings and queens? Is all this part of what is meant by an "imperial presidency"? Certainly all the trappings of royalty were present—even for us—and John and I were far removed from the "throne." I could sense that people who are treated so royally for long periods could easily come to the view that they are entitled to it all.

The cabins at Camp David are not plush, but they are oh so comfortable. In the large main rooms there are double and twin beds, a night stand, and lots and lots of telephones. Off the main rooms, there is a good-sized bathroom, and then a small, cozy room with sofas and a desk and bookcases. And there is a television set—color, of course.

The Laurel Lodge—where we had dinner every night—is enormous. And lovely. I remember a large wooden coffee table, overstuffed sofas, and lots of wingback chairs.

Naturally the telephone rang shortly after we arrived. But I was so giddy with delight at being away for a few days with John that I didn't even frown—or groan. Again the operator said it was the President calling, and then I really began to wonder what was going on. What was so important and so secret that the President of the United States had to talk to John twice in little more than an hour, the second time before we had even begun to follow his orders to "relax"?

But it was not President Nixon. Instead, Bob Haldeman came on the line. I paid no attention to John's side of the conversation once I learned it was Haldeman on the telephone. He was always calling, wherever we were.

But that call was just the beginning. John was on the telephone constantly the entire time we were there. "We'll talk about it," he said once. "Soon. But not right now."

At Camp David I just looked around while John talked from the telephone in our cabin. I saw a navy blue jacket with a Camp David insignia over the left pocket that seemed just my size; I put it on, and modeled it for John while he talked. There was a jacket for John, too, and we were supposed to take them with us when we left. But we didn't know it. (We each got one later, anyway.)

At last John was free. We ordered cocktails, and then told the dining room what we wanted for dinner. The ensign had told us we could have anything—absolutely anything—we wanted.

That night, I dressed up for dinner, even though there would just be the two of us. I wanted to be alluring to my husband. In the lodge, the fireplace was ablaze and there were several huge paintings. It had sort of a Williamsburg look.

The stewards all wore red jackets, white shirts, black pants. I remember John saying: "You couldn't pay for such services." It's true.

We dined at a table for four. There was soft, melodic stereo music during the meal, which was exquisite. I loved the fresh flowers and the candles on every table, but thought it rather extravagant to have them on every table when only one was occupied.

Strangely, it was almost an intimate atmosphere, despite the size of the lodge. Everything seemed so perfect, so right. But one tiny little question constantly ran through my head: Why are we here?

I was on the verge of breaking my resolve not to initiate "shop talk" but decided against it. John would be no help. I was getting one-word responses to any and all topics that I brought up.

But at last he did stop staring into space and trained his eyes on me. His look was tender and loving. I melted. For a moment, he had cast aside the worries that possessed him, and at last his focus was me and not the President. His look said it all, but there were a few words to go along with it.

"I'm sorry I'm not mentally here," he said in that deep, soft voice. Our hands touched.

That was all I needed.

"I don't want to pressure you, honey. I know you have enough problems already. I don't want to be another one."

He squeezed my hand, stared into my eyes for a moment, and said: "No way."

For a long time, John had been preparing me for bad news—how bad I simply could not imagine. "Things are getting rough, dear, and they're going to get a whole lot rougher," he would tell me.

His warnings about stormy days ahead seemed to be coming more often, and he was more emphatic each time. My assumption was that there would be a lot more attacks like the one by Pat Gray, and that there would be a lot more newspaper stories trying to link John to the Watergate cover-up.

Only once before we went to Camp David had John become more explicit. He told me things were getting so rough that he might even have to go to prison. I put that out of my mind so completely that I have no memory of it at all. John does, though. He remembers everything. It was the night of March 20, 1973, and he recalls telling me very bluntly and that I cried in his arms. It's always difficult for me to accept unpleasantness, but it's especially so when I'm in bed with my husband and facing the possibility of losing him.

So that night at Camp David I told John that everything would work out, and I just enjoyed the Long Island duckling, the baked Alaska, and the delicious wine. And my husband's company, most of all, even though he wasn't his often scintillating self.

John has a great sense of humor, but obviously he wasn't overworking it that night. I do remember one funny comment, though, that he made earlier that evening, after we had ordered another bottle of wine to be brought to our cabin: "These people aren't used to the Deans after serving Haldeman and Ehrlichman and that crew of teetotalers." Somehow, the stewards got the message. They brought over a bottle of Scotch with lots of ice, and several bottles of wine.

After dinner that night, and the next three days and two nights, John worked in another cabin, equipped with typewriter and desk. Now I realize what he was trying to do. After he had told President Nixon on March 21 that there was "a cancer on the presidency," there had been a meeting on March 22 of Nixon, John Mitchell, Bob Haldeman, John Ehrlichman, and John. John had thought the President would try to get at the truth and then bring a quick end to the cover-up. But, instead, the talk was about writing a report that would "clear" just about everybody of involvement in Watergate—a report that would be vague and incomplete. John must have been simply aghast, but if all these older and more powerful men believed the problem could be solved this way, he was willing to try. It beat going to prison.

So that's what he was doing at Camp David—trying to write a report that was impossible to write.

While he worked, I was alone and not liking it one bit. The stewards continued to anticipate my every wish. I played pool with myself. I thought I would slowly go crazy. I looked at the books. They were all old and dull.

Then I remembered the movies! Thank heaven. John had told me that Bob Haldeman had said that Larry Higby had all the dirty movies up there, if we wanted to see them. I rushed to a large book in the movie room that contained the names of all the movies that were available, and I saw five movies in three days. I remember *Avanti* (which to Haldeman may have been a dirty movie) because it was the only one that John saw with me. I also saw *The*

Poseidon Adventure and *Deliverance* and two others I can't recall.

Most often I'd just stretch out on a huge leather sofa with a pillow and a blanket, and a bottle of wine in an ice bucket. The sofa was nine feet long! I measured it.

I slept late in the mornings, and I slept a lot during the days while John worked on the "Dean Report." One afternoon I took a nap by the blazing fire. John came by, tucked the blanket around me, kissed me, and said he wanted me to know he cared, and that he was still alive. I was happy to get both messages.

Nature abounds at Camp David. It's a great place for getting your head together, if you can keep from getting too heady. Presidents since Franklin Roosevelt (who named it Shangri-La) have loved it, and I hoped that just being there would help John to see things clearly and to work out his problems. He took long walks in the woods—alone —when he wasn't working. Of course, I knew that what he was going through was heavy. And I did not enjoy being neglected. But I believed in my husband and loved him very much. Whatever he had to do, he had to do. So I stayed away.

There was nothing to do other than enjoy the beauty and the luxury. I collected the cigarette packages with the Camp David seal. Both of us rode around the place in golf carts. I remember riding up to take a look at the old Eisenhower swimming pool, which was then being used by the staff, since President Nixon had ordered a new, smaller but much fancier pool for himself adjoining his lodge.

On the third day, John's secretary, Jane Thomas, came up to do some typing, but he didn't keep her very busy, so we had great fun together. Her presence gave me the courage to examine the President's own lodge. I'm really brave when I have someone with me. We looked in every door and window. We saw absolutely nothing! Darn. I especially wanted to see the President's huge stereo system, because John told me that some of the Camp David staff had been whispering that Nixon often stood before the stereo and—all by himself—"conducted" a symphony. I hope it's true. It would make him seem more human.

Jane is a tall, slender, attractive woman who has been with John since he worked for the House Judiciary Committee in the 1960s as counsel to the minority. At first I resented Jane because she was so overly protective of John, but I came to really love her. She's got a super head—and she never violates a confidence.

Jane brought lots of papers and folders up for John, and she did a little typing. But since he wasn't getting much writing done, she had plenty of spare time. We saw two movies together.

But the fun and games were drawing to a close.

Ron Ziegler notified John by telephone that the *Los Angeles Times* was about to break a story saying John had been involved in the planning of the Watergate break-in. John was outraged. So was I. But I couldn't help being a little bemused by the thought that if a false newspaper report could snap him out of his melancholy, it couldn't be all bad. Of course, as the melancholy melted away, it was replaced by a fit of anger, something I would not ordinarily welcome. But at that time I was ready for a change—any change.

John shouted, and I tried to calm him down a bit. He was particularly perturbed because he had tried in his own way to abort the illegal surveillance scheme that G. Gordon Liddy had presented to John Mitchell, Jeb Magruder, and himself. Such a plan should not even have been discussed in the office of the attorney general, John had said, and he never heard any more about it until the burglars were arrested in the Watergate headquarters of the Democratic National Committee.

John knew he couldn't stop the *Times* from printing the

story. He said he would sue the newspaper for libel. He said he would call an attorney. I suggested Robert Mc-Candless, who used to be his brother-in-law and whom I liked very much then. But John said no—he would call Tom Hogan, and he did. I heard him tell Tom, "There'll be a lot more later," and I asked him what he meant.

He said, "It's time for your husband to hire a good lawyer, because one thing I will not do is lie."

I'm great at biting my lower lip.

Thank goodness he left me quickly. He went for a walk in the woods. I sank into a chair, and let the tears flow. By the time he returned, I had regained my composure and what I thought was my sanity.

John walked in the woods a lot, most often alone, sometimes with me. Thoughts were racing through my mind. John was in deep trouble and I couldn't be of help. I couldn't do a thing for him. I wanted to throw my arms around him—to hold him close. It wasn't the time for that, either.

I thought of Richard Nixon. Then I thought of Camp David. And I remember saying to myself: What a lovely place. Wouldn't it be great to come back here at the invitation of some President other than Nixon? Even then, knowing so little, I was beginning to sense that John's troubles, whatever they were, flowed directly from Nixon.

John reached the point we both knew he would, but it had to be his timing. He knew I was at the point where further easing would not do. Nothing could be easy now, and perhaps would never be again.

"I have serious legal problems, Mo," he said gently, and very persuasively, as we walked into the woods. "I'm sure I've been involved in things for which I have a criminal liability."

John W. Dean III—my beloved husband, the President's counsel, a criminal?

I could not, would not, believe it, even though he was telling me so himself.

We talked some more. My eyes became blurred by tears, my head was spinning, and my defenses against unpleasant truths were working overtime. John—the kindest, gentlest, most thoughtful, dearest man I had ever known—a criminal? No.

John knew I had had enough. We walked further and further into the woods, and then we returned, and somewhere along the way he had begun to talk of other things. And then it was time for dinner, and afterward, John did not leave me. We held each other closely, and soon that merry, tinkling laugh of his reappeared between his sentences, and somehow I felt comforted and lulled back into the realm of the possible, where thoughts of my husband ever going to prison simply could not exist.

Our evening together had been the tenderest ever, and we had had many tender ones. As I dropped off to sleep, I just knew that John would never go to prison.

For that was impossible.

16
"Moser—Have Gone to Meet the Man..."

First there had been the Watergate break-in and the need to keep it quiet until after the election, and then there had been the election and the need to keep it quiet longer. Next there had been the mysterious meetings with Segretti and the urgent calls that interrupted our honeymoons and Thanksgiving, and next there had been the second inauguration, John's face-to-face meetings with the President, John's resolve to awaken the President to a "cancer on the presidency." Then there had been the Gray hearings, the "Mr. Dean lied, didn't he?" accusation, and then Camp David, and the dreadful story in the *Los Angeles Times* saying John Dean had prior knowledge of the Watergate break-in, and John's threatened libel suit because that simply was not true.

And then there was the night at Camp David when my husband told me he might have criminal liability, and might have to go to prison.

It was all too much for me. My head was in a constant whirl. I could not bring all this into focus. When I tried to sort out the facts of one incident, another one, more sensational, swept them out of my mind.

This much I could grasp:

Whatever John had done, he had done out of misguided

loyalty to a man who, like all men, turned out to have feet of clay.

Whatever John had done, he was my husband, I loved him, and whatever the future had in store, it had in store for both of us.

In the rare moments of reflection that were possible in this dizzying situation, my mind turned from the question of what had happened to why it had happened. It seemed so clear to me now—why hadn't it all along? Had I asserted myself, had I followed some of the precepts that have been engrained in me, I might have spared my husband some of the awful hurt he was now undergoing, and had all the wives of the Watergate principals rebelled against being relegated to insignificant roles everywhere but within the home, their families, like ours, might have been spared the years of trauma, bitterness and lasting shame that none of us will ever shed. The country, too, would have been infinitely better off.

But men in government are oblivious to their families for long periods. I have seen it so often, firsthand, in this country and on my trips abroad. These men work long hours, longer than they need to. Several hours after the workday should have ended, they still do not go home, because that would imperil their own sense of importance, and, what they fear even more, it might make them appear a little less significant to their peers. It's a heady atmosphere—at the office, the telephones are ringing, the messages are coming in and going out, the underlings are being suitably deferential, and the next morning the men of power will be able to lean back in their swivel chairs, stifle yawns, and say to an impressionable visitor: "Excuse me. Didn't get away from here till nearly eleven last night. It's been that way for weeks now."

If they go home when they should—and can—what is there for them? Most often, there are children, who need help getting ready for bed, or who beg to stay up for one more television show, or who want help with homework, or who have been arrested for speeding or smoking marihuana. And then there is the wife, who after struggling alone for weeks with the problems of the children and the home may not seem quite so sparkling as some of the nearly always attractive secretaries who work at the office.

I say all this from personal observation. I have been pinched, patted, squeezed, and hugged by some of these men of power, and so has every other moderately attractive woman who has worked for them. Most were men with families who should have been with their families, but preferred the company of pretty girls and the atmosphere where their own personal importance was always being confirmed.

Men should realize—perhaps some of them will now— what they are missing, and that it is not only more precious but even more practical for them than the system currently in vogue in high government circles and many an executive suite.

It's the sustaining power of love and it's the candor that comes with love.

What wife will *not* tell a man—even a man who is the President of the United States—that he is wearing one brown sock and one black sock? Will his secretary? Will his top aide? No—they look the other way and pretend that everything is fine. What wife will *not* tell a man that he looks funny, that his hat is on crooked, that he needs a haircut?

And what wife will *not* tell a man to realize that he is not the best companion when he takes her along on a trip and spends much of his time thinking of how irresistible he would be to other women if he were alone. Richard Nixon, Henry Kissinger, and Walter Annenberg, when all were at the height of their power, thought that every female in sight would swoon at the least sign of interest from any of them. They were only three among hundreds of victims of this side effect of power.

Not only will a woman tell a man that his orange tie clashes with his burgundy shirt, she will also tell him his lying to cover up for the boss is going to force him into additional lies, that he'd better stop the thing before it gets started. Things like this really may not occur to him.

But women do not often hear of the "shortcuts" being taken, because they play such an insignificant role in power, whether in government or business. Men talk to each other, not to their wives. The wives are home, and when the men get there, it's too late and they are too weary for shop talk. The wife and the husband live, think, act in separate compartments.

Only when difficult times arrive do the men have any concept of the fact that *love*—however expressed or not expressed—is not the only essential ingredient of marriage. Married couples must also be *friends*. Each should be the other's best friend, and best friends share.

In Washington as in Hollywood and as in big business, everything seems so baffling to those on the outside—a reason, I suspect, that many men don't talk to their wives. She wouldn't understand, she wouldn't be interested, they feel. Well, nine times out of ten, she would understand, and she would be interested. She would also discover that the inside is not so baffling as it had seemed to her, that a great deal is superficial pomp and circumstance, and that when decision-making time comes, the fundamental things apply—or should. And if they were applied, there would be much less grief and anguish.

A wife can say to a husband: "You've got that title, and people fawn over you, because they are impressed by what you are. But both of us know *who* you are, and what you should and should not do."

In fact, many wives, myself included, may say far more

than is necessary, may be far more critical than is warranted. And we don't know everything, of course. We are often wrong. But if we are overly critical, that at least gives the man an opportunity to open up and discuss things. An argument is better than no discourse at all.

I like to think—I do think—that if the wives of the men who held the top positions in the Nixon administration had known what was going on, at least some of them (myself included) would have said: "Get out of it. It's wrong." One or two of the men—maybe more—might even have listened.

I knew this intuitively, but in the confusion of the circumstances, I was most often too frightened to think.

And after Camp David, I was very often frightened.

With John seeking out a lawyer so soon after he had tried to convince the President to remove the "cancer," it was clear that the part of our life that revolved around the White House was nearing an end. Under other circumstances, I would have been ecstatic. In fact, after the re-election, when John was considering some opportunities outside government (he had offers to become vice president and general counsel of several large companies, as well as an offer to become a partner in the law firm of Colson and Shapiro), I rather hoped he would accept one of them. But both of us wanted to live abroad before settling down, and he had mentioned that he had a chance to become ambassador to a small, French-speaking country. (In fact, he went to Berlitz and I went to the Alliance Française to learn to speak French.)

But right after the election Haldeman had persuaded John to stay on. "The loyalty bit," John explained.

Now it was all ending—this way. That it was coming to an end didn't dismay me. That the security of a job and income was disappearing frightened me a great deal. Although I still could not believe John would ever be found guilty of a crime or would ever have to go to prison, I knew that when the time came for him to leave the White House, it would not be under favorable circumstances, and he might have difficulty finding something else at a level that would challenge his interest and abilities.

But I couldn't brood on that for long. Too much was going on. I had to help.

On the very day that a White House car brought us down from Camp David, John went on to the White House, and the copies of documents used at Camp David came home with me.

"I want these all at home for a while—where I know nothing will happen to them," he said. It was a statement that made me aware for the first time of the rampant mistrust and suspicion that now existed among the President's aides. John is not paranoid. He never suspects something without good reason, and now he obviously was thinking that a time could come when one or more of his close colleagues might raid his files. He brought home more files and memos from time to time, but not in great volume and, as it turned out, he didn't bring enough.

It was Bob Haldeman whose actions first prompted John to look after his own flanks, because Haldeman was so obviously looking after his. When Jeb Magruder and John Mitchell were trying to decide how to explain their meetings with Liddy prior to the break-in, Haldeman insisted that John meet with them. When John said he did not want to meet with them, and that if he were asked about the Liddy meetings, he would tell the truth, his old "friend" Haldeman virtually ordered him to go and said that he—Haldeman—didn't wish to get involved.

Imagine!

"There are more rough times ahead," John told me after the encounter with Haldeman. He needn't have. By this time I could look down the road ahead, and see rather clearly how rough it was.

What John and I were going through was difficult, and again it got so we practically never saw each other.

On one of the few occasions when we did have some time together, he told me that Tom Hogan, whom he had consulted on the libelous *Los Angeles Times* article, was not a criminal attorney and that he was trying to get Charles Shaffer, whom he had met on a hunting trip, to represent him.

Shaffer was a tall, slender, crisp-talking, no-nonsense lawyer who had served in the Department of Justice under Robert Kennedy. He has a very commanding, confident manner and great intelligence. I also thought he was rather cold and stuck on himself, though that feeling evaporated rapidly. Now he and John were spending hours and hours together, John telling him—to Charley's amazement and near-disbelief—all that he and the others in the White House had been involved in over the past few years. Between talking with Charley and fending for himself in the intrigue-filled White House, Mr. Dean had little time for Mrs. Dean, who understood fully and hated it thoroughly.

John was looking increasingly haggard. No one knew better than he how bleak his future looked, and the present was not exactly a bargain, either. The areas around his eyes turned black and then blacker. He was nervous and high-strung. Later, a look of relief would take command of his features. Now he was, by standards of the power establishment, just a "punk kid" who was biting off more than he could chew. He was getting ready to tell the Watergate prosecutors everything he knew, without knowing if even a word he said would ever be corroborated. He was preparing to butt heads with the former attorney general of the United States, with the White House chief of staff, with the President's top domestic counselor, with his former special counsel, and with a half dozen others who were or had been on the White House staff or that of the Committee for the Re-election of the President. And John was increasingly distressed because the more he talked with Charley Shaffer, the more he realized he could not spare the President once he began talking with the prosecutors. It may be difficult to believe now, but John agonized, even at that late date, over the wounds he would have to inflict on President Nixon, because he still admired the President (in many respects he still does). He also feared the consequences, foreign and domestic, of weakening a President of the United States. And he also knew that Haldeman, Ehrlichman, Mitchell, and Colson—and Nixon himself—were shrewd, cunning, and, with their backs to the wall, capable of a great deal. Would there be a single paper that John would be able to produce to corroborate any essential part of his story?

He of course never dreamed that there would some day be something even better than paper—tape recordings.

At this point, let me say that to me, my husband was and is an honorable man. And let me add that I realize there are people who do not share that point of view.

And most of those say, "He was only trying to save his neck." Without the word "only" that statement is true to a degree. But it was bigger than that. John tried to save everyone's neck, yours and mine included, when he made his decision. It is said that you have to love yourself before you can love anyone else. Maybe it is equally true that you have to save yourself before you can save anyone else.

During those long, lonely days and nights when John was either with Charley Shaffer or at the White House, I hardly knew what to do with myself. I cleaned the house a lot, more than ever before or since. Two or three times a week, I would even clean out the fireplace. I also read a lot, mainly Catherine Cookson novels, and every bestseller, fiction or nonfiction, that I could get my hands on.

But I preferred fiction—I didn't want anything that dealt with the problem. More escapism.

I spent most of my time alone, but Maria Fielding came over frequently to make certain I was bearing up. I'm sure that one reason I *was* bearing up is that I wasn't spending those seventeen or eighteen lonely hours a day thinking about John's situation. I did needlepoint, I went shopping, I planted azaleas and chrysanthemums in our garden, I went window-shopping with Maria. There was virtually no social life, except for an occasional dinner with the Fieldings, or with Pete Kinsey, or with Susan and Barry Goldwater.

I was waiting, waiting. I knew that this matter would come to a head. I couldn't hurry it, or slow it. I could only wait for it.

March 1973 is history now, but it contained more history than anyone suspected at the time. On March 23 James McCord had provided the first solid, believable confirmation of the involvement of higher-ups in Watergate when he wrote to Judge Sirica just before McCord and the other six defendants were sentenced for the break-in.

April looked as if it would be rather historic, too, and it didn't disappoint anyone. John met with Shaffer and briefed him (Tom Hogan sat in on most of the early sessions, too, some of which were held in Heidi's apartment). Once I drove John to one of the meetings, then picked him up five or six hours later and brought him home. It was better than not seeing him at all. John had told Hogan and Shaffer in the beginning that he wanted to go to the prosecutors, but needed their advice on his own situation before doing so. When Shaffer, who is a staunch Democrat, finally agreed to represent John, Hogan, who had represented Colson and felt he had a conflict of interest, dropped out.

John's "own situation," as he explained it to me, was this:

"I can try for immunity," he said—meaning that by becoming an essential witness, willing to disclose fully his own involvement and that of others, John could hope to be granted immunity from prosecution. "Or," he said, "I can plead guilty to one charge, testify, and the prosecutors will probably drop everything else they may have against me."

"But you'd go to prison that way!" I cried.

John looked at me a long time.

"That's right," he said softly. "Maybe that's the only way I can clear my conscience."

I wouldn't hear of it. "You'll be a witness, nothing more," I said. "They just have to have your testimony." And with that, I again confidently excluded from my mind any possibility that my husband would ever go to prison, a self-delusion that lasted up to the moment, almost a year and a half later, when the marshals picked him up and took him away.

On April 2, Charley Shaffer talked with the prosecutors, telling them some of the information John had and was willing to impart to them. Charley asked for total immunity for John, much to my delight. "I'm not going to let you go up there [to the prosecutors] with their machine guns blazing at you," Charley told John. I thought he was right. John thought he was wrong. Charley settled the issue: "If I'm going to be your attorney, you're going to let me run the show. You are a witness, not a defendant." By that time, John was sure of one thing: he wanted Charley to be his attorney.

By April 8, John was talking to the prosecutors himself. Names that were unfamiliar to me suddenly were appearing in John's conversations, and their owners were calling on the telephone. Earl Silbert, Seymour Glanzer, Donald Campbell—the original Watergate prosecutors—had been absolutely astonished by what John was revealing to them. Later, all of them insisted that they had known all along that higher-ups were involved, that they had intended to prosecute only the burglars at first, then grant them immunity and get them to tell all they knew. I think John, who is slow to criticize anyone (a fault, sometimes), is hard put to believe this, based on the reactions of the three prosecutors when he began to tick off the details of his own involvement, and that of everyone else except the President. Those reactions can only be described as wide-eyed.

I found myself fulfilling the traditional female role later when the Senate investigators began coming to the house: I served them cheese and crackers, hors d'oeuvres, iced tea, lemonade, coffee. I suppose I should have been disturbed at not participating in the discussions, but by then things had progressed to a thicket of legalisms in which I was totally lost. I didn't mind the housewife role: at least John was at home, and at least I was doing something to ease his burdens—even if only slightly.

Suddenly John stopped dealing with the Watergate prosecutors and began working with Sam Dash, Terry Lenzner, Scott Armstrong, and others on the staff of the Senate Watergate Committee. All he said was that the prosecutors didn't have any damn idea of what was going on and how to deal with it. All I could think was poor John—for hour after hour, they would ask him questions. They would go over the same ground, again and again. Obviously, they were all skeptical about the story he was telling—because no story quite like it had ever been told in the history of the United States government. The White House and the President's reelection committee involved in break-ins? burglaries? illegal wiretapping? perjury? obstruction of justice? conspiracy? And who knows what else?

Silbert, Glanzer, and Campbell had not simply been surprised earlier by what they were hearing—they also seemed to John a little bit dismayed. Now that the true dimensions of the Watergate scandals were confronting them, they must have sensed how weak it would sound later if they said (as they did and had to): "We were just about to get on to all this." I felt sorry for them, because even if that story were true, it would be a hard one to sell. Their task was difficult because of pressure being brought on Assistant Attorney General Henry Petersen and the entire criminal division of the Justice Department.

By April 12, personal salvation—for me—presented itself in the forms of Elizabeth and Jack Garfield. Jack is my dentist, but more than that he is a friend from years and years ago in Beverly Hills. I had not met his wife, Liz, but when I telephoned Jack with a question about a loose filling (I was falling apart in every way), he knew of the events swirling around John and told me that he and Liz were planning a vacation. I suggested they come to Washington and stay with us. Friends often think you want to be alone when a chasm is opening in front of you, but you don't. At least I don't. I told Jack I would meet their plane and they simply had to stay at 100 Quay Street.

Jack had some difficulty persuading Liz to stay with us, because she was naturally apprehensive about meeting me under such trying circumstances. Suspecting this, I went up to Liz first at the airport, to put her at ease, then turned to Jack. Liz and I were friends from that moment on.

Jack "borrowed" the office of a nearby dentist, took care of my filling, and then we had two fun-filled days just sightseeing, talking (Jack and I must have bored Liz with our reminiscing, but if so, she didn't complain).

Just having them there was the most marvelous therapy for me—I could even take my mind off John for brief periods. As for their getting to know John—well, that was slightly out of the question. He was almost never home. He would arrive late, just before we were ready to turn in. He'd have a nightcap with us, say little, and then collapse in bed himself, sleeping only fitfully despite his exhaustion.

But I had high hopes for some activity for all of us for Sunday, April 15. Doc and Penny Saffer (Doc was another Staunton Military Academy classmate of John's) had invited us to go to the races at Middleburg, Virginia, and I thought it would do John a world of good to get away from investigators and prosecutors. That was naive. A government was toppling. The man who was opening a crack here and a crack there could hardly run off for a day while the loose bricks were beginning to fall off.

Jack and Liz wound up going to Middleburg to visit the Saffers with Susie and Barry Goldwater. When they returned, I joined them for dinner at a restaurant, and when we came back to the house after dinner, there was a note on the coffee table. It read:

> *Moser—have gone to meet the man. See you later.*
>   *Love,*
>   *John.*

" 'The man' must be the President," I told Jack and Liz.

I handed the note to Jack, who glanced at it and then said simply:

"Wow!"

17
The President Calls—
One Last Time

N.Y.
John fired
from W.H.

(From my calendar, April 30, 1973)

Liz and Jack Garfield had heard my husband speak approximately ten words in the three days they had been staying with "us."

It was April 15, 1973, and John, looking and acting strangely animated, appeared at the door about 10:30 or 11 P.M. I am almost certain he came through the back door, because Washington was awash with rumors that night, and reporters were lurking everywhere, including on our doorstep.

The President had been in meetings all day—with Attorney General Kleindienst, with Henry Petersen, with Haldeman, with Ehrlichman. Most of these were private. But when something big is happening in Washington, the air is electric. Maybe only a handful of people know what is going on. But everyone, the press in particular, knows that *something* is going on.

John apologized for having had so little time to spend with the Garfields, and Jack insisted that no apologies were necessary; they understood perfectly. After all, one of them observed, when a man is summoned to meet with the President of the United States, he'd better go.

Then Jack ventured a timid probe:

"I hope all went well."

"I really can't discuss it," John replied.

And he didn't. But he was so keyed up he discussed everything else under the sun. When John starts talking at a fast clip, so fast you simply can't cut him off, you know he's very nervous and anxious about something.

I just let him run on and on until finally he ran down. It's good therapy for him, his method of unwinding.

As soon as John reached a point where he was talking only two-thirds of the time and listening the other third, I realized the worst was over, took him by the arm, said goodnight to Liz and Jack, and we went upstairs to our bedroom.

"What *was* it all about?" I asked excitedly when we were alone.

"A real surprise. I didn't really expect it."

When you are counsel to the President, and when at the same time you are telling prosecutors about criminal acts that have gone on in the White House, well—what *does* one expect? I think John anticipated being accused of disloyalty and being fired on the spot. The moment he entered the house, I could tell that that had not happened, simply by observing the expression on his face. But I couldnt imagine what had taken place.

Before he told me any more, he slumped in a chair, and muttered wearily: "I've got to have another drink." Suddenly, he was entirely wound down. He looked drained, spent.

"Mo—I don't know how much longer I'll be at the White House. And it won't exactly be my own decision when I leave."

I wasn't surprised. At this point, I was incapable of

being surprised. Absolutely nothing could shock me. Revelations had come at me so fast I was numb. In a few short months, I had regressed from the bright-eyed bride of a young White House aide, caught up in the excitement of a presidential administration in which I believed and of which I was at least a tiny part, to a thoroughly disillusioned and saddened and frightened woman. It was as if John and I had been living on a luxury yacht, safely moored. Then suddenly we had awakened and found the yacht had been cast adrift and was being tossed up and down, back and forth, in unbelievably stormy seas. Not even the captain knew the directions. Already the word was getting around to abandon ship, and I knew that whatever lifeboat John and I landed in, security would be a long way off—if it were there at all. I wanted to cry. But I didn't.

Disaster was inevitable now, for the country, for the President, for us and so many others. The remaining question was the extent of it. The only thing worse than facing up to it would be for everyone to cling to the ship, refuse to admit it was lost, and refuse to admit that the present captain would never be able to guide it back into calm seas.

I looked at John. He was saying, "It's a frightening thing to be taking on the President of the United States," but that night he had begun to realize he would have to. He told me things would be tight financially. There would be huge legal fees, and he did not know, once he was off the payroll, when he would be on one again.

"John—I can get a job," I said.

"No. Not now. It won't be necessary for a while."

We sat there, each with our own thoughts. I had a burning desire to get away—anywhere, the two of us, just so we could be together, any place where it didn't seem like the walls were crumbling in on all sides. A wild thought flashed through my mind—why *didn't* we just pack up and get out of here?

But no. John would never agree to that; that would be running away. And I wouldn't go without him.

On Monday, things were not as bad as they had been on Sunday. They were worse.

By then, at least Haldeman and Ehrlichman knew some of the details, perhaps all, of John's visit with the President the night before. They knew he was "off the reservation," and would not be back. In fact, each had talked with President Nixon later on Sunday night. I have often wondered if the President did not play for them a tape recording of the meeting, although, months later (when the taping system had become publicly known), the White House claimed that the tape recorder had run out of tape that night and that the Nixon-Dean conversation was "never recorded."

This seems very strange to me, for the President that night was being terribly self-serving, as if in his talk with John he were attempting to obtain a recording that could, if needed, establish his own ignorance of or noninvolvement in some of the crimes that had been committed.

John wrote the following as part of his statement for the Senate Watergate Committee:

> The President almost from the outset began asking me a number of leading questions, which was somewhat unlike his normal conversational relationships I had had with him, which made me think that the conversation was being taped and that a record was being made to protect himself. Although I became aware of this because of the nature of the conversation, I decided that I did not know it for a fact and that I had to believe that the President would not tape such a conversation.

Had John not made that observation, and had a Watergate Committee staff member not asked Alexander Butterfield if it were possible that White House conversations were taped, the existence of the White House taping system might never have become known, and President Nixon probably would have completed his second term.

But why—if the President wanted this conversation on record for his own purposes—did the White House later claim the machine had run out of tape? I have always felt that either the White House was telling the truth, or that some damaging statements that the President probably all but whispered to John were picked up clearly on the tape.

For example, John also testified about that meeting: "The most interesting thing that happened during the conversation was, very near the end, he got up out of his chair, went behind his chair to the corner of the Executive Office Building office, and in a nearly inaudible tone said to me he was probably foolish to have discussed Hunt's clemency with Colson." If those words were on a tape, there should be no mystery as to why the tape could never be located.

John received a call quite early on Monday morning that the President wanted to meet with him again. Oh, dear! Now what? John didn't say because he didn't know, but he was well aware—as was I—that at one or another of these meetings soon, the ax would fall. He kept hoping it would be as part of a general housecleaning that might spare the President.

By this time, neither of us had any thoughts of John's staying on at the White House. I don't want to leave the impression that even while he was peeling away the layers of secrecy that had covered the activities of the Nixon White House, John wanted to go on in the administration. He has much more character than that. But he did have hopes that at some point the President would say to him: "All right, John. The time has come to make a clean breast of everything. I'm a damn fool for not having done so before. I don't know what will happen to me, to the country, to you, or to any of the others. But we've reached the point where all we can do is lay it all out, and if the reaction is national outrage and a demand that I resign, so be it. It's all coming out some day, so we'll just put it out ourselves and hope for the best. I'll need your help."

He would have settled for even less. He would gladly have submitted his resignation and taken his share of the blame and perhaps a bit more than his share. He was resolute on only one point. He would not take it all.

In fact, John told me—as he had told the President—that he thought there still was a chance to save the Nixon administration if he, Haldeman, and Ehrlichman resigned from the White House staff, went before the grand jury, and testified about everything except matters he thought were protected by national security or executive privilege. In that way, the President might be spared the shame and disgrace that would befall his closest aides. It was no longer "simply a case of saving Richard Nixon the man," John told me one troubled evening (we had nothing but troubled evenings), "but it is important to save the President. I don't think the country could stand having its President under investigation for crimes. How could he function?"

We talked only briefly on that Monday, April 16. John was in meetings or writing proposed presidential statements the entire day and on into the evening. The one brief telephone conversation I recall was when John called from the office and told me, "The President wants me out, but I told him I won't go without the Big Two. So we may all be gone by tomorrow, or we may all still be here. Everything is completely up in the air."

Several weeks later, when I was helping type John's Watergate Committee statement, I learned that President Nixon on that day (April 16) had given John two letters of resignation to sign. One read: "Dear Mr. President, In view of my increasing involvement in the Watergate matter, my impending appearance before the grand jury and the probability of its action, I request an immediate and indefinite leave of absence from my position on your staff." The other: "Dear Mr. President, as a result of my involvement in the Watergate matter, which we discussed last night and today, I tender you my resignation, effective at once."

Even today, I find it difficult to believe. The one high-ranking aide to the President who was willing to shoulder much of the blame for Watergate was being asked to shoulder it all! I don't know which bothers me more— the President's callousness, or his stupidity. The letters amounted to confessions to an unlimited number of crimes, apparently committed by John Dean alone. The game of finding scapegoats was running its course, and it had reached John. Of course, he would not sign!

Jack and Liz had begun to feel terribly uncomfortable about being in our midst at a time of constant crisis. They felt that John needed to concentrate all his resources on resolving the urgent matters that kept him at the White House day and night, and they correctly sensed that while he was doing just that, he also was concerned about being such a poor host. As long as they were there and he was aware of their presence, it was an added worry, one that he obviously didn't need. So they announced that they were cutting their visit short and heading for their next stop—Miami. They both urged me to join them.

I couldn't think of leaving John at a time like this— until I began to reflect. He had to be worrying about me, too. And there really wasn't a blessed thing I could do at this stage. When I gently raised the subject, he said: "Go. For God's sake go and get away from this madness, which isn't going to get any better for a long while." He would be much more at ease, he said, knowing I was with friends, rather than sitting at home alone waiting and waiting for him. I made him promise that if things came to a head, or if I could help or comfort him in any way, he would call me.

It *was* better. The very thought of sitting alone in that house until ten or eleven or twelve night after night, with the shades and draperies drawn because of the ever-present press, was more than I could bear. With Jack and Liz, I could at least endure my "prison." All alone, I was not certain that I could.

So one afternoon in the middle of that hectic week, Jack and Liz and I and our suitcases emerged from 100 Quay Street. It had been sunny and quiet, but soon it seemed as if the sky had miraculously been bathed in the brightest, whitest light since the advent of lightning. There are only three television networks, but it seemed to me that at least a half dozen camera crews started grinding away at us, and some of them even followed us and our bewildered cab-driver to the airport. The others stayed to continue the futile watch for John. His ability to slip in and out the back way kept them from knowing even when he was and when he was not in the house.

It isn't difficult to imagine the reports that went out on the air and made their way into print. They went something like this: "Mrs. John Dean, the wife of President Nixon's beleaguered White House counsel, fled from the couple's suburban Washington town house tonight, accompanied by an unidentified man and woman. The three boarded a Florida-bound jet at nearby National Airport, giving rise to speculation that Mrs. Dean and her husband may be separating at this juncture of the tangled Watergate affair, in which Dean's personal involvement is thought to be extensive."

It was the first but by no means the last of a series of rumors that had John and me separating, or divorcing, or being seen with other people. I have decided there is only one way to prevent such false rumors from circulating, and that is never to go anywhere and never to do anything. Early on, I rejected that idea—and so did John.

We left in such a rush that all we had time to do was notify Lance Cooper that we were on our way and ask him if he could help find us a place to stay. *Dear* Lance. By the time the plane landed, he had moved out of his own apartment and arranged to stay with a friend. He turned his apartment over to me, and somehow borrowed another apartment for Jack and Liz. Don't ask me how he did all this on such short notice. I never asked him. I was just so grateful.

Anyone who ever gets caught up in a maelstrom such as the one that wrapped itself around us will wind up with an enhanced appreciation of friends, as John and I did. Jack and Liz were so concerned about my need to get away that they even insisted on buying my plane ticket for the trip to Florida. But John wouldn't allow it. However, they and Lance did stay right with me, and worked over-time trying to take my mind off the terrible and only half-understood goings-on in Washington. We went to good restaurants, and to the Palm Bay Club, and everything was going along as well as possible—considering. . . .

One morning, I flicked on the radio in Lance's apart-ment. Suddenly, the music was interrupted for a news bulletin. "Oh, no—what now?" I groaned, knowing full well that whatever it was would concern Watergate, be-cause there just wasn't *any* other news during this period. I was correct, of course. The bulletin was about Watergate, and the first two words of it, not entirely to my surprise, were: "John Dean. . . ." The announcer went on to say that John had just released a statement through his secre-tary, bypassing the White House press office, to the effect that he would not be made a "scapegoat" for Watergate and that anyone who thought that he would just did not understand the American system of justice.

It was one of those news bulletins that, as you listen, you

tell yourself isn't true. And yet you know it is. But I couldn't understand what was happening. John had never issued press statements. And he rarely spoke to anyone in the press, which was one reason he had been so highly valued in the White House. What was he thinking of with this wholly uncharacteristic act?

I was trying to call his office as these thoughts churned around in my mind. One thing I understood very well: everything had come apart in the White House, or John would not be turning even this far toward the press. Things had moved further and faster than I had expected. At what level was John being made the scapegoat? It had to be one of two possibilities at this stage of the game, and maybe both: the Haldeman-Ehrlichman level and/or the presidential level.

I was still so in awe of the presidency and the power it controlled that I was almost overcome by fright. Could they do something to my husband? Could they have him thrown in jail? Could they blame everything on him, so that he would have to go to prison and none of the rest would? Could all this happen in a free country? I told myself that it could not, but I needed more reassurance than my own confused self could offer.

I was trying to pull myself together when the telephone was answered by Jane, John's secretary. John was not in his office.

"What on earth is going on?" I demanded.

As she responded, I noticed that her voice was quivering. Then I remembered that there was a quiver in it under the best of circumstances. But it was much more pronounced now.

"I don't know," Jane cried. "John just phoned me his statement from home and told me to call the AP and the UPI." She said she was so startled she had to ask him to repeat it to make certain she had heard him correctly. She had.

"Well—please have John call me the moment he returns, or the moment you hear from him," I said. Jane promised she would.

A few minutes later I reached John.

"What's happening?" I asked.

"Things are really rough," he replied, then paused.

"But why didn't you forewarn me? About the statement? I heard it on the radio."

"I didn't know I was going to do it. I decided at the last minute. And then I did try to call but I couldn't get through."

"John—you've never issued a public statement before. I'm in total shock. I'm scared. I know something terrible is happening."

He tried to soothe me, using the fewest possible words. The gist of what he said was that he thought Haldeman and Ehrlichman were jointly trying "to set me up." He did not mention the President. Even at that late date, even after the President had virtually dumped the entire Watergate scandal in his lap, John would not tell even his own wife that it was the President as well as Haldeman and Ehrlichman who were trying to set him up.

I remember mumbling something like: "It's the point of no return, isn't it?" John didn't respond.

Lance and Jack and Liz were concerned about John, and also wondering how (or if) I was going to be able to hold up in the pressure cooker. I had been there a long time, but the valve had not been turned on full force. Now it was, and friends who know that I am shy, hold things within myself, and am deathly afraid of insecurity were touchingly worried that the last blow might have felled me, or that the next one surely would.

To them, I made no attempt to conceal my fright, but I also thought I should reveal something they may not have been previously aware of: my apparent fragility is only apparent. Beneath it, there is enough reinforcing steel to keep my various parts from flying off in all directions under conditions of stress. I'm not being boastful. It's nothing I have accomplished. It's something my Irish ancestors passed along to me. I think I was able to reassure everyone that, come what might, I could handle it. Everyone except myself, that is, and only I knew of my failure in that area.

Easter Sunday fell on April 22, and I planned to fly home, as I thought that surely this was one day John and I might have together. But John insisted I stay in Florida because he was going to be interviewed the entire day. So I missed being present when he received his final telephone call from the President.

John told me that it was about midday when the White House operator rang and announced that the President was calling for Mr. Dean. My disillusionment with Richard Nixon had not progressed far enough to overtake my still illusionary view of the presidency. For a few moments at least I was able to put out of my mind the Richard Nixon who had tried to trap and completely undo my husband (Haldeman and Ehrlichman must have been behind all that). Once again I returned to the view of this man that I had held for so long—the President, the nation's leader, the man my husband had always felt was so worth working for and fighting for. The majesty of the presidency is not something that disintegrates suddenly. At least not then.

The President's call had come in on our special white telephone directly linked to the White House switchboard. John said the President had called mainly to wish us a happy Easter. John's response wasn't rude, but he admitted he was a little cool, something he had never been before in talking with the President. He still retained a great deal of respect for the President, but in the "every man for himself" atmosphere then prevailing in the White

House, John was skeptical about every communication and every contact he had with White House people from the President on down.

I can't say I was elated about the call, but I was interested—and hopeful. The eternal optimist, I always expected the President would some day call John, tell him he had been right all along, and assure him that everything would be worked out satisfactorily, especially for John W. Dean III.

John continued: "He mentioned 'your pretty wife,'" but mostly he just called to wish us a happy Easter." He also said, "You're still my counsel." Of course, I thought, it was a calculated move on the President's part, a last-ditch attempt at "stroking" John, yet another application of, another misuse of, the aura in which the presidency is cloaked.

"What did you think," I asked, "when the operator told you it was the President calling?"

"For a moment it felt like old times," said John. "But then I knew there had to be something behind it."

Richard Nixon had sought to re-ignite the fires of loyalty that had burned within John for so long, and at such personal cost. But those fires by then had been put out. The gesture was futile. And, at bottom, ridiculous.

He never called again.

Something else was happening to me that I really did not need. I was coming down with the flu. By Monday I was really miserable. It wasn't simply the flu—it was the flu on top of everything else. And it was the flu at a time when I felt I desperately needed to regenerate myself for whatever the future might bring. By this time, Jack and Liz's vacation time had expired and they had flown back to California the previous Saturday. Feeling so weak and miserable that all I wanted to do was crawl into my own bed and die peacefully, I had Lance put me on a plane, and I flew home alone.

Once there, I just collapsed. My private world was crumbling all around me. For all I knew the Republic itself was in its death throes. My husband was in an ever-tightening vise. And there I was—out of it. Out of it all. John was as solicitous as he could be, which doesn't come within the definition of the word at all. A call occasionally —and a cool hand on my fevered brow when he climbed into bed at eleven or twelve or later. That was it. In a way, I suppose my illness was something of a deliverance for me. When you are suffering physically—and I was, for this was one of the worst cases of the flu I have had—you simply cannot be as concerned about other things. Sometimes you say to yourself that all you want is to get well— that you don't care if the Republic stands or falls so long as you get well. A half week was almost totally lost to me.

In my near-delirium, I had a recollection that President Nixon had made a public declaration that "as a result of serious charges that came to my attention . . . on March 21," he had begun "an intense new inquiry into this whole [Watergate] matter." March 21. I'm not very good about dates, but that one stuck in my mind somehow. I thought that was the date when John met with the President and told him there was a cancer on the presidency, but I wasn't certain, and by the time John came home at night I was either asleep or still too drained to ask him. Nor could I now kindle much interest within myself, while I was sick, as to what had gone on since the President's statement.

Then, as suddenly as it had struck, my health problem began to disappear; I felt weak, but at least I was mobile.

While I continued to recuperate, Fred and Maria Fielding, and Pete Kinsey all stopped by to talk and to comfort me, and when they were there, everything seemed less bleak, although I must say that both Fred and Pete, who were on John's staff in the office of counsel to the President, were both bewildered and frightened. Each had been frozen out of so much bearing on Watergate, as had Jane and everyone else on the staff. This was frustrating, particularly to Fred, John's deputy, who was wise enough to know that a great deal was going on, and, at least during the early stages, fearful that he was missing out on something. With only a few exceptions (for example, John confided in Fred when John Ehrlichman told him to "deep six" some materials from Howard Hunt's safe), John tried to keep his staff removed, both for their own protection and because that is the way the Nixon White House worked: on a "need to know" basis. That is the only way, really, that the extensive scheme of paying off the Watergate burglars could have gone on for so long, undetected.

April was slipping away in this manner: with John away constantly, with me gratefully receiving succor from very, very close friends. When John was not at his office, he was with Charley Shaffer. Or he was with the prosecutors. Or he was with the staff of the Watergate Committee. I was sustained only by the certainty within me that nothing so hectic could last very much longer, and by the fact that these were such crucial days for the country as well as for John, days when all other considerations simply had to be set aside.

On the following Sunday, April 29, John kissed me goodbye and said he had to make a quick trip to New York. A grand jury investigation was under way, and the prosecutors needed his testimony.

"Couldn't it wait?" I asked. "They seem to need your testimony here in Washington, too."

"That's why I'm going up on a Sunday," he said, a bit wearily.

Later I learned that it was the so-called Vesco grand jury that had called him to New York—the one investigating a $200,000 campaign contribution from Robert Vesco, a financier who was suspected of bilking hundreds of people of millions of dollars. John Mitchell and Maurice Stans were involved in arranging for the contribution, were later indicted, and acquitted.

Again I had a foreboding—or perhaps it was just a continuation of foreboding during those days that were so exciting for the press and others, but so devastating to those of us whose lives were being disrupted constantly. I didn't want John to leave me. Frightening things were happening. Even though he was seldom home, it was a great comfort for me to know that at least he was in Washington, reachable by telephone, and able to be at my side within thirty or forty minutes if I asked him to come (I never did).

"I know how you feel, Mo. But we're in a period of no options."

No options. How true that was, had been, and would continue to be.

"Fred and Pete are going to look in on you," he added. "You'll be okay. Won't you?"

I managed a half smile and a weak: "I guess." Then I braced myself for what was to come. I had no idea what it was, but I knew there would be something. By no means was I disappointed.

On Monday, the telephone rang incessantly. I had half determined not to answer it any more, but every time it rang, I just had to pick it up. It might be John. It might be my mom, or it might be about my mom, who was seriously ill in California.

It was about 11 A.M. when the call I had been dreading came. I did not know what I had been expecting, or from whom the call would come, but I knew I would recognize it for what it was the moment I lifted the receiver. And I did.

It was Jane Thomas calling from John's office, and her voice was not simply quivering this time. It was filled with

fright, unmistakable fright, and with sorrow, bewilder-
ment, and panic.

"John's been fired!" she cried. "The White House has
men in here sealing everything up—all the files, all the
papers, everything. I don't know what to do!"

I'm afraid I was no help. I didn't know what to do,
either—except for one thing. Find John. I told Jane to be
calm, not to worry, to stay where she was as long as she
could. Then we both tried to locate John in New York.

He had left the number of his hotel with me, but I
just knew he wouldn't be there, and I had no idea of how
to get in touch with him if he was testifying before the
grand jury—nor did I know if I would be allowed to talk
to him even in a crisis such as the one I was experiencing.

I could only call the hotel and hope that every time
John got a break, he would check the hotel for messages—
his usual practice. Thank God he followed his usual practice.

After leaving an urgent message, I just sat by the telephone. I was shaking all over, wondering what was going
to become of us, wondering what was happening to the
country. Men sealing the files of the counsel to the President? I had visions of officers in hobnailed boots. What
would they try to do next? Was John's life in danger? Was
mine?

That last question made me realize I was becoming
hysterical. Why would my life be in danger? With John
it was different—he knew so much, so many details about
so many powerful men who were clinging to their power.
He could be in real danger. I was not and would not be.
So cool it, girl, I told myself. See if you can be of some
assistance to your husband.

The telephone rang. I reached for it so anxiously I
almost sent it clattering to the floor. Yes—thank God—it
was John.

"Honey—you're fired, and they're sealing off all your files, and Jane and I are so upset. What can we do?"

The voice on the other end of the line was not that of a man fearful of being gunned down in the streets. John was so calm and rational that I immediately heaved a sigh of relief and began to collect my own wits.

"You . . . you knew this was going to happen?"

"Yes. I just wasn't sure when."

"What's going to happen to us?"

"Nothing right away. But listen carefully. There's something you must do for me. You know that big box full of papers and memos that I brought home from the office? Well, get it, Mo, and take it to the attic right away. They may be coming after it."

"Oh, no, John," I cried. "I can't!"

"Why can't you?"

"I just can't. It's too heavy. I've never even been in the attic. I'm afraid to go up there. Maybe when Pete comes by . . ."

"Mo. There's not enough time to wait. Someone could be at the door any minute. You've got to take that box to the attic. If anyone comes to the house and sees that, that's the first thing they'll grab. They'll say it's government property, and they'll take it back. This is *terribly* important, Mo. Especially that thick envelope on top. Hide that separately when you get the box to the attic."

Well, as John had said, this was a period of no options. Somehow I struggled to the attic, carrying the box of photostated documents, some of which might help prove that my husband was not a liar. Under normal circumstances I could not even have lifted that box. I was afraid of encountering a spider or a mouse (either would have finished me off) in the attic, and I was equally fearful of a knock on the door before I could complete my mission. I hurriedly pushed the box into a far corner, rushed downstairs, and placed the envelope under the mattress of our bed.

Then I scurried back to the kitchen and pretended to be quite busy preparing a meal. I waited and waited for the FBI or the Secret Service. The bell did ring several times, but it was always the press. No representative of either the FBI or Secret Service ever approached the house.

I stayed there alone that day, jumping at every actual sound and several imaginary ones. Pete and Fred came by for just a few minutes, and they were terrified by the implications of John's firing. They knew that the battle lines had hardened, that the President would make no real disclosures, that he would fight every inch of the way to retain his office, his power, his place in history. Fred and Pete, I could tell, thought the adversaries were terribly unequal—that in taking on the President of the United States, reluctant as he was to do so, John was hopelessly overmatched. "It will be his word against the President's," Richard Nixon had once told Bob Haldeman, and Fred and Pete could see that that was about what it would come to. How many people would take the uncorroborated word of a 34-year-old lawyer and accomplice, accusing the President of crimes when no President of the United States had ever been personally implicated in crimes?

When the President went on the air that night to announce the resignations of Haldeman and Ehrlichman, "two of the finest public servants it has been my privilege to know," and also to disclose the fact that the counsel to the President, John Dean, had also resigned, John was in New York and I watched the historic telecast at home.

As I listened to President Nixon, I knew that although John would be very cynical about much the President was saying, he would also be very hurt. Something and someone he had believed in with his whole being had crumbled and turned out to be quite different from what he had thought. And now the hopes he had for his future, for his own reputation, for his own life, could never be retrieved.

He had had such blind faith in this President that he had committed crimes for him, had had such faith in the power of a man and an office that he had forgotten the power of the law, and the fact that it applies to every man, no matter how exalted or humble.

That night, when John called, he did not bad-mouth President Nixon, nor did he later. His thoughts were and are his own. But I could imagine the hurt he must have felt when the President praised Haldeman and Ehrlichman, conspicuously omitting Dean so everyone would know who was, in the President's eyes, the true culprit of Watergate.

John tried hard to show no emotion, but I detected a heaviness in his voice—not because President Nixon found him unworthy of praise, but because unfolding in front of him was the shambles his dreams had become. Sure—what had happened was Nixon's fault, and Haldeman's fault, and Ehrlichman's fault, and the fault of many others.

But when John returned the following day, and our eyes met, I think I understood the message that was in his.

I could almost sense him struggling to say:

"I'm a grown man, honey. You know who's at fault for what is happening to us, for what is yet to happen to us? I am."

18
Imprisoned by the Press

Everywhere, a big black headline. And all so impersonal. "Dean Fired." "Dean Expected to Testify." "Dean Said to be Seeking Immunity." "Dean Watergate Role Extensive." And then the truly nasty statements: Because of his "boyish" good looks, John Dean was afraid to go to prison where he felt certain he would be subject to homosexual attacks. John Dean had been dismissed from a private law firm for unethical conduct. John Dean had a woman friend in Georgetown—his car was frequently parked in front of her home all night long. John and Maureen Dean were separating. Maureen Dean was preparing to sue John Dean for divorce. John Dean had "taken" his first wife, Karla, for a million dollars. John Dean was the real "mastermind" of Watergate—now he was trying to involve others in the hope of saving his own neck. The prosecutors doubted the truth of what John Dean was telling them. John Dean was a squealer—so desperate he would lie even about the President of the United States to make a better deal for himself. John Dean's sources of income were being investigated—how could he have bought two town houses in Alexandria on his government salary? This type of statement was always misleading, slanted, or untrue.

I'll never again feel the same about headlines. Once you are in them, or once someone you love is in them, you know how distorted they are. They subtract the "human" from "human beings." Readers do not think of headline personalities in terms of families, homes, emotions. They aren't people who eat, sleep, love, hate—who have children, dogs and cats, mothers and fathers, bills to pay, leaky water faucets to fix, mirrors to look into every morning, feelings that can be hurt. In the cascade of words written about Watergate, barely a trickle indicated even an awareness of the flesh and blood of which "Dean" and "Nixon" and "Haldeman" and "Ehrlichman" and members of their families were composed.

Most people reading those headlines, those names, would understandably think in terms of disembodied individuals, the whole of whose lives consisted of tapping telephones, plotting dirty campaign tricks, and otherwise subverting the Constitution. If any consideration was given to the suffering they and their families were experiencing, it probably most often was followed by the thought: "Well, they deserve it." And there is some truth in that.

I cannot speak for the others whose lives were abruptly and permanently altered, but deserving or not, I was thrust into what seemed the nearest thing to prison, short of actually being there. First of all, there was the frustration. I hated the impression of my husband that the headlines and the false stories were creating. But we were helpless to do anything about them. We knew where some of the rumors were originating—in the White House itself, where a massive campaign to discredit John was under way. Chuck Colson was no longer on the White House staff, but he was still a master at circulating innuendo and falsehood—as he would now be the first to admit. The false stories about John and about us infuriated me. And so did the depiction of my husband as the man behind the entire scandal, who was now "ratting" on his friends in order to escape punishment. I wanted to shout in a voice that would go from coast to coast and around the world: "These are lies, all lies. John Dean is not like that. You've got to believe me." But I couldn't do that. I couldn't do anything, except feel trapped, and tell myself that some day the country would realize the truth about John. The truth always emerges.

There were other aspects to my personal prison. The reporters camped on our doorstep were only the most obvious. One Saturday early in May I escaped from the house to go to the supermarket, and again the press caught me, filmed me, and somehow made me the only woman in the country whose grocery shopping excursion was something people from coast to coast would want to see. I could not go anywhere with my husband, and I could not be with him when I wanted to. I couldn't go into the garden, I couldn't walk around the neighborhood, I couldn't go into town for lunch, I couldn't go window-shopping.

There was one overwhelming concern the headlines did not and could not reflect: my own terrible fear about the future. Would my husband go to prison? I wouldn't let myself think so, but John kept telling me that that was a possibility. Would our friends desert us now? What would Johnny think of his dad? Would John Dean go down in history as a squealer and a liar? How would we be able to live? Would anyone hire John? Would anybody hire me?

John's final checks from the White House came in the mail, including the two weeks' pay the government holds back at the start of employment. And John told me that he had about $12,000 of his own contributions to the federal retirement program that he could withdraw. That information both comforted and hurt: to think that we were being forced to spend retirement income at the ages of thirty-four and twenty-seven.

"Many families live on a quarter of that amount of money a year," John told me.

"With our mortgage?" I asked.

No, he said. But we could sell the house at a profit. We could sell the car. We could sell our half interest in a boat. We would have to resign ourselves to a markedly lower standard of living. But we'd get by. We'd survive.

Sell the house we were married in? Sell the Porsche—John's most prized possession? Yes, of course we could do those things. But the thought of having to do them in order to live brought a lump to my throat.

I felt terribly insecure, and to me, marriage is supposed to be synonymous with security. I'm usually reasonably calm. Now I was nervous. Suddenly there was no stability to my existence. My whole world had come apart.

Strangers kept coming to our house—lawyers, investigators, prosecutors. When they didn't come to our house, my husband went to them. I felt so terribly lonely and frightened and neglected—as if I were being asked to suspend all human emotions and feelings for the foreseeable future.

And in addition to the presence of reporters—forcing us to disconnect our doorbell, to cover the window of our garage, to draw our shades and draperies—who chased us everywhere we went, now there were telephone calls, letters and telegrams from people like Walter Cronkite, John Chancellor, Mary McGrory, and dozens more, wanting interviews, each insisting that he or she (and no one else) was entitled to see John and ask him questions. John had two lawyers now, Charles Shaffer and his former brother-in-law, Robert McCandless, and Bob was spending virtually full time fending off the people demanding interviews. But Bob was also trying to persuade John and Charley that John should come forth and be interviewed —that the White House was destroying John with leaks that were false, with the impression that John was hiding, slinking around and not daring to show his face; the

impression was growing and Bob felt it could hurt John
and injure his credibility.

On the same Saturday that my grocery shopping became
network news, John peeked out the window and saw that
the press had left temporarily; he grabbed a toothbrush
and a clean shirt, and escaped, leaving me alone as a
prisoner. He went to Bob and Marie McCandless' apartment in southwest Washington, because he had an appointment the following morning with the prosecutors
and didn't want the press to follow him.

I didn't like this one single bit. I was able to endure all
else I was being asked to endure, but was it also necessary
that I be abandoned? That I spend the night in that big
house alone? It was, John said. Sorry, dear, a time of no
options.

This brought me near to the breaking point. Alone with
my thoughts that Saturday night, I tried to read, I tried
to watch television, I tried to talk to my mom on the telephone, I tried to keep doing something that would take
my mind off the dreadful truth of our situation. But it
was no use. My feelings of insecurity, uncertainty, friend-
lessness, and hopelessness simply intensified. What was
happening to me? to us? This was not a nightmare—no
mere nightmare could be this bad.

Sunday. Gloomy Sunday. Maria called. Pete came by.
So I wasn't friendless. I always knew that no matter what,
I would never lose those two. Then—alone again. More
fussing around. Why didn't John call? Still with the prosecutors, I guess. Didn't they have families? Didn't they ever
take a day off? Would they never run out of questions?

At last John did call. It was evening, and he had spent
the whole day either with the prosecutors or with Charley
and Bob. He was bushed.

"Where are you?"

"At Bob's. Press outside the house?"

"Naturally."

"Well, I think I'd better stay here again tonight, then."

I couldn't believe my ears. I had been the good soldier, doing what was required of me without complaining, but this was too much. Another night alone in the prison our home had become was more than I could bear.

"John. You're coming home. You're not leaving me here alone another night."

"Hate to. But I can't run that press gauntlet."

"Why can't you? Why can't you stand up and face the press? What are you afraid of?"

"I'm not afraid. It's just damned unpleasant."

"It's also damned unpleasant for me to be here alone. You're being very childish."

With that, I slammed down the receiver. I don't believe I had ever hung up on my husband before. Nor have I since.

Shortly after, the telephone rang and I was sure it was John, ready to apologize and to tell me he was leaving for home. Instead, it was Marie McCandless, urging me not to be upset with John, and to understand why he and Bob felt it was important that the press not grab John and put a microphone in front of his face at this particular time—these were the wrong circumstances under which to go public. When she finished trying to soothe me, I said:

"Marie—there is no reason why John can't come home."

Perhaps an hour later, someone knocked on the front door. I looked out. It was Marie. Again, she did her best to convince me, and when she concluded her arguments, I said: "I won't put up with this, Marie. I'll put up with a lot of things, but not this. I'm just not going to be shoved out of the way." My life had suffered enough ruptures— I was not going to let matters disintegrate to the point where my husband was unable or unwilling to enter and leave our own home.

Another hour passed. Again the telephone rang. This time it was John. This time he did apologize. This time he did say he was leaving for home. He made it through the back way, without being spotted by the press, and the press failed to keep me incarcerated without my cellmate —that time.

The incident served to remind John both of my existence and of the frazzled state of my nerves. His weren't in the best condition, either. Nor were the constant presence of the press and the restrictions it imposed on us conducive to peace of mind and a harmonious relationship. We began to plot an escape. The urgency of it was reinforced for both of us the following day, when John spent seven hours in our bedroom, with the telephone receiver pressed against his ear, talking to lawyers. He was anxious to begin preparation of his statement for the Senate Watergate Committee, something he clearly could not do, or even think about doing, unless we could get away. We knew we could not go far, but even ten miles, assuming the press did not follow, would take us right to heaven.

Bob McCandless suggested we go to Bethany, a beach town in Delaware, about two and a half hours away. He made arrangements for us, and when he told us the name of the motel, I began to suspect that Bob had a perverse sense of humor. It was the Atlantic Watergate.

Would we never escape?

I began to think that we would have to move to Nebraska or somewhere else inland where there isn't much water and hence there is little temptation to name buildings "Watergate."

We waited until nightfall to leave. As John looked out to make certain no reporters were by our back door, he noticed that a light was on at the back of our next-door neighbor's house. We called and got them to turn it off. Then we crept through the small yard, down an alley, into Fred and Maria's house, out their front door, and into Pete's waiting car, a silver BMW. It was a delicious triumph. The icing for the cake came the next day when the press spotted our Porsche, followed it all the way to the Atomic Energy Commission headquarters, collared the driver, and discovered that it was Pete.

"Isn't this John Dean's car?"

"Yes."

"Where is he?"

"They're out of town."

"Why do you have their car?"

"Mine's broken down."

End of "interview."

Meanwhile, life at the Atlantic Watergate was a drag. We were right on the beach, but there was no sun, there were no people, there was no television, and no radio. The weather was so miserable we stayed inside a lot and read. Occasionally, we would walk along the beach together, and sometimes John would take walks alone, preparing in his mind his disclosure statement. He had so much to think over—how could he find corroboration for the story he was telling? Where was there a document, a memo, a log, a letter—anything to support him? John was very troubled, distant at times. He did not relish playing the role of informer, although he was resigned to it, convinced that only the truth could pave the way for a restoration of confidence of the people in their government.

At times, we would just look at each other and ask ourselves: Is this all really happening? How did we—a couple of very private people—ever make our way to the forefront of a never-to-be-forgotten slice of history? How did we—two people content with only each other and perfectly willing to pass through life unnoticed—become the objects of constant attention by the press? The world seemed so unreal.

Bob McCandless was becoming increasingly disturbed by the attacks on John, which had increased in frequency and vehemence, and John's "disappearance" added to the impression of him that the White House was trying to

create: of a frightened, mousy, turncoat, a liar whose character was such that he could not be believed, especially in
his desperate, self-serving versions of conversations he had
had with the President of the United States. Bob finally
convinced John and Charley that it was time to "go
public" to a limited degree—not to talk about John's
forthcoming Senate Watergate Committee testimony, but
to let the public know that John W. Dean III was an
intelligent, articulate, sincere, and repentant human being, not a serpent spewing venom on decent and honorable men in order to save himself.

Accordingly, we left the Atlantic Watergate (we were
both becoming weary of that place and wanted to return
to our own home) for Easton, Maryland, where Bob was
waiting with a good friend of his, John Lindsay, a correspondent for *Newsweek* magazine. We met at the Tide-
water Inn. The interview lasted nearly two hours, during
all of which Wally McNamee took pictures of us for
Newsweek and Bob took pictures he said were for *Time*
magazine, but nobody believed him. He wasn't kidding,
as we all thought. The pictures turned up in *Time*.

That afternoon we drove to Bellevue, Maryland, and
went sailing on our boat—for the last time. It was also the
last time for days and days that we had any time together.
After this, the lawyers and investigators co-opted John
again, and I sometimes spent hours and hours sitting
outside a law office while John gave a deposition. When
at last he emerged, it was only to go to another office, to
meet with someone else while I again sat outside.

My feeling of insecurity once more became overpower-
ing, and so did my feeling that I was being neglected. I
was sick of all the moves we were making. "Why can't we
just stay put for a while?" I wrote in my diary for May 12.
"All this moving around and lack of privacy is really getting to me . . . I need help . . . I need to feel loved right
now . . . I suppose I can write off the rest of the day as

far as affection and attention go. For now I'm sitting in some stranger's office waiting for JWD to emerge from his meeting—it may take hours! Then he has a 2 P.M. meeting (with whom I don't know or can't remember) and then a 6 P.M. meeting with the same group!" But I ended on a hopeful note: "Maria Fielding said that there were no press outside the house. Maybe we can go home today —please!"

We did—or at least I did. John went to his 6 P.M. meeting and arrived home at 12:30 A.M. I had something to tell him—something that surely would capture his attention. I thought I was pregnant, and I just knew that when I told him, he'd take me and hold me and say: "That's wonderful!"

It didn't work out quite that way. He said: "Oh? Well, I guess that's all right; I mean it's O.K." End of reaction. Ten minutes later he asked me what I had for dinner. Thirty minutes after that, he asked if he could fix me a drink. Then he went to bed, leaving me to write in my diary:

"Oh, Lord, what is happening to us? Me? Where are we headed? I feel myself turning off out of hurt and self-defense. I pray that it won't happen—I need strength now. If only there wasn't a Watergate . . . !"

I never thought of leaving John—not once, not for a moment. But our relationship was more strained during this period than at any time before or since. The next night he stayed with Bob McCandless again—so the press wouldn't follow him to court in the morning, he said, but the increasing tension between us no doubt was another reason.

That morning he called me at seven-fifteen. He had left for Bob's so hurriedly he had neglected to pack his shoes and had nothing to wear on his feet except the tennis shoes he happened to have on when he left. The incident provided me with needed comic relief. I could just picture

John—always so meticulous about his dress—arriving at the courthouse wearing his conservative pin-stripe suit, button-down blue shirt, modest tie—and tennis shoes!

Barry Goldwater, Jr., came to the rescue. John had called Barry and asked him to pick up the shoes from me, and Barry had to fight his way through the assembled press and try to make a sensible explanation of what was in the brown paper bag he had picked up from me. The press was so curious that some of them followed Barry to the McCandless apartment, and when he came out they followed him again, thus allowing John—now wearing his wing tips—and Bob to escape undetected. John came back home that night.

But the tension returned with him. John was going from meeting to meeting, and was too preoccupied to be more than vaguely aware of my existence. Once Bob McCandless called, trying to work in an interview for John with the *Chicago Sun-Times*. John didn't want to do it because he was exhausted, but soon he was yielding to Bob's pleas, and I just shouted: "No."

John shouted back: "You stay out of this."

"I will not. If you can't stand up to Bob, I will. Or else you can go live with Bob and let him hear you complain about being so tired and so drained all the time." We didn't speak for a while after that, but John didn't agree to the interview at that time either.

But shortly after—and with my enthusiastic approval— Bob did arrange for Walter Cronkite to come to our house and interview John, with me sitting beside him. This sounded really exciting. But John was still awfully crotchety—when I started to wash my hair about ten o'clock the night before the interview, he ordered me not to—it was "too late" and why didn't I start such activities earlier? Okay, I said. I won't wash my hair, and I won't be present at the interview, either.

Suddenly, John was so sweet and understanding. But I

found myself wondering if he was really sorry, or just worried that his "image" might suffer if his wife were not at his side during the interview. "These last few months," I wrote in my diary, "have made me very aware of people's ulterior motives! Including JWD's and my own."

I loved Walter Cronkite. He was so easy to talk to, such a genuine person, delightful and easy to be with. He put me totally at ease. He even invited us to go sailing with him and his wife off Martha's Vineyard during the summer.

John and I watched the interview that night, and I thought it went well. But it was so strange to be looking at myself on television—it was almost as if I was watching some other person, someone much heavier than I. Fred Fielding called as soon as it was over, and I was once again in a good mood—which I like to think is my normal mood. I asked Fred if he wanted my autograph. He said no—he wouldn't consider keeping the autograph of someone who got in only five words in a thirty-minute telecast.

After the Cronkite interview and one with Hays Gorey of *Time* magazine, John resumed the role of recluse. He had to, really, because the Watergate hearings had begun, and by middle or late June it would be time for him to give his testimony.

What a frightening prospect! We knew that any error that John might make, no matter how minor, would be pounced on and exploited in the hope of discrediting all of his testimony. We spent several days at Bethany, John writing out his testimony on yellow pads, going through whatever documentation he could find, racking his brain, remembering little details that would make his testimony more convincing.

It was during this period that I became completely disenchanted with Bob McCandless, who until then I had looked upon as "family." One day, to my utter astonishment, Bob whipped out an agreement for John to sign.

A part of it was a retainer for his legal services, but he also wanted John to sign a paper naming Bob as John's exclusive literary agent for the rest of John's life!

So that was it. Bob's service to John, his friend and former brother-in-law, was not completely altruistic. I was sick. John was locked in a struggle to salvage something of his reputation and, if possible, to avoid being sent to prison. He was also struggling to get the truth of what had been going on in government out to the American people, and in the midst of this enormously difficult period, here was Bob McCandless, who seemed to me to be primarily concerned with getting John's name on the dotted line. I could never feel the same toward him again.

This was the time for long-held impressions of people to be shattered. As John completed page after page of testimony, he would give them to me to type, and the people who emerged from those pages—Bob Haldeman, John Ehrlichman, Chuck Colson, Dick Moore—were not the people I had known, or thought I had known. Strangely, even at this late date, I still retained some belief in President Nixon, but reading the accounts of his meetings with John—the same accounts that would mesmerize the nation a few weeks later—I became increasingly disillusioned.

I also realized for the first time exactly what John had been going through for so many agonizing months, and I couldn't understand why he had not acted before he did. Neither could he—now.

One day I heard John talking with Charley Shaffer and Bob McCandless, and was startled to hear Charley ask: "Does the President have all his marbles?" John's response startled me even more:

"I don't really know," he replied, softly and earnestly. He obviously meant it. He was not certain that the President of the United States was not mentally unbalanced. How frightening!

Day by day, I was learning how wrong some of my perceptions had been, and how little I had known of events that actually were taking place all around me. My altered views of the President and his top assistants saddened me more than anything.

John was so busy preparing his testimony, and I was so busy helping him that we saw very little of the televised Watergate Committee hearings. I do recall one day when we tuned in just long enough to hear Jack Caulfield testify that John had told him to talk to James McCord about the possibility that McCord would receive executive clemency if he did not talk. John muttered: "That's true. I was passing along 'guidance' from Ehrlichman." When Caulfield went on to say he had the impression John Dean was not acting on his own, John heaved a sigh of relief. "I'm glad he said that."

The days zipped by this way—with almost unrelieved sameness: John writing, me typing, Charley coming by, Sam Dash stopping in, staying until one or two in the morning.

As the time for John to testify drew near, Chuck Colson —probably because the President was becoming increasingly fearful that John's testimony might have some impact—went on television and told several blatant lies, all of which added up to a thesis that John W. Dean III was the real Watergate culprit and everyone else—especially the President and Colson—was innocent. I could have cried. Chuck and Patty had been such good friends, and had been so nice to me during the inauguration and on other occasions.

It was a time of ugliness all around. Senator Hugh Scott was interviewed one day and described John as "a turncoat and embezzler." I was outraged. Scott obviously was being a patsy for the White House, something he continued to be almost to the day Richard Nixon left office. The program of vilification was proceeding on schedule.

Jack Anderson was even working on a libelous story that John and Barry Goldwater, Jr., were homosexual companions.

Finally, it was Saturday night—the Saturday before John would begin testifying. I felt I just had to get out of the house, but John had so much work to do that he wouldn't take me anywhere. So Susie Goldwater and I went out together, had a couple of drinks and dinner, and I got my first rude awakening to the fact that I, too, was now a public figure—a status I didn't want.

Someone recognized me and pointed me out to a woman who works as a secretary for the *Washington Post*'s gossip columnist, Maxine Cheshire. She approached me, and I explained to her that Susie and I were old friends, that I just had to get out of the house, and that I hoped nothing would be printed. She said she understood and that I need not worry.

Of course, we made it big in print the following day.

John was not amused. Senator Barry Goldwater was furious. He told Susie: "When you girls want to go drinking, you come to my apartment, understand?"

My days of being a "private person" were over.

19

Watergate Witness and the Unforeseen Corroborator

Much of the nation sat on the edge of its chair on Sunday, June 24, 1973.

John and I slumped in ours.

Long before, John had decided to tell the truth, the entire truth, and there were no misgivings or second thoughts at this late date. But the emotional wrench involved in making revelations about old and, in some cases, very dear friends hit both of us again the day before John's public testimony: Herb Kalmbach, the gentle, thoughtful, trusting soul with the mournful eyes and the naive faith in everyone he met; Dick Moore, the mold from which the stereotype of the kindly father must have been cast; Fred LaRue, whose whole life had been filled with tragedy since as a youth he had accidentally shot and killed his father; John Mitchell, a brilliant and successful lawyer whose once unblemished reputation would soon be in tatters. Jeb Magruder, Bob Haldeman, Bob Mardian, Dwight Chapin, John Ehrlichman, Gordon Strachan, Bart Porter, Ken Parkinson, Paul O'Brien, Dick Kleindienst, Pat Gray, Henry Petersen. These were among the names mentioned, some of them several times, on the three hundred pages of John's testimony.

And Richard Nixon.

Because Leonid Brezhnev, the Russian leader, had been visiting with the President in Washington, John's testimony was delayed for a week to spare President Nixon the embarrassment his former counsel's revelations were expected to cause. The delay simply intensified the anticipation with which John's appearance was awaited. The final draft of his statement was not completed until Sunday, and then John had to take it to Charley Shaffer's office in Rockville, Maryland, for final typing. Sam Dash had a crew on hand to run off copies that night so they could be distributed to the press Monday morning. There were things that had to be done, but John and I still had time to sit, look at each other, and wonder about the thoughts running through each other's mind. Neither of us had any regrets that at last the truth would emerge. But we could not help wishing that the damage to so many people's lives could in some way be minimized. Of course, there was no possibility that it could.

We also thought and talked about the immediate ordeal facing John—several days of testifying before an audience of millions, hostile questions from some of the senators and committee staff lawyers, embarrassing revelations from John's not unsullied past, and so much public airing of our finances and other aspects of our private lives. How would the committee and the country react to John? Would he come through as a Johnny-come-lately to truth only because it at last suited his purposes, or as a "turn-coat," or as a sincere convert to the thesis that justice would have to be done to all who had played a role in subverting it, including himself?

There had been virtually no discussion of whether I would be with him at the hearings. I really didn't know for certain if he wanted me there. The prospect of facing all those cameras was an unsettling one, and I had no difficulty in thinking of a thousand and one places I would rather be. But several days before John was scheduled to begin testifying, he was talking with someone and I heard him say, "When Mo and I go up there . . ."

"Am I going?" I asked.

He gave me a startled look.

"Of course," he replied. And that was that.

Being preoccupied with the statement he was going to make, and being a man, John of course had given no thought to the fact that a woman about to go on view before thirty million people must concern herself with what she is going to wear. At least this woman must.

"Just look like a wife," he said.

Not knowing his precise notion of what "a wife" looks like, I relied on my own fashion instincts, choosing a very high collared tan dress to wear the first day. On Tuesday I picked out a combination that I loved—a brown linen dress and a white silk blouse with brown polka dots. Wednesday I wore a floral blouse with a melon red suit, Thursday a white blouse with a bright yellow linen suit I had purchased in London when I was working for the marihuana commission. On Friday, I wore a burgundy blouse with white polka dots, a white skirt, and a navy blue blazer.

My hair was in a bun, the way I most often wear it, so it did not occur to me that there was anything unusual about it. But Sam Dash's office started getting calls from television viewers who wanted to know where I had my hair done!

On Thursday morning, I was all ready to go to the hearings—I thought. I had put on a new turban I had bought—and John drew the line. "That won't go well with Middle America," he said, sounding as if he were still a member of the Nixon administration.

"I'm not dressing for Middle America or anyone but myself," I told him.

He asked me to get rid of the turban. I refused. We argued. He left without me!

It took me half an hour to find something else to wear, but I managed, and, as John knew I would, I appeared—late—at the hearings.

But on the Sunday night before the hearings began, after we had talked about the people involved, John was absolutely silent. I realized he wanted no company other than his thoughts, so I went to bed early. But I couldn't sleep. I was tense, keyed up, fearful that I would not wake up early enough in the morning. John came to bed very late, and dropped off quickly. Thank goodness. He needed his sleep a lot more than I needed mine, but I had reason Monday morning to wish I had been able to get more. I felt just dreadful.

Before 7 A.M., I was downstairs, having coffee. No breakfast, for either of us. My own major decision—what to wear—had been made the night before.

Also the night before, two deputy U.S. marshals had moved in with us. They stayed in the recreation room, one of them awake at all times. I felt really safe with them there. So did John, although he made wisecracks to the contrary, suggesting that we might have to stop making love because they would hear us.

We left in a car with the two marshals at about 8:30. As we weaved through the heavy early morning traffic, I was busily trying to steel myself for the ordeal ahead. Suddenly it occurred to me that a much greater ordeal was ahead for John. I should be thinking of ways to calm him. I took his hand and started to say something soothing and then sensed that there was no manifestation of nervousness whatsoever. There he was—a man who fully realized that his words could topple a President, that whatever the outcome the words would never be forgotten—and he sat there, cool, collected, stoic.

"How can you face this so calmly?" I asked. "I'm frightened to death."

"It's something I have to do," he said matter-of-factly, then fell silent again.

We arrived at the Senate Office Building shortly before 10 A.M.—the marshals had had difficulty finding the place —and headed for the historic Caucus Room, where so many famous hearings have been held. But none of them were quite so crucial for a national administration as the Watergate hearings had been and would be. By this time, I should have been used to cameras, but never before had I been confronted by so many. We were bathed in bright lights, and I'm sure I looked startled and bewildered because I was. There must have been a hundred cameras clicking away, and the chaos of cameramen stumbling over each other, jostling for position, was terrifying. Inside the Caucus Room, which seemed much smaller than I had imagined from seeing it on television, I was vaguely aware of a blur of faces—reporters, spectators, and, in front, some of the senators and staff members.

At last the marshals were able to get us to our seats. Bob McCandless and Charley Shaffer were there, and it seemed to me that they were both enjoying the publicity immensely, a fact I envied. I wished I felt as comfortable.

Soon a big man with white hair, bushy eyebrows, and jelly-like jowls took his seat at the center of a long table and gaveled the hearing to order. Unmistakably this was Senator Sam Ervin, and my first impression of him was both harsh and untrue, and I was sorry for it later. I thought he was senile. His eyes had sort of a wild look, he had difficulty coming up with the right words when he talked, he looked even older than he was. I had not had enough exposure to his wit and wisdom to realize that he was very much in command of himself and of the committee.

Howard Baker, the tiny Tennessean with the big voice, was the only senator I recognized instantly. I had never thought a great deal of him, and his cloying, sanctimonious posturing during the hearings did nothing to alter my impression.

Senator Edward Gurney of Florida, who, John had told me, would ask the most hostile questions, and who did, reminded me of Dan Duryea. He angered me with some of the insinuations in his questions (at one point he tried to discredit all of John's testimony because he had referred to the Mayflower Hotel when he meant the Statler-Hilton), but I also felt sorry for him. He had been wounded in World War II and seemed to be in such pain when he walked.

When the questioning began, Senator Lowell Weicker of Connecticut impressed me more than any of the others. He was the best prepared, knew what questions had been asked already (something several of the others did not know), and seemed more anxious to elicit a truthful answer than one tailored to his preconceptions.

Senator Joseph Montoya of New Mexico had the most difficulty. I had been around Capitol Hill enough to sense that his staff had prepared the questions for him, and the staff didn't have enough understanding of Watergate to prepare intelligent questions. During a recess one day, Mrs. Montoya introduced herself to me and offered me words of encouragement.

Senator Herman Talmadge of Georgia made no impression on me at all.

Next to Lowell Weicker, Senator Daniel Inouye of Hawaii struck me as the most forceful. He also paid very close attention to the questions of others.

But Senator Ervin quickly became the most interesting one of all to me. On the first day of the hearings, I noticed that his eyes were absolutely riveted on John. He stared at him with unwavering intensity, as if examining the depths of his soul. When I first became aware of this, I couldn't understand why he would never look anywhere else. The second day of the hearings he did the same thing —stared and stared. About midway through the third day of the hearings, he suddenly sat back in his chair, his whole body seemed to relax, and he no longer stared at John. The tone of his questions softened, and then it dawned on me: Senator Ervin had been concentrating totally on John's expressions, his voice, the look in his eye, his manner. After two and a half days, he had made up his mind: John Dean was telling the truth.

But on that first day, neither the senators nor the country had made up its mind about John Dean. As I sat there watching and listening, conscious of the history being made, my mind wandered occasionally. What were we doing here? How did we get here? How could we get out of here? What did the future hold?

Occasionally, I became aware of the photographers massed in front of us, and of the big television cameras blinking away in all directions. But I did not realize— could not have imagined—the footage they were devoting to me. Every time I scratched my nose, touched an earring, or made any sort of a motion I could hear the cameras click all around me, and I was annoyed, because it seemed the photographers were interested only in getting pictures that would make me look ridiculous.

At the end of the long, long day (John had been reading his prepared statement from 10 A.M. until 6:15 P.M.) I felt he had done well. His sincerity and truthfulness had come through—not to everyone, I realized, but to many. We were both so weary, he from testifying, I from the emotional strain of being present and in the spotlight I abhorred so much. So I was glad when the marshals whipped us out of the Caucus Room and took us home. The two marshals staying with us round-the-clock made the press keep its distance from our doorstep, for which I was grateful.

Bob and Charley followed us home, but left early. I

cooked cheeseburgers, a mistake, because we were to have cheeseburgers in Sam Dash's office every single day of the hearings. Pete came by with some pizza, and we were just starting to have a bite to eat when Mom called.

"Darling, you looked just beautiful on TV," she gushed. I told her I was glad she'd caught a glimpse of me, and she burst into laughter.

"A glimpse? You were on all day."

I wilted. It was a case of nerves after the fact.

It hadn't occurred to me that I had been on camera so frequently and for so long. I was naturally curious about how I looked, so we turned on the television and watched the network news. Well, I may have looked beautiful to Mom, but to me I looked like a large size 12—double my normal 6. I went very easy on the pizza and cheeseburgers that night.

We couldn't get the educational television channel on our set, so we didn't watch the rebroadcast of the hearings. We didn't have the stomach for them anyway. All day was enough. We just wanted to relax. Pete, who had taken a week off work to watch the hearings, relaxed with us.

For the next four days of the hearings, I just sat, listened, studied the senators and their reactions—and apparently impressed the reporters more with my impassivity than anything else. That is what most of them wrote about, making me wonder what they expected me to be doing—laughing? smiling? joining in with testimony of my own? I didn't want to give anyone the impression I was taking the hearing as a joke, for I certainly was not. Impassivity seemed the wisest course, but I realized I was in a no-win situation, and that some people would assume I just didn't grasp the situation.

One situation I did grasp: being on national television several hours a day for five consecutive days had put a complete end to my cherished anonymity. I was public property now, and this fact was driven home to me by the first of many terribly and highly impertinent questions that were to be put to me. This one was from Sarah Mc-Clendon, the powerful-lunged Texas newspaperwoman who has startled many a presidential press conference with her blunt questions.

During one of the recesses, she came up to me and, in a loud voice, bellowed:

"Didn't you used to be a go-go dancer in Dallas?"

"No," I said softly, smiling sweetly and seething within.

I must say I was completely unprepared for the attention, especially for the nasty prying by reporters and for the falsehoods that were printed and broadcast. Some reporters, I quickly learned, will stop at nothing. A certain few could scarcely conceal their disappointment when rumors that John and I were divorcing turned out to be untrue.

Naively, I thought all the publicity was a temporary thing that would not last much longer than the hearings. When Ann Blackman of the Associated Press asked me for an interview, I told her maybe in a week or so, thinking that her interest would fade.

Each day, the hearings became more difficult to endure. Senator Gurney was no longer questioning John at all— he was badgering him. He went over the fact that John had taken money that was not his for our honeymoon. Then he went over it again, and again. It was almost all that interested him. He cared little for any of the facts. Once I asked John why he didn't snarl back at him occasionally. John just shrugged. But a year later when Gurney was indicted in Florida for accepting payoffs, John said: "Well, as you now know, I didn't have to snarl back at Gurney." John knew at the time that Gurney had a number of legal problems and would shortly be discredited.

I sensed that Senator Inouye had made up his mind that

John was being truthful. Senator Montoya seemed to have believed that all along. Senator Talmadge was very cold and unemotional and gave no indication of his feelings.

Senator Baker was so busy being charming and playing to the television audience that he seemed to lose sight of what the hearings were about. I thought John was much too easy on him. He knew about Baker's general pro-administration performance behind the scenes at the committee, and I was dying for him to say something, but he wouldn't.

As the week wore on, I began to fear John wouldn't get through it. He was so tired, and more tired each day than he had been the day before. I began to wonder how anyone could go on answering questions like that for four full days, which was how long that phase was supposed to last. And Senator Gurney's attempts to discredit John were getting so wild I became a nervous wreck every time it was his turn to do the questioning. He focused on our personal finances, read from our bank statements, and on one occasion his eyes lit up as if he had just stumbled on a gold mine.

"Who's Jane?" he demanded, smacking his lips, as if he had just discovered the name of John's mistress.

"That's Jane Thomas, my secretary," John replied, and Gurney sank back in his seat, looking like a balloon that had just been deflated.

John did get through the hearings, of course, and at last the dreadful week was over. Riding home, we were so relieved and happy that we must have shocked the marshals with our behavior: hugging and kissing, laughing and generally letting our hair down. When I got to the house, the first thing I did was climb out of my color-coordinated outfit and into some blue jeans and a sweater, an outfit I generally reserve for cleaning the house and gardening. But now—what a relief!

It took us until four in the morning to wind down

sufficiently to be able to sleep. John was marvelous the next morning—he did three loads of washing and vacuumed the house, leaving me free to pack for both of us— because we were going to Florida, where a private house, away from the Senate, away from the press, away from everything and everybody, awaited us.

Accompanied by a marshal, we flew south that afternoon, provoking double takes and whispered conversations among airline passengers. But not a bit of hostility. Everyone was so kind and encouraging. People asked us for autographs. And while we waited in the lounge for a plane change at Atlanta, someone shouted: "Hello, Mrs. Dean. Good luck!" Two more marshals met us in Atlanta and flew with us to Orlando, where ten Eastern Airline mechanics formed a line, cheered, and applauded John while one took his hand and said simply: "Thank you, Mr. Dean, for restoring my faith in humanity."

If it could be like this all the time, being a celebrity wouldn't be so bad after all.

I was happier than I had any right to be. I completely shut out from my mind any possibility that John would be going to prison. After such impressive testimony, surely he would be granted complete immunity. It was now two months since he had been fired, and we were spending money from our dwindling reserves, but I also managed to put that out of my mind. We could still sell the house when we had to, and John could make some money writing. The future did not look so bleak now as it had earlier.

But my usual "Florida luck" was still with me and soon brought me back to earth with a thud. First, Heidi called from Washington to tell me that Maxine Cheshire had written a nasty column about my "past"—my first and second marriages, implying that John didn't even know about my marriage to George Owen. I had not reported it when John and I took out our marriage license, she noted. Of course, I hadn't. The marriage was annulled and there was no need to. She also wrote about my various jobs in Washington and Beverly Hills, with several of the details wrong, and told of my having lived with a "German girl" (Heidi) in Washington, and she was all mixed up on Heidi, too. She said Heidi was the daughter of a Nazi U-boat captain. Untrue! The article upset me terribly. I hadn't yet learned to ignore such things.

But critical articles and comments about John hurt even more. One night on television, Howard K. Smith absolutely infuriated me when he asked: "Would you buy a used car from John Dean?"

After several luxurious days at the private home in Melbourne, Florida, John received a telephone call from Sam Dash. Dash wanted John to return to Washington, and would not say why; all he said was that it was important. John tried to get out of it, but Sam was insistent.

"I have to leave for a day or two," John told me.

"Here we go again," I replied.

Could we *never* come to Florida and stay for a complete vacation?

It had been so wonderful to be alone together. We had become reacquainted. Once again we were husband and wife, lovers, best friends. We had had so many laughs together, the biggest one when I went swimming in the nude in the pool at the home where we were staying, knowing no one would be coming by. But I looked up in horror as a car pulled up and the biggest U.S. marshal in the entire world—one of the two who had met us in Atlanta—emerged, stole an appreciative glance, and then discreetly delayed coming to the door until I had a chance to recover—and cover. He had just come by to see if we were all right.

Neither of us knew it at the time of Sam Dash's call, but the Watergate Committee had just learned of the existence of the White House taping system. Alexander Butterfield would testify publicly about it on Monday, but before he did, Dash wanted to use his new knowledge as a test of John's truthfulness.

Therefore, Dash insisted John fly back on Sunday. Dash met with John alone, and their conversation went something like this:

"Do you think there could be a tape recording system in the White House?"

John thought a moment and said:

"There could be. I'll tell you how you could find out." He suggested that the committee ask Butterfield, the Secret Service, and the White House Communications Agency.

"What if I told you that all the conversations you have told us about happen to be on tape?" Dash asked, studying John's reactions closely.

John's eyes lit up. He smiled joyfully.

"Great," he cried. "Then there would be corroboration."

Sam Dash grinned. He had no way of knowing whether the committee would ever be able to get those tapes from the White House. But he did know this: he had no reason to wonder any longer about the truthfulness of his star witness.

20
The Debt Is Repaid

One day in October 1973, John Wesley Dean III rose to his feet in the courtroom of United States District Judge John J. Sirica. "How do you plead?" asked the clerk.

"Guilty," John replied.

Moments later, Judge Sirica adjusted his black robe, declared the court in recess, and strode from the bench. Special Prosecutor Archibald Cox and his associate, James F. Neal, slid some documents into their briefcases and walked out a side door. Reporters dashed to their telephones or clustered around John. In ten minutes, the event over which we had agonized for seven months was over, as far as most people in the courtroom were concerned. For us, it would, of course, never be over.

John Dean was now a felon (how I hate that word), guilty of "conspiracy to obstruct justice and to defraud the United States." John had made up his mind in March of 1973 that there were two essential elements to his "cleansing" process: telling the truth was one, and accepting his punishment was the other. In all honesty, I cannot say even now that I agreed with him. I'm too selfish and self-centered, some might say. Unwilling to pay my share of the price: long separation while John served his sentence, and the never-ending shame of my husband's prison record. No one can view someone he or she loves objectively. I fully realize that. But to me John was and is a man of great courage, who told the truth when the President of the United States would not, who changed the course of history, who challenged the most powerful men in the land to end their and his criminal conspiracy, and when they would not, he forced them to.

After all this, why should he go to prison? Call it my emotionalism or my unwillingness to face facts. No matter what you call it, I could not accept the idea of prison. But John had made his decision months earlier, and it was final.

We were down to our last $500 and had a growing mountain of debts. Friends were coming over at night to have dinner with us, bringing the steaks. For seventeen months, we had had no real income other than witness fees. For seventeen months, John had been cooperating with the special prosecutors, the courts, committees of the House and Senate. He had been disbarred. We had no life of our own. For the last six months two deputy U.S. marshals had lived with us, following us wherever we went, to protect the government's key witness. Once we hopped on our motorcycle, drove along a desert road, savoring our aloneness. Then we turned our heads and saw the marshal's yellow Pinto following along behind us. Whenever any government investigator wanted to interview John, John would drop everything and fly across the country, stay for days or even weeks, helping in any way he could. When Bantam Books offered John a $250,000 advance for his Watergate book, the Special Prosecutor's Office asked him to reject the offer until after all the trials at which he would be a witness were over, and he did. It did not seem to me that he—and I—had totally escaped punishment.

And here I was, having been taught self-defense by a deputy U.S. marshal so I could protect myself against rapists and robbers during the time my husband would be in prison—for telling the truth.

Mother was now dying of cancer and wanted us near her; and we wanted to be near, so we sold the house on Quay Street to Senator Weicker and bought an unfinished one near Beverly Hills. Poor Mom—she was bedridden, could not even visit the house we lived in. But she would not let us lose our courage and she would not lose hers. After we had sold our home, our car, and our boat, she gave us $2,000 so I would not have to sell my jewelry, every piece of which has a sentimental value. I bought no new clothes whatsoever.

John, who had genuinely feared he was becoming an alcoholic during the weeks following the Watergate hearings, no longer drank at all, and when he was home, he jogged every morning at UCLA with Jack Garfield and movie actor Gary Conway. We both worked on the house (John and Gene Adcock, an old friend, even sandblasted the ceiling), and it was good therapy for both of us—kept our minds off our precarious financial status, and off the prison sentence that drew ever nearer.

My disillusionment with Richard Nixon was complete, and the country's was fast becoming so. One night in May, John and I sat with Jack and Liz Garfield, watching the increasingly desperate President releasing transcripts of taped conversations that he said would tell the "complete story" of Watergate. All I could think was: What a total liar. And this was a man in whose presence I used to virtually swoon. John's reaction to the President was quite restrained. Once during the telecast he made a rather formal-sounding observation:

"That's not quite an accurate accounting of what took place."

Another time he said:

"The White House hasn't changed a bit—it still believes its own propaganda." But not a single other word did he say about the President.

I was not so skillful in holding my feelings back. By

then I hated Richard Nixon, and said so. I had absolutely no respect for this man who was, in effect, looking the country in the eye, and lying to it. He had lied to the Congress, to the people who worked for him, to the people who elected him, and even to his daughters. As I looked at him that night, I thought of his situation as compared to ours: he was still in the position of the highest honor and trust the people can bestow, and the man who out of blind loyalty to him had tried to cover up crimes would soon be behind bars.

But as I watched, I felt that some day there would be an abrupt end to the presidential term of Richard Nixon. He wouldn't be impeached—he was not the type to wait for impeachment. But he couldn't possibly remain in office another two years, I felt certain. Now it was simply a matter of time. He would resign, probably because of ill health, I thought. John never felt this as strongly as I did. He was not one to underestimate Richard Nixon's capacity to change, lose, or withhold evidence, including tapes, that would incriminate him. John had accurately forecast the resignation of Vice President Agnew the very day the fact that Agnew was under investigation appeared in the press, but he thought for a long time that President Nixon might manage to survive. Even after all that had happened to him, John did not have enough faith in the one dictum I have always had complete faith in: the truth always emerges.

Meanwhile, my primary concern was with what had happened and would still happen to us. We had made some money on the sale of the house in Alexandria over and above what we had had to pay for our new home, and John also had received an advance from Bantam to write a novel, *The Nomination,* about the first black woman to be named to the Supreme Court. His greatest concern during that period was to free me of financial worries by the time he would begin serving his sentence.

Looking back on this entire period now, I can't understand how an easily frightened, terribly insecure person like myself could have gotten through it. At times I would be so overwhelmed by John's situation and by the prospect of fending for myself for a year or more that almost anything could make me cry. Often I would be watching a television commercial and suddenly I would burst into tears. In retrospect, I suppose that I was bolstered in part because I am an escapist: I still would not allow myself to believe that John would really go to prison. Something would happen to prevent it.

In August 1974, reality, which eventually overtakes us all, began to catch up with me. We had almost lost Mom a couple of times, and now her condition was very bad again. On August 2, Judge Sirica imposed a one- to four-year sentence on John, completely undoing me. On September 3, he would be going away.

It was just over a week after the sentencing when the full meaning of what my husband had done for the country received a new and overdue emphasis: Richard Nixon resigned. Would this man who had so abused the powers of the presidency ever have been compelled to step down had there not been a John Dean? I think I know how historians will some day answer that question.

For us, as for most of the country, the end came almost as an anticlimax. The week before, the House Judiciary Committee had voted three articles of impeachment, and three days before the resignation President Nixon had been forced to release the tape of June 23, 1972, on which he and Bob Haldeman were agreeing to get the CIA to halt the FBI's investigation of the Watergate break-in and bugging.

With our dear friend Gene Adcock, we listened to the President's speech in our bedroom. We were not shocked. We were not sad. We were not overjoyed. John had had some impacted wisdom teeth pulled that week, and the effect of the extractions was that his face had ballooned up until he was almost unrecognizable. With his face so swollen, it was difficult to read anything from his expression during the historic moment he had done so much to bring about. He said very little—just listened, and when it was all over, I turned to him and asked:

"Why didn't he tell the truth?"

"He's still not able to," John replied. Then he added: "I must say I didn't expect him to go out that way— delivering a campaign speech."

And a campaign speech is what it was—boasting of his administration's accomplishments, admitting "mistakes" but no wrongdoing, blaming his downfall on the erosion of his political support in the Congress.

My thoughts wandered to Pat Nixon, and Tricia and Julie, what they must be thinking, and how terrible they must be feeling. Of course, they would be supportive of Nixon, for I'm sure they all loved him dearly, and always would. And now, leaving office in disgrace, Richard Nixon needed them so much. They were all he had. And still, as I looked at John, I wondered if Pat and the girls could really be proud of the President. Whatever John had done —and he had done a great deal that was terribly wrong— he had at last told the full truth about it. Whatever Richard Nixon had done—and he, too, had done much that was terribly wrong—he was still unable to tell the truth to the country and even, I felt sure, to his own family. I understood fully what John meant about the "cleansing" effect of telling the truth. Even though he was going to prison, even though—as he himself said—he would wear the "scarlet W of Watergate" the rest of his life and down through history, I knew that the man sitting beside me had greater peace of mind than the man whose image had just faded from the TV screen. Richard Nixon would be tormented for the rest of his days unless he, too, should decide some day to tell the truth.

Now it was a time of "subconscious lasts" for us. Still clinging to the hope of a last-minute reprieve for my husband, I nonetheless found myself thinking this is the last time we'll go shopping together, the last time we'll visit Mom together, the last time we'll watch a TV movie together, the last time we'll go to a party together. And then even some of the precious few days left to us were co-opted by the special prosecutors, who needed John in Washington for ten days of interviews before he surrendered to the U.S. marshals. So back we went to Washington.

And then suddenly it was a night late in September. Some friends had taken me to a party, and I was being introduced to someone, someone who apparently did not catch the name, because she was saying to me: "Delighted to meet you. Is your husband with you?"

"No," I replied, having long known a moment like this would arrive but not knowing how I would handle it. Then I blurted: "My husband is in prison." It sounded so unreal.

And I was living alone in Heidi's apartment in Chevy Chase, reading and writing through the long, dreary week, and traveling to Fort Holabird, Maryland, on weekends to visit my husband in the room to which he was confined and in which he would remain until he went to a different prison when he was no longer needed as a witness. Thank God the room was not a cell. But it was a prison, nonetheless, a prison with more physical comforts than most, but imprisonment is not primarily a physical situation. It's mental and emotional—if you are to be deprived of your freedom and rendered helpless to do anything for yourself or the people you love, the fact of your confinement is primary, the place of secondary importance.

Every Saturday and Sunday, I would drive the Baltimore-Washington Freeway one hour each way in order to spend two to three hours with my husband, to sit in his room and talk with him with the door wide open and a marshal sitting just outside. As the days went by, the effects on John were more and more visible. He was losing weight. He felt the full force of the shame he had brought upon himself, his family, and his name, and more than anything, he felt helpless and hopeless. Now it was his turn to burst into tears while watching a television commercial, and he did.

Not long after John's imprisonment, Pete Kinsey telephoned one Sunday morning to tell me that President Ford had granted a full pardon to former President Nixon. Having gone through so many emotion-draining events over the past several months, I had very little left for this one. Knowing how painful the experience of prison had been for us in just the short time John had been there, I could not wish it on anyone. But it struck me as so unfair that the President, for whose benefit the crimes had been committed, had been singled out for a pardon while even pitifully minor participants in the scandals, such as Bart Porter, had been compelled to pay their penalties.

I made up my mind that I would try to convince President Ford that the shame and pain suffered by other Watergate families was no less than that suffered by the Nixons. Senator Lowell Weicker, who by now had become a close friend, told me to wait. So did Senator Barry Goldwater, through his son, Barry, Jr. I waited—approximately twenty-four hours. Then I tried to get through to the White House, but the entire country seemed to have been outraged by the pardon, and the White House lines were constantly busy. Finally I reached an aide, told him who I was and that I hoped to arrange an appointment with the President. He told me the President was in Pittsburgh, and that I would have to convey my request through a Mr. Robert Hartman, one of President Ford's principal assistants.

Perhaps it was just as well. It gave me time to compose my thoughts.

I was not going to ask the President point-blank to pardon my husband. I was going to ask him where the justice was in pardoning one member of a criminal conspiracy and none of the others, and in not even demanding that the person pardoned tell the country the full truth, no matter how painful that might be. It was no easy task for John Dean or Herb Kalmbach or Egil Krogh or Jeb Magruder either, nor for their families. At length I decided to issue a statement to the press, one in which I reminded the President that the men who were in prison and whose families were also suffering were the ones who had spoken the truth, "something we have yet to hear from Mr. Nixon."

My statement was widely and erroneously printed and broadcast as a plea that the President also pardon my husband, and in responding to it, the White House press office said that the President was considering pardons for all of the Watergate defendants. Then it retracted that announcement, declaring that it had meant to say only that formal requests for pardons would be considered on an individual basis. This performance did nothing to bolster my confidence in the Ford White House.

As the weeks dragged on and the tension and insecurity weighed more heavily on me, I felt I simply had to get back to my own home, if only for a few days. I also had to get back to Mother, who was worrying so much about me that she wasn't doing herself a bit of good. I wanted her to see me so she'd know I was just fine.

But you cannot trick your own mother. She saw what she suspected—that I was exhausted and drained. At her insistence, I went to a psychiatrist. He found me on the verge of a nervous breakdown and ordered me to get to a hospital.

"Oh, great," I said. "This is just what John needs—to receive word while he is in prison and helpless that his wife has been hospitalized with a nervous breakdown three thousand miles away." But I really had no choice. Under the name of Maureen Biner (so the press would not learn of it) I was admitted to St. John's Hospital in Santa Monica, but was unable to telephone John. That night at Fort Holabird, John used one of the two telephone calls he was allowed each week to tell a friend he had never known such frustration: his wife ill—he knew not how seriously—and he unable to do a single thing to help.

Several days later, I managed to pull myself together— I had to. Two weeks after that I flew back to Washington, staying this time with Susie and Barry Goldwater, again visiting John on weekends—and on Thanksgiving Day we sat together in his tiny room (with the marshal near the open door) and had Thanksgiving dinner together.

About this time, Charley Shaffer was preparing an appeal to Judge Sirica, asking him to shorten John's sentence, or at least to fix it for a definite period. Sam Dash, Lowell Weicker, and many others had written letters to the judge, emphasizing John's major role in uncovering the Watergate scandals and his complete cooperation with the courts and the prosecutors for nearly two years. But there was something missing from all these letters, something needed from the person who knew John Dean best —his wife. So for several days I struggled to put together the most important letter I had ever written or would ever write, and then I hand-delivered it to the judge's chambers. I wrote:

Dear Judge Sirica:

I am writing to you with the hope and prayer that you will reduce the heavy prison sentence you have given my husband, John Dean, for his involvement in Watergate.

My renewed hope stems from the fact that before you sentenced John, the materials presented to you were not complete. Since that time in early August so much more of the case has come to light and more and more of what my husband testified to before the Senate Watergate Committee has been substantiated. In light of this I cannot believe that you would not give every consideration to my request.

I have had occasion to discuss your sentencing of my husband with a number of people familiar with this case, people connected with the Special Prosecutor's Office, the Senate Watergate Committee, members of Congress, and people who are and have been following the events of Watergate closely ever since June of 1972. Every person I have spoken with felt that John received the harshest punishment of all those involved in Watergate, especially since he and he alone came forth and told all in order to bring the truth of the matter out for the American people. He did this with no ulterior motive, as only I can say and say with the conviction of a wife who knows her husband's character—and knows it well.

Your honor, I still have not recovered from the shock of the sentence which you imposed on my husband. I can only ask if you have considered the difficulty and enormity of the decision my husband made to tell the truth, and the price which he has had to pay for telling the truth?

I feel I must explain to the court about this price and the impact of the decision to tell the truth and about the punishment it has been in itself. Once John decided to cooperate with the government in righting the wrongs of Watergate, we lost our freedom. Since April of 1973 until today, John has been helping with his incredible memory to unravel Watergate and also matters he was not even involved in.

For the last sixteen months before he was incarcerated— virtually every day—John has been working, meeting, and testifying on and on to assist the government. My own personal diary reflects that during this time, that all or at least part of each day was consumed with John's efforts to cooperate and assist the various forces seeking to put the pieces together— the Senate Watergate Committee, the Special Prosecutor's Office, the Southern District of New York, the House Judiciary

Committee, and the Commerce Committee. John unselfishly gave . . . and gave honestly. It virtually ruined our lives; and has been a tremendous financial, emotional and physical strain and burden. But, John believes it was and is essential to repay to society the debt he believes he owes for his misguided loyalty during his days at The White House.

Another point I feel I should make about his cooperation; he told me he was going to plead guilty to the offense he had committed, despite the fact that his attorney, Charles Shaffer, believed strongly that if anyone could beat the charges, John had a technical case of—I think it is called tainted evidence—and Mr. Shaffer said that it would take years to even get a case before a jury if the government ever could. But, long before mid-October of 1973 when the government asked John if he would plead, he had decided to do so. In fact, he had reached a decision even prior to his Senate testimony in June of 1973. And, when Mr. Shaffer asked him what Judge he wanted to plead before, he chose you, because he felt you had done so much to break the case.

Thus, John not only spent some sixteen months cooperating with the government prior to his sentencing, he even cut short by ten days the time you had given him to get his affairs in order because the government needed him back in Washington. And consistent with this belief that he owed his cooperation, he refused to tie the government in legal knots and delay the ultimate resolution of Watergate for years by not pleading.

It is because of this painful sixteen months of total cooperation of which the last six months before he surrendered have been virtual imprisonment because of the presence of Deputy U.S. Marshals twenty-four hours a day, that I now find it difficult to believe that Your Honor has not appreciated the fact that John had served almost sixteen months before you even sentenced him to prison. Does not a Judge consider the impact of such cooperation? Should our system not encourage people to cooperate? If Your Honor saw how time consuming and difficult my husband's cooperation has been, I do not believe that you would have given him the sentence that you did. I only fear that I have not fully presented what this time has meant to John in terms of it being a tremendous penalty in and of itself.

Finally and lastly, I would like to tell you of the devastating impact your sentencing of John has had on our family. While I believe that my husband is capable of accepting his punishment I know that we cannot believe that he may be imprisoned for a full year or two years or even three. I can as only a wife knows, tell that he believes that justice will prevail. That he will not be faced with a long sentence, when the man for whom he did his wrongful acts was excused. That as the one person who cooperated first, and of his own decision before being charged, and who has cooperated the most—is the recipient of the heaviest sentence. John always expected to go to jail, but please, Your Honor, don't break him with a sentence that is more punishment and retribution than any society would demand.

The possibility that John may be faced with another year or more than the sixteen months he (we) went through already has been more than I am capable of handling. With my mother suffering from terminal cancer and John being the only person who has been able to keep her alive, I find myself emotionally incapable of facing life. I am currently trying to keep myself together by receiving psychiatric treatment, after being committed to a hospital following a total breakdown in early October.

Frankly, I have written this letter not only because I feel that if Your Honor knows what I know, you will view John differently, but also this letter will give me the hope in my heart that I need to go on. Thus, I pray that it is God's wish and your reconsidered fair judgment, that will release my husband from jail at the end of this trial in which he is presently assisting.

Thank you, for I must believe you will consider the matters

I have told you and cannot believe they will not affect your judgment accordingly.

Sincerely,
Mrs. John W. Dean III

On December 23 I flew to California again to be with Mom—we both knew it would be her last Christmas. I promised John that I would return to Maryland by the second weekend of January.

One morning early, John called to ask me how I was feeling. I felt terrible—a headache, nervous tension, anxiousness about getting back to see John again, and worry about leaving Mom.

"Get some rest," he advised me. "Take the telephone off the hook."

I did. And later that morning, Judge Sirica terminated John's sentence—and John couldn't even reach me to tell me about it!

He did reach Mom, though.

"Irene. I'm free!" he told her.

She wept with joy. Finally, I started answering the telephone again, and when Mom told me the wonderful news, I, too, wept with joy.

A crushing weight had been lifted from both of us—from all of us.

John and I again had all we really needed—each other.

We didn't know—don't know—what the future will bring.

But we do know we'll face it together, and we'll be fine.

Mom knew that, too.

On February 5, three weeks after John came home, she knew it would be all right to leave us.

She died that day—peacefully—in her sleep.

Index

About the Author

HAYS GOREY *was born in Salt Lake City, Utah. He received his B.A. in English from the University of Utah and was a Nieman Fellow at Harvard University.*

Mr. Gorey was a reporter, city editor and finally news editor for the Salt Lake City Tribune. *He received the Service to Journalism award from the University of Utah and served as American Specialist Abroad for the U.S. State Department in Tehran, Iran.*

Since 1965 he has worked as Washington correspondent for Time *Magazine and has contributed to such other publications as* Harper's, Fortune, Life, Sports Illustrated *and* People *magazine.*

Mr. Gorey and his wife, Nonie, have four children and live in Washington, D.C. He recently published a study of Ralph Nader entitled Ralph Nader and the Power of Everyman.